W9-ACB-449

OXFORD TEXTBOOKS IN LINGUISTICS

Series editors

Keith Brown, Eve V. Clark, April McMahon, Jim Miller and Lesley Milroy

A Practical Introduction to Phonetics

Second Edition

OXFORD TEXTBOOKS IN LINGUISTICS

General editors: **Keith Brown**, University of Cambridge; **Eve V. Clark**, Stanford University; **April McMahon**, University of Edinburgh; **Jim Miller**, University of Auckland; **Lesley Milroy**, University of Michigan

This series provides lively and authoritative introductions to the approaches, methods, and theories associated with the main subfields of linguistics.

PUBLISHED

The Grammar of Words
An Introduction to Linguistic Morphology
by Geert Booij

A Practical Introduction to Phonetics
Second edition
by J. C. Catford

Meaning in Language
An Introduction to Semantics and Pragmatics
Second edition
by Alan Cruse

Principles and Parameters
An Introduction to Syntactic Theory
by Peter W. Culicover

A Semantic Approach to English Grammar
by R. M. W. Dixon

Semantic Analysis
A Practical Introduction
by Cliff Goddard

Pragmatics
by Yan Huang

Diachronic Syntax
by Ian Roberts

Cognitive Grammar
An Introduction
by John R. Taylor

Linguistic Categorization
Third edition
by John R. Taylor

IN PREPARATION

Natural Language Syntax
by Peter W. Culicover

Translation: Theory and Practice
by Kirsten Malmkjaer

A Practical Introduction to
Phonetics

Second Edition

J. C. Catford

OXFORD
UNIVERSITY PRESS

OXFORD

UNIVERSITY PRESS

Great Clarendon Street, Oxford OX2 6DP

Oxford University Press is a department of the University of Oxford.
It furthers the University's objective of excellence in research, scholarship,
and education by publishing worldwide in

Oxford New York

Auckland Cape Town Dar es Salaam Hong Kong Karachi
Kuala Lumpur Madrid Melbourne Mexico City Nairobi
New Delhi Shanghai Taipei Toronto

With offices in

Argentina Austria Brazil Chile Czech Republic France Greece
Guatemala Hungary Italy Japan Poland Portugal Singapore
South Korea Switzerland Thailand Turkey Ukraine Vietnam

Oxford is a registered trade mark of Oxford University Press
in the UK and in certain other countries

Published in the United States
by Oxford University Press Inc., New York

© J. C. Catford 1988, 2001

The moral rights of the author have been asserted

Database right Oxford University Press (maker)

First published by Oxford University Press 1988
Reprinted with corrections 1994
Second edition 2001

All rights reserved. No part of this publication may be reproduced,
stored in a retrieval system, or transmitted, in any form or by any means,
without the prior permission in writing of Oxford University Press,
or as expressly permitted by law, or under terms agreed with the appropriate
reprographics rights organization. Enquiries concerning reproduction
outside the scope of the above should be sent to the Rights Department,
Oxford University Press, at the address above

You must not circulate this book in any other binding or cover
and you must impose this same condition on any acquirer

British Library Cataloguing in Publication Data

Data available

Library of Congress Cataloging in Publication Data

Catford, J. C. (John Cunnison), 1917-
A practical introduction to phonetics.
Bibliography: p.
Includes index
1. Phonetics. 2. Grammar, Comparative and
general—Phonology. I. Title.
P221.C33 1988 414 88-12546

ISBN: 978-019-924635-9

9 10

Typeset in Times and Stone Sans
by RefineCatch Limited, Bungay, Suffolk
Printed in Great Britain
on acid-free paper by
Antony Rowe Ltd,
Chippenham, Wiltshire

Preface

It may be worth drawing attention to the fact that the title of this book is, designedly, 'A Practical Introduction to Phonetics' and not 'An Introduction to Practical Phonetics', for it is, indeed, an introduction to general, or theoretical, phonetics, though it proceeds towards that goal in a highly practical way.

Readers are introduced to the phonetic classification of the sounds of speech by means of a series of simple introspective experiments carried out inside their own vocal tracts, their own throats and mouths. By actually making sounds (very often silently) and attending to the muscular sensations that accompany their production one can discover how they are produced and learn how to describe and classify them.

At first sight 'making sounds silently' may appear contradictory, but, as Abercrombie (1967) has aptly pointed out, speech is 'audible gesture' and the principal aim of this book is to enable the reader to discover and to analyse the gestural aspect of speech (upon which most phonetic classification is based) and to bring it under conscious control. This must be done, to a large extent, in silence, since the auditory sensations of loud speech tend to mask the motor sensations, which are the perceptual accompaniment of the gestural aspect of speech.

That this kind of experimentation is an effective means of acquiring a knowledge of the categories and principles of general phonetics I know from personal experience, for this was precisely how I learned phonetics as a boy, without a teacher, eagerly reading Sweet's *Primer of Phonetics* and constantly experimenting in my own vocal tract.

Although, as this reference to boyhood experience suggests, phonetics is a fascinating hobby for young people, it is primarily an indispensable tool for all those adults who have to work with language: students of linguistics, teachers and students of languages, teachers of the deaf, the hearing-impaired themselves who may be striving to acquire intelligible speech, actors, and many others. Armed with the understanding of the basic principles of phonetics which this book seeks to inculcate, they should be able to read and fully understand any specialist work on whatever aspect of phonetics is of special interest to them.

Much of the material of the book has been used for some years past at the University of Michigan, in teaching phonetics to large groups of students of linguistics, speech pathology, anthropology, languages, education, drama, and many other fields. I am grateful to all those students who contributed comments and suggestions, and I should also like to thank Dr Harriet Mills who read most of the text and made numerous valuable criticisms.

Some readers have suggested that it would be useful to have a set of recordings of the experiments, or at least of the sounds that should result when each experiment is carried out. This might be helpful, but it also carries the risk that some readers might be induced to try and learn sounds merely by imitation of heard examples. This would tend to defeat the purpose of the book, which is to inculcate an understanding of the mechanism of speech and of phonetic taxonomy by experimentation in one's own vocal tract.

However, it may be useful for some to be able to hear examples of many of the unfamiliar sounds that they have been led to produce in these experiments.

A recording is now available of all of the sounds represented on the latest chart of the International Phonetic Alphabet, which can be found on pages 114–15 of this book. This demonstration, *The Sounds of the IPA*, spoken by John Wells, Professor of Phonetics, and Jill House, Senior Lecturer in Phonetics, at University College, London, is available on audio cassette or CD. For further information write to Listening Centre, Department of Phonetics and Linguistics, UCL, 4 Stephenson Way, London NW1 2HE, UK (Fax: +4420 7383 0752. Email: mary@phon.ucl.ac.uk).

This new edition contains additions and corrections, and most importantly, presents an expanded and updated list of items for further reading, on pages 217 to 219. I am particularly grateful to Jimmy G. Harris and Professor John Esling for the many helpful suggestions that they provided, and to John Davey and Jo Stanbridge of Oxford University Press for their guidance and careful editorial work.

J.C.C.

Ann Arbor,
August 2001

Acknowledgements

The International Phonetic Association has kindly given permission for the reproduction of the IPA chart and the International Phonetic Alphabet. For further information, please write to: The International Phonetic Association, c/o Department of Linguistics, University of Victoria, Victoria, British Columbia, Canada.

Permission to reproduce figs. 1, 19, 21, 22, 23, 24, 25, and 35, which originally appeared in *Fundamental Problems in Phonetics*, has kindly been granted by Edinburgh University Press.

Contents

List of Figures

1

Introduction

1. The uses of phonetics

Phonetics is the systematic study of human speech-sounds. It provides means of describing and classifying virtually all the sounds that can be produced by human vocal tracts. How this is done is the principal subject-matter of this book. But before we begin to investigate the sounds of speech it may be useful to say something about why it is interesting and useful to do this: in other words, to review some of the *uses* of phonetics.

Over a century ago, the great English philologist, linguist, and phoneti-cian, Henry Sweet (who, as Shaw tells us, was in part the prototype of Professor Higgins in *Pygmalion*—perhaps better known nowadays as the musical, *My Fair Lady*) described phonetics as '. . . the indispensable foun-dation of all study of language—whether that study be purely theoretical, or practical as well . . .' (Sweet (1877), p. v).

This is as true today as it was in the time of Sweet. Any person who works with language would do well to have a basic knowledge of phonetics. The teacher of languages, for example, including the teacher of English as a second language, must be able to diagnose the pronunciation errors made by students, and to devise means of correcting them—this is impossible without both theoretical and practical knowledge of phonetics.

Phonetics is also useful to those concerned with various aspects of the mother tongue: the phonetically trained teacher of reading will have a bet-ter understanding of orthographic problems and the relationship of spell-ing to the spoken language; in the teaching of speech-production phonetics is obviously essential—actors, particularly those who wish to master numerous dialects and foreign accents, certainly ought to have a thorough knowledge of phonetics, which, alas, they usually lack.

Speech pathologists have an obvious need for phonetics, which they

readily acknowledge, both for a general understanding of how the vocal apparatus works and for the diagnosis and treatment of minor articulatory defects.

Communication and computer engineers and other 'speech-scientists' working on the improvement of speech transmission systems, on speech synthesis, and on automatic speech recognition, also need to have a considerable knowledge of phonetics.

Another important application of phonetics is to what Sweet calls 'scientific philology'—or what we would now call 'comparative-historical linguistics'. In his words: 'Without a knowledge of the laws of sound-change, scientific philology ... is impossible, and without phonetics their study degenerates into a mere mechanical enumeration of letter-changes' (p. v).

And of course phonetics is absolutely essential to the student of linguistics. It is virtually impossible to do serious work in linguistics without a thorough knowledge of phonetics. Clearly, without phonetics, field-work, the most important source of linguistic data, is impossible, and phonological rules become (like the sound-laws referred to above) meaningless and unmotivated rules of letter-substitution. Even in the study of syntax and morphology questions of phonetics frequently arise.

Now, it is perfectly possible to acquire a good *theoretical* knowledge of phonetics by reading, and even more so by working in a phonetics laboratory where aspects of the physiology and acoustics of speech are investigated instrumentally. But the kind of superficial, purely intellectual, knowledge of phonetics that is acquired in this way is quite inadequate as a basis for carrying out many of the activities referred to above. What the competent phonetician *must* acquire is a deep, internally experienced, awareness of what is going on within the vocal tract—an ability to analyse, and hence describe and ultimately control, the postures and movements of organs that produce the sounds of speech. It is fairly obvious that this kind of practical ability is essential for those, like language learners and teachers, or actors, who have to identify and produce exotic or unaccustomed sounds. What is not so obvious, but is undoubtedly the case, is that the acquisition of these 'practical' skills is by far the best way of acquiring a deep understanding of phonetic theory—of the principles underlying the description and classification of the sounds of speech—and is consequently of the greatest importance also for more 'theoretical' uses of phonetics.

Thus, the nature of a historical sound-change can usually best be under-

stood by those who can actually carry through the change in their own vocal tracts and internally, introspectively, *experience* its mechanism; and the interpretation of physiological or acoustic instrumental records of speech is most efficiently carried out by speech-scientists who possess the same kinds of skill—investigators who cannot themselves pronounce, and internally experience, most of the phenomena they are investigating sometimes misinterpret their data.

It is because of the great importance of this kind of introspective awareness of the phenomena of speech that in this book we introduce the reader to the principles and categories of phonetic classification not only by means of descriptions, which can produce a merely intellectual comprehension of phonetic theory, but by means of *experiments* which readers are asked to carry out in their own vocal tracts. In this way, they will acquire that deep understanding of phonetic theory which is the indispensable stock-in-trade of the competent phonetician.

2. The phases of speech

Before we begin the experimental approach to the subject, in Chapter 2, it will be useful to consider the nature of the speech-event, and what particular aspects of it are, or may be, the domain of phonetics.

When someone speaks to someone, the sequence of events is, in outline, as follows. In response to the need to communicate about some *event* (which may either be in the world at large or within his own consciousness) the speaker *conceptualizes* the event in a particular way and then *encodes* that conceptualization in a form laid down by the grammar of his language. The linguistically encoded utterance is *externalized* and apprehended by the hearer through the agency of a series of events that we term the *phases* of speech. These phases start in the speaker, and culminate in the hearer *decoding* the utterance and arriving at a *conceptualization* which, assuming he is familiar with the speaker's language, closely matches the speaker's conceptualization, which was the start of the process.

The processes of conceptualization and coding/decoding are outside the domain of phonetics. The purely phonetic part of the speech process begins, we assume, with the execution of a short-term neural programme in the central nervous system, which is triggered by the lexico-grammatical structure of the utterance and determines the nature and the sequencing of everything that follows. We may call this the *neurolinguistic programming* phase of the utterance.

Thereafter, in a sequence no doubt determined during the stage of neuro-linguistic programming, specific 'motor commands' flow out through motor nerves to muscles in the chest, throat, mouth, etc. As a result, these muscles contract—in whole or in part, successively or simultaneously, more or less strongly.

We call this whole process of motor commands (the outflow of neural impulses from the central nervous system), together with the indissolubly related muscle contractions, the *neuromuscular* phase.

As a result of the muscular contractions occurring in this neuromuscular phase, the organs to which these muscles are attached adopt particular postures or make particular movements—the rib-cage may contract, the vocal folds in the larynx may be brought close together, the tongue adopt a particular configuration, and so on. In short, the sequel to the neuro-muscular phase is a posturing or movement of whole organs in the vocal tract. We therefore call this the *organic* phase.

The movements of organs during the organic phase act upon the air contained within the vocal tract. They compress the air, or dilate it, and they set it moving in various ways—in rapid puffs, in sudden bursts, in a smooth flow, in a rough, eddying, turbulent stream, and so on. All of this constitutes the *aerodynamic* phase of speech.

As the air flows through the vocal tract during the aerodynamic phase the things that happen to it set the air molecules oscillating in ways that can be perceived by our sense of hearing. In other words, the aerodynamic events generate sound-waves, and these constitute the *acoustic* phase of speech. In the acoustic phase, an airborne sound-wave radiates from the speaker's mouth and reaches the ear of anyone within hearing distance, including the speaker himself.

The sound-wave, impinging on the hearer's ear-drum, sets it vibrating in step with the wave-form, and these vibrations are transmitted, by the little bones of the middle ear, to the inner ear, or cochlea, where they stimulate sensory endings of the auditory nerve. Neural impulses from the nerve-endings travel up the auditory nerve to the brain, where they give rise to sensations of sound. We call this whole process of peripheral stimulation and afferent neural transmission the *neuroreceptive* phase.

Finally, an interpretative process occurs in which the incoming neuroreceptive signals are identified as this or that particular vocal sound or sound-sequence. This is the phase of *neurolinguistic identification*, which we can regard as more or less the obverse of the neurolinguistic programming phase with which the phonetic event began. Though there may always be some awareness of sound in this phase, the identification as particular speech-sounds is usually below the threshold of consciousness. In the actual exchange of conversation, attention is directed more to the meaning of what is said than to the sounds by which that meaning is manifested.

The final steps in the process—the hearer's decoding and ultimate conceptualization—are outside the domain of phonetics, just as were the matching conceptualization and encoding in the speaker.

We can now summarize the phases of speech as follows:

(1) *Neurolinguistic programming*: the selection, sequencing, and timing of what follows.
(2) *Neuromuscular phase*: transmission of outbound (motor) neural impulses and the contraction of individual muscles.
(3) *Organic phase*: postures and movements of whole organs.
(4) *Aerodynamic phase*: dilation, compression, and flow of air in and through the vocal tract.
(5) *Acoustic phase*: propagation of sound-waves from speaker's vocal tract.
(6) *Neuroreceptive phase*: peripheral auditory stimulation and transmission of inbound neural impulses.
(7) *Neurolinguistic identification*: potential or actual identification of incoming signals as specific speech-sounds.

In addition to all this we must take note of two other phases, or aspects, of the speech process. These are the two kinds of feedback: *kinaesthetic feedback* and *auditory feedback*.

As the organs of speech posture and move about in the performance of speech, sensory nerve-endings within the muscles and on the surfaces of the organs are stimulated by muscle contraction and by contact and pressure. We may be, but often are not, conscious of this feedback as *proprioceptive sensations* (feelings of muscular contraction and tension) and *tactile sensations*. As a general name for these proprioceptive and tactile sensations we use the term 'kinaesthesis', hence *kinaesthetic feedback*.

The second type of feedback consists of the stimulation of the speaker's peripheral hearing organs by the sound-wave issuing from his own mouth which reaches his ears both externally, by air conduction, and internally, by bone conduction. This is *auditory feedback*.

These feedback systems monitor and control speech by inserting into the motor system information concerning the continuing muscular, organic, aerodynamic, and acoustic events. Much of phonetic training involves making these feedbacks, especially kinaesthetic or proprioceptive feedback, *conscious*. Analysis, and conscious control, of the activities of speech must be based upon awareness of what the vocal organs are doing and this awareness is derived from the feedback systems.

Of the seven phases of speech described above only three lend themselves conveniently to categorization for general phonetic purposes: these are the organic phase, the aerodynamic phase, and the acoustic phase. Traditionally, phonetic classification has been based on the *organic* phase. This was the basis of classification of the earliest phoneticians—the Indian grammarians of 2,500 years ago—and also of the ancient Greek and Roman grammarians, the medieval Arab grammarians, and the English phoneticians from Elizabethan times onwards. The acoustic phase has only been fully accessible since the development in the twentieth century of electronic devices for acoustic analysis, such as the cathode-ray oscilloscope and the sound spectrograph in the 1930s and 1940s. Nevertheless, since such instruments became available an enormous amount has been learned about the acoustic phase, and the study of this phase of speech is known as *acoustic phonetics*. The aerodynamic phase is also accessible to instrumental investigation and aerodynamic data have been used since the nineteenth century, chiefly as a means of acquiring information about the preceding, organic, phase: by looking at variations in the rate of airflow out of the mouth, measuring intra-oral pressure, and so on, one can make many useful inferences about the organic activities that give rise to these aerodynamic effects. It is only recently that the suggestion has been made that there should be a more or less independent *aerodynamic phonetics*, parallel to acoustic phonetics.

General phonetic taxonomy, however—that is, the general or basic classification of speech sounds—is still based on the *organic phase*, with some contributions from aerodynamic and acoustic phonetics where helpful. This type of phonetics is often called *articulatory phonetics*, a term which is somewhat inaccurate, since, as we shall see, articulation is only one (though a very important one) of the components of speech sound production.

3. The vocal tract

All the sounds of speech are produced in the vocal tract. For the purpose of this book we take the vocal tract to consist of the entire respiratory tract, from lungs to nose, plus the mouth. This is a somewhat wider application of the term than is found in most other works, where 'vocal tract' means only the tract from the larynx up through the mouth and nose. It is, however, more useful for phonetic purposes to use the term in the wide sense of all those tracts within the human body that normally participate in the production of vocal sounds.

The student of practical phonetics does not require a very detailed knowledge of the vocal tract and vocal organs, and in this book we shall introduce such detail as is necessary as and when it is needed. However, it may be useful in this introductory chapter to outline the structure and phonetic functions of the principal organs in the vocal tract. Figure 1 and the following description are primarily for reference, and at this stage need not be deeply studied, but should be apprehended in a general, impressionistic, way.

As we have seen, the function of the organic phase of speech is to create certain aerodynamic conditions—to set the air in the vocal tract in motion, and to control the flow of air in ways that ultimately generate sounds. The vocal tract can thus be regarded as a pneumatic device—a device consisting of a bellows and various tubes and valves and chambers whose function is to set air in motion and to control its flow.

Figure 1 is a sketch of this 'pneumatic device' alongside a somewhat more naturalistic sketch of the vocal tract with lines connecting the two to show the relationships between their parts. The brief account of the vocal tract that follows should be read in close conjunction with a study of the figure. The bellows (lungs) can expand to draw in half a gallon or so of air, and can contract to blow out a like quantity: in speech they contract quite slowly. There are two tubes leading from the bellows (the bronchi) which unite in a larger tube (the trachea, or windpipe).

Near the upper end of the windpipe there is a piston (the larynx) that can slide up and down for an inch or so. You can feel the front of the larynx-piston as a projection in the front of your neck (the 'Adam's apple') and you can also feel that it can slide up and down—this is specially noticeable when you swallow. The larynx is usually more prominent in men than in

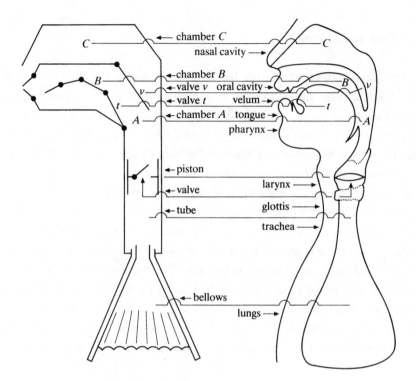

Fig. 1 The vocal tract

women but the swallowing movement can easily be felt by both. Within the piston there is a valve (the glottis—that is, the space between the vocal cords, or vocal folds, as we shall call them). The glottis-valve can be tightly closed or opened to varying degrees or else rapidly and rhythmically opened and shut in the course of speech.

Above the larynx there are three chambers, *A* (pharynx), *B* (oral cavity, i.e. mouth), and *C* (nasal cavity), which can be put into communication with each other, or separated off from each other by the valves *v* (velum, or soft palate) and *t* (tongue). The tongue-valve is highly mobile and can control airflow through chamber *B* (mouth) at a number of different places and in a number of different ways. Finally, the outer end of chamber *B* (mouth) is provided with a double valve, namely the upper and lower lip.

Study of this brief description of the 'pneumatic device' and the corresponding sketch of the vocal tract in Fig. 1 should make clear the main parts of the vocal tract and their major phonetic functions.

As we said earlier, phonetic taxonomy is primarily based on the organic phase; but it requires contributions from the aerodynamic phase. This is inevitable, since the production of speech-sounds is an aerodynamic process. The organic postures and movements do not themselves generate sounds; they merely set the air in the vocal tract in motion, and it is the flow of air through the vocal tract that generates sounds.

4. The functional components of speech

From the organic-aerodynamic point of view the production of speech-sounds involves two essential *functional components*: (1) some method of *initiating* a flow of air in and through the vocal tract—that is, some form of **initiation**, as we call it; and (2) some method of shaping or *articulating* the air-stream so as to generate a specific type of sound—that is, some form of **articulation**. There is a third functional component of speech-production, present in most, but not all, sounds, and consisting of certain types of modulation of the air-stream as it passes through the larynx—that is **phonation**. In order to understand the mechanism of speech it is essential to have a clear conception of these three functional components—of the forms that they can take, and of how they interact to produce speech-sounds.

The following chapters introduce the reader to these three basic functional *components* of speech, and to the various *parameters*, or ranges of variation, of the sub-components or features that characterize each of them. Because of its concern with these two aspects of phonetics, the phonetic theory expounded in this book may be called *componential-parametric phonetics*.

These components and parameters and other features of speech production are introduced in a series of experiments to be carried out in the reader's own vocal tract. These experiments will not only provide a deep, personally experienced insight into phonetic theory, but will also develop the motor and auditory skills that are essential for the competent phonetician, and which cannot be developed by the mere reading of descriptions and explanations.

2

Basic Components of Speech

1. Initiation and articulation

The first step in the study of phonetics is to discover, experimentally, the *basic components* that go into the production of any speech-sound.

We begin by producing a prolonged [f]-sound—the first sound in the words 'first', 'four', and last sound in 'huff', 'puff', and so on. While making the sound one must think about what is going on—that is, one must *analyse* the production of the sound introspectively, by taking note of the kinaesthetic sensations, the feelings of contact and movement associated with it.

1   Begin by comfortably filling the lungs—that is, take in a deep, but not excessively deep, breath—then start up a prolonged [f]-type sound: [f f f f f f]. On one full intake of breath you will no doubt easily be able to keep the sound going for 5 to 10 seconds. Repeat this three or four times—breathe in, say prolonged [f f f f f f], then relax—concentrating your attention upon what is happening, upon what you are doing in order to produce that sound.

It will quickly become clear from introspective observation that the production of this prolonged [f]-sound requires the simultaneous occurrence of two events; in other words, the production of the sound has *two components*. These components are (*i*) *deflation of the lungs*, which sends a stream of air up the windpipe and out through the mouth, and (*ii*) *contact between the lower lip and the upper teeth*, forming an obstacle to the flowing air, which forces its way through in a turbulent stream that generates the specific hissing sound of [f].

2   Now carry out the same experiment with a prolonged [s]—the first sound in *see*, the last sound in *hiss*. Breathe in, start up a prolonged [s]-type sound [s s s s s s] lasting for 5 to 10 seconds or so. Repeat several times—breathe in, say

[s s s s s s], relax—concentrating your attention all the time upon what you are doing to produce that sound.

Once again, it will be clear that there are two simultaneous components: (*i*) deflation of the lungs, initiating an upward and outward flow of air, and (*ii*) an obstacle to the flow, past which the air forces itself in a turbulent stream that generates the specific hissing sound of [s].

Any speech-sound that we care to examine will always exhibit these two components in some form or other namely:

(*i*) An activity (lung-deflation in the examples just studied) that *initiates* a flow of air, and is consequently called *initiation* (or 'air-stream mechanism')—the organ(s) used for this purpose being called an *initiator* (the lungs in the present case).

(*ii*) An activity that modulates or *articulates* the air-stream, thus generating a specific type of sound. The process itself is called *articulation* and the organs utilized in articulation are *articulators*.

For [f] the articulation was formed by the juxtaposition of the lower lip and the upper teeth, which thus were the articulators. For [s] the articulation was formed a little further back, by the juxtaposition of a part of the tongue, just behind its tip, and the ridge that you can feel behind the upper teeth.

> Now repeat Experiments 1 and 2 saying both [f f f f f f] and [s s s s s s] again, several times, and consciously introspecting about what the two basic components, initiation and articulation, feel like.

Figure 2 is a simplified diagram of the vocal tract, showing the locations of the two basic components of speech-production for the two sounds we have studied so far, [f] and [s]. For many other types of sound both articulation and initiation would be located elsewhere, as we shall see.

The next two experiments demonstrate that it is essential for *both* basic components to be present in order to produce a specific sound. In these experiments we first *remove the initiation* (i.e. stop the air-stream) but keep the articulation intact (Experiment 3) then *remove the articulation*, keeping the initiatory air-stream intact (Experiment 4).

Figures 3 and 4 show these processes diagrammatically. The double line labelled 'articulation' represents the juxtaposed articulating organs being held together through time. In Fig. 4 the removal of the articulation is indicated by the separation of the juxtaposed lines representing

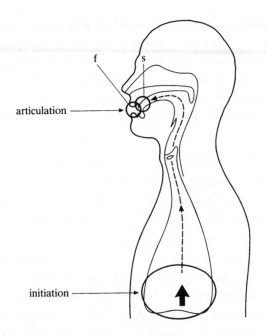

Fig. 2 Basic components of speech-sound production

articulation, disintegrating into broken lines when the articulation has thus been abolished.

The lowest line labelled 'initiation' symbolizes deflation of the lungs and resultant airflow, and in Fig. 3 the cessation of initiation is indicated by a short vertical line.

The irregular scratchy-looking line labelled 'sound' represents the hissing noise of [f] or [s]: it is, in fact, taken from an actual instrumental recording of the sound-wave of a hissing [s] sound.

Now continue with Experiments 3 and 4.

3   *Removing initiation.* Breathe in, and start saying [f f f f f f] as in Exp. 1, only this time, while carefully maintaining the lip–teeth articulatory contact,

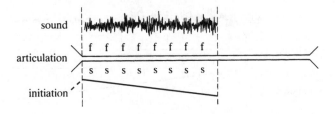

Fig. 3 Experiment 3: Remove initiation

suddenly stop breathing out—i.e. abolish the initiatory air-stream. (See Fig. 3.) Take care to retain the articulation for at least 5 seconds after you have abolished the initiation. Now repeat the experiment with an [s]-articulation. Breathe in, start up [s s s s s s] then, while carefully maintaining the [s]-articulation, suddenly abolish the initiation—i.e. stop breathing out. Retain the [s]-articulation for another 5 seconds or so after you have abolished the initiation.

In both cases it is quite clear that the moment the initiatory air-stream stops the sound of [f] or [s] ceases: there is only silence—silently held articulation.

This experiment demonstrates that both of the components, initiation and articulation, must be present to produce a sound like [f] or [s]. Remove the initiation, and, even though the articulation is still maintained, the result is silence. Incidentally, this is a first example of a procedure of very great use in the study of phonetics: the formation of *silent articulation*. As we shall see repeatedly in what follows, the production of 'silent sounds', that is, the formation of silent articulation with introspective analysis of the kinaesthetic sensations, is by far the most powerful way of learning about articulation, and we shall use it frequently.

The next experiment, 4, demonstrates a second way of breaking down a sound into its components, namely, by *abolishing articulation*.

4   *Removing articulation*. Breathe in and then start up a prolonged [f f f f f f] but, this time, suddenly abolish the articulation while taking care to keep the initiatory airflow going as long as you can. This will probably be only a very few seconds, because, when the retarding effect of the articulation is removed, the residual initiatory air flows out very rapidly.

Do the same with [s s s s s]. (See Fig. 4.)

In the case of [f f f f f f], 'abolishing the articulation' means removing the lower lip from the upper teeth. This can be done forcibly, by taking the lower lip between finger and thumb and then when the sound of [f f f f f f] is well

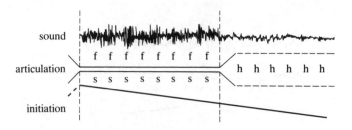

Fig. 4 Experiment 4: Remove articulation

established, suddenly pulling the lip away from the teeth, taking care to keep the air-stream going as long as possible.

Both of these experiments, 2 and 4, demonstrate that the presence of both *initiation* and *articulation* is essential for the production of the specific sounds of [f f f f f f] and [s s s s s s]. In Experiment 3, the abolition of the initiation (complete cessation of airflow) simply resulted in silence—silent maintenance of the articulatory posture. In 4, the abolition of articulation resulted, not in absolute silence, but in the immediate loss of the *specific* sound of [f f f f f f] or [s s s s s s]. For the short period of time during which airflow continued, the unmodified sound of exhalation, the non-specific hushing sound of exhaled breath, could be heard.[1] We can represent this non-specific exhalation sound by [h]: thus, the process of holding and then abolishing the articulation of [s] may be transcribed [s s s s s h h h].

The last two experiments demonstrated the necessity of both initiation and articulation by means of what may be called a process of *analysis*: resolving the production of a sound into its two component parts.

The next two experiments, 5 and 6, involve the opposite process, namely *synthesis*. We can synthesize a sound by starting with one component, and then adding the second one, and it will be clear that no specific sound is produced until we have both components in place.

5   *Adding initiation*. Synthesize a [f]-type sound by starting with the articulation (which, by itself, produces no sound) and then adding initiation (at which time the specific sound of [f] becomes audible). Breathe in, form, and hold, the articulation—that is, put the lower lip firmly against the upper teeth— then, after silently holding that articulation for a few seconds, start up the

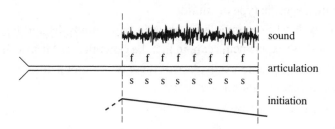

Fig. 5 Experiment 5: Add initiation

---

[1] This statement will do for the present but, as we shall see later, strictly speaking this is not the 'unmodified sound of exhalation', but, more accurately, exhalation modulated by passage through the larynx, where the turbulent flow of air generates a laryngeal, or glottal, fricative sound. (See Chap. 5.)

initiation, i.e. release the breath and let the initiatory air-stream flow pass the articulation generating the usual specific hissing sound of [f f f f f f].

Do the same experiment with [s]. Breathe in, hold breath, form, and silently hold, the [s]-articulation, release the breath and note how the addition of the initiation generates the specific sound of [s s s s s s].

In Experiment 6 we start with the initiation, and then, after the initiatory air-stream is going, we add the articulation.

6   *Adding articulation.* Breathe in. Start up the initiation, i.e. begin to exhale, and then, before you have lost too much air, suddenly place the lower lip firmly against the upper teeth: the sound of exhalation is immediately replaced by the specific sound of [f], thus: [h h h f f f f f]. (See Fig. 6.)

Repeat the same experiment with [s]: [h h h s s s s s].

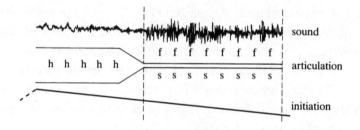

Fig. 6 Experiment 6: Add articulation

These initial experiments, 1–6, were designed to demonstrate that the production of speech-sounds requires the simultaneous presence of two basic components: *initiation*, or the production of a flow of air, and *articulation*, or the formation of some kind of obstacle that modulates the airflow to generate a specific type of sound.

So far, we have experimented with only two sounds, [f] and [s]; but the findings of these experiments can, in fact, be generalized. All speech-sounds require the simultaneous occurrence of these two components, *initiation* (or air-stream mechanism) and *articulation*.

2. Fricative and stop articulation

There are different varieties of both components: an enormous number of different varieties of articulation, and several different varieties of initiation; and we will make a detailed study of these in due course. So far, however, we have discovered only one variety of initiation (involving the exhalation of air from the lungs) and two examples of articulation, [f] and [s]. Both of these articulations involve turbulent airflow through a narrow channel, resulting in a hissing noise. This type of articulation is called *fricative*. The sounds represented by the symbols [f] and [s] are both fricatives, but they are articulated at different places. As we shall see later, articulations can be described and classified in terms of their manner of articulation, or 'type of stricture' (in this case 'fricative'), and their place of articulation within the vocal tract. Another manner of articulation—another articulatory stricture type—involves complete closure, and hence complete momentary blockage of the air-stream, with the consequence that pressure builds up behind the closure as the air tries to continue flowing. When the blockage is removed, the somewhat compressed initiatory air bursts out in a small explosion. This type of articulation is known as *stop*, and examples of stop sounds, or *stops*, are the sounds of [p], [t], [k], represented by the initial letters of *par*, *tar*, *car*. The final sounds of *lop*, *lot*, *lock* are also stops, but in the pronunciation of many English speakers, particularly in America, they differ quite noticeably from the initial stops. The difference is that, while the initial stops of *par*, *tar*, *car* are explosively released, the final stops of *lop*, *lot*, *lock* may (in some persons' speech) not be noisily or immediately released at all.

We now experiment with the production of stops, and, in order to get an insight into their nature, we start by superimposing them upon an air-stream.

7   First, silently make and release the stops [p], [t], [k] several times, and then proceed to the following experiment. Breathe in, and then start up the initiation; that is, begin to exhale through the open mouth. Very soon after the exhalation has started, and while trying to keep the exhaled air-stream going, close the lips and suddenly open them again after a very brief period of closure, and continue to exhale until the air in your lungs is exhausted. Throughout this operation you must strive to keep the initiating air-stream going all the time. Think of it as a continuous stream of initiatory air, with a stop articulation [p] momentarily superimposed on it. If this is done properly, the effect should be a slight pressure buildup behind the closed lips, so that when they are suddenly opened again a moment later there is an explosive release of the high-pressure air that had been pent up behind the stop. We can represent the process as [h h h p H h h], where the capital H represents the momentary explosive release of air. Fig. 7 indicates what is going on.

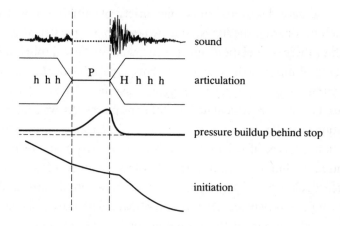

Fig. 7 Experiment 7: Superimpose stop on air-stream

Now carry out the same experiment with the stops [t] (tip of tongue making momentary contact with the ridge behind the upper teeth), and [k] (back of tongue making momentary contact with the velum or soft palate—the soft back part of the roof of the mouth): [h h h t H h h] [h h h k H h h].

In each case, strive to keep up a *continuous* initiatory effort and consequent exhalation, in order to get the feeling of the stop articulation as being a momentary closure superimposed on the air-stream.

Repeat the experiment several times, and note, of course, that you can superimpose a stop articulation on the initiatory air-stream at any point in time. Try, for instance, starting the initiation with the closure already in place. Breathe in, form the stop articulation, start the initiation, then, as pressure builds up behind the stop, suddenly release it: [p H h h h] [t H h h h] [k H h h h].

3. Pulmonic pressure and suction initiation

We have now experimented with two types of articulation: fricatives ([f] [s]) and stops ([p], [t], [k]), but still with only one type of initiation: namely, one that involves exhalation—a stream of air forced out of the lungs under pressure, and propelled up the windpipe and out through the mouth. Since it makes use of the lungs, this type of initiation is called *pulmonic*—we shall see shortly that speech-sounds can also be initiated at other places in the vocal tract. And since it involves deflation of the lungs and consequent compression of the air contained in them, it is pulmonic *pressure* initiation.

It is not at all difficult to use *inhalation* in place of exhalation as a form of initiation. To do this, we dilate the lungs, thus lowering the pressure within them and so sucking air down the windpipe and into the lungs: not surprisingly this type of initiation is called *pulmonic suction*.

8   In this experiment we initiate the air-stream by pulmonic suction. Begin this time by emptying the lungs. Now form the articulation for [f] and begin to inhale. The articulation is exactly the same as for a 'normal' [f], but this time the hissing sound of [f] is generated by air flowing from outside, through the articulatory channel into the mouth (and down the windpipe).

Repeat with [s]. Empty the lungs, form the [s]-articulation and hold it while inhaling, drawing air into the mouth and through the articulatory channel.

Now experiment with alternating pulmonic pressure and pulmonic suction initiation. There are no special phonetic symbols for pulmonic suction sounds, so we will represent them by means of an arrow pointing downwards next to the regular symbol. Thus pulmonic pressure [f] = [f], pulmonic suction [f] = [f↓].

Breathe in, start up an ordinary pulmonic pressure [f] and when the lungs are nearly empty, reverse the air-stream so that you end up making a pulmonic suction [f↓]: [f f f f . . .] [f ↓ f ↓ f ↓ . . .]. Continue alternating pressure and suction [f] [f↓].

Carry out the same experiment with pulmonic pressure [s] and pulmonic suction [s↓]: [ss] [s ↓ s↓] [ss] [s ↓ s↓] etc.

These experiments demonstrated that more than one type of initiation can be used in the production of fricatives. It is easy to discover that the same is true of stops.

9   Just as you alternated [f] [f↓] and [s] [s↓], now start alternating pulmonic pressure and suction stops. Make pulmonic pressure [pH], then close the lips again and generate pulmonic suction (i.e. attempt to inhale while the lips are closed), so that on the release of the stop air rushes into the mouth [pH↓]. Then continue to alternate: [pH] [pH↓] [pH] [pH↓] [pH] [pH↓] etc.

Now do the same with [t] and [k], i.e. alternate [tH], [tH↓] [kH] [kH↓].

If we return for a moment to Experiment 8 and produce the pulmonic pressure and suction fricatives [f] [f↓] and [s] [s↓] we get an interesting insight into the aerodynamics of fricative production.

10   As in Exp. 8, alternate pulmonic pressure and suction [f] [f↓] [f] [f↓] . . . several times. Notice that the sound generated by the suction [f↓] is very much the same as that generated by the pressure [f]. Now alternate pressure

and suction [s]: [s] [s↓] [s] [s↓] . . . several times. Notice that the sound generated by the suction [s↓] is considerably different from that generated by the pressure [s].

Experiment 10 showed that the direction of the airflow—out of the mouth (egressive) for pressure [f] and [s], into the mouth (ingressive) for suction [f↓] and [s↓]—has a noticeable effect on the hiss-sound in the case of [s], but *not* in the case of [f]. Indeed, while the pulmonic suction [f↓] sounds fairly normal, the pulmonic suction [s↓] hardly sounds like an [s] at all. Why?

The reason for this difference is easily explained, with the help of Figs. 8 and 9. Fig. 8 shows how the air-stream, whether egressive as for pressure [f]

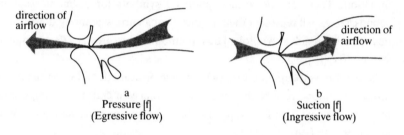

Fig. 8 Pressure and suction varieties of [f]

(8a) or ingressive as for suction [f↓] (8b), squeezes through between the teeth and lower lip and through the interstices between the teeth, becoming turbulent and noisy as it does so. But the articulatory channel through which the air squeezes is of much the same shape whichever way the air is flowing—so the turbulent airflow and the resultant hiss-sound are much the same for each direction of flow.

If we look now at Fig. 9 we see that the aerodynamic conditions are quite

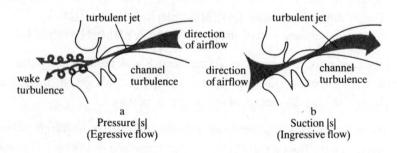

Fig. 9 Pressure and suction varieties of [s]

different. In the pulmonic pressure [s] (Fig. 9a) the egressive air-stream first squeezes through a narrow channel between the tongue and the ridge behind the upper teeth (alveolar ridge). As it passes through this channel it is accelerated, becomes turbulent ('channel turbulence'), and issues from the channel in a high-velocity turbulent jet. This jet strikes the teeth, and this imparts further turbulence to it: beyond the teeth, 'downstream' from the teeth, there is a turbulent *wake*, full of swirling movements or 'vortices'. The turbulence of the wake ('wake turbulence') contributes an additional rather high-frequency component to the hiss-noise of [s].

In the pulmonic suction [s↓] (Fig. 9b) however, the ingressive air-stream coming from outside of the mouth flows rather slowly and non-turbulently past the teeth and inwards through the narrow [s]-type articulatory channel. Once again it is accelerated as it passes through the channel, and emerges as a turbulent high-velocity jet. But this inflowing, ingressive, jet, as it shoots into the interior of the mouth, meets with no obstacle comparable to the teeth, and so acquires no additional wake turbulence. Because of the absence of wake turbulence the ingressive, pulmonic suction, [s↓], sounds noticeably different from the egressive, pulmonic pressure, [s]. (See Fig. 9a,b.)

Experiment 10 and Figs. 8 and 9 provide a simple and easily observed example of the importance of what we called in Chapter 1 the 'aerodynamic phase' in the production of speech.

We have now discovered two different forms of *initiation*. Both involve the use of the lungs and are thus called pulmonic—pulmonic pressure and pulmonic suction. But the lungs are not the only organs that can act as initiators. The pressure-change and consequent airflow necessary for speech can be initiated by other organs than the lungs.

One of the most important other initiatory organs is the *larynx*. The larynx, or 'voice-box', will be referred to again in the next chapter, where we study *phonation*. Here it will suffice to point out that the larynx is located in the throat—the front of it can be felt, and often seen, as a forward projection in the neck—the 'Adam's apple'. Within the larynx are located the vocal cords, or, more descriptively, the vocal folds—two shelves of cartilage and muscle that run from back to front, and which can be put into various positions. For the moment we need only note that the vocal folds can be quite widely separated, as in breathing, and as in the various sounds we have experimented with so far. They may also be tightly closed. Now, the space, or passage-way between the vocal folds is called the *glottis*.

Therefore, another way of putting what has just been said is to say that the *glottis* can be wide open, as in breathing, or it can be tightly closed.

We close the glottis tightly when we 'hold the breath' or when we cough. In a cough, we build up a strong pulmonic pressure below the tightly closed glottis, then release the closure explosively. If you cough, rather gently, two or three times, introspecting about what you are doing, it will be clear that a cough is a strong stop-type articulation—what is called a *glottal stop* (phonetic symbol [ʔ]). The glottis is functioning as articulator, just as the lips do in [p].

4. Glottalic initiation

We must, however, now turn to the larynx not as the locus of a type of articulation, but as an initiator. If the glottis is tightly closed, and there is at the same time a closure in the mouth, say between the back of the tongue and the soft palate (a [k]-closure), a small quantity of air will be trapped between the closed glottis and the oral closure. If, now, the larynx is slightly raised, the air trapped between the closed glottis and the oral closure will be compressed. Then, if the oral closure is suddenly released, the entrapped high-pressure air will momentarily burst forth in a short sharp explosion. Here the air-compression, and eventual airflow when the articulatory closure is released, are initiated by the larynx. The larynx is thus the initiator, and because of the importance of the glottal closure within the larynx this type of initiation is called *glottalic*: and since the larynx rises, in the initiation of this sound, and compresses the air trapped above it, this is an example of *glottalic pressure* initiation.

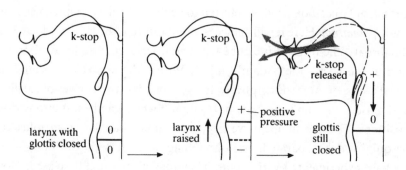

Fig. 10 Three stages in the production of glottalic pressure [k']

Figure 10 shows, somewhat schematically, three stages in the production of a glottalic pressure stop, [k']. Note that sounds with glottalic pressure initiation are indicated by an apostrophe, thus: [k'], [t'], [p'], etc.

The first step towards learning to make glottalic pressure stops is to make certain that you can tightly close your glottis and hold it closed for some time. If you are not sure if you can do this, develop it from a cough, as in Experiment 11.

11   Make a series of quiet coughs; that is, a series of glottal stops [ʔ], [ʔ], [ʔ] . . . Now, make the closure for [ʔ], but don't release it; hold it for some time. In order to make the beginning and end of the period of glottal closure clearly audible, begin with a momentary exhalation, [h], which is abruptly cut off by the closing of the glottis, thus, [hʔ]. Then release the glottal closure again into an exhalation, [ʔh]. Now produce the whole sequence again a number of times, [hʔh] [hʔh] . . . progressively increasing the duration of the [ʔ]-closure until you are sure that you are able to hold glottal closure for 5 seconds or longer.

One way of testing whether your glottis is really closed is the following. Open your mouth and make sure that your soft palate is raised, closing entry to the nose, and that your tongue is not touching the roof of the mouth at any point; there must be a clear passage from the larynx through the mouth. Now, while holding the mouth open and unobstructed in any way, close your glottis, and, keeping it closed, flick a finger against your neck either on the side of the larynx or just above it. If you do this properly you should hear a moderately clear note of a definite pitch; you can change the pitch by lip-rounding or tongue movements. If the glottis is open the clear note sounded by the tapping is replaced by a dull sound of indefinite pitch. In this way you can test whether your glottis is really closed or not. We shall find another use for this larynx-tapping later, in Chap. 8, p. 163.

Having learned to close the glottis, and to keep it closed for some time, you can proceed to the next step—learning to raise and lower the larynx at will. This is important, because in glottalic initiation it is the vertical displacement of the larynx, with the glottis closed, that compresses or rarefies the air trapped above it. The larynx acts as a piston sliding up or down in the neck.

12   To capture the sensation of raising and lowering the larynx, and to learn to do this at will, start by uttering the *highest* note you can reach, on the vowel [a] = 'ah'. Now descend very rapidly to the *lowest* note you can reach. We can symbolize this as \ [a]. Then go back up to the highest note: / [a]. Repeat this

rapidly, several times, with a finger or fingers lightly touching the neck at about the 'Adam's apple'. As you repeat / [a] \ [a] / [a] \ [a] many times you can feel your larynx shooting up and down inside your neck. The next step is to raise and lower the larynx many times *silently*. *Imagine* you are singing rapidly up and down the scale but make no sound; thus: / \ / \ / . . . While doing this, introspect about what it feels like to raise and lower your larynx. To test your ability to raise and lower the larynx, relax for a moment, then say to yourself, 'Now I'm going to raise my larynx,' and then do so, confirming that you actually are doing so by lightly touching your neck with your fingers. Repeat this, deliberately raising and lowering your larynx several times.

You now have control of all the elements of glottalic pressure (or suction) initiation—you can close your glottis, and hold it closed for a reasonably long time, you can raise and lower your larynx at will, and, of course, you can make a stop-articulation in your mouth. If you carry out the steps described in Experiment 13 you will synthesize a [k]-type stop with glottalic pressure initiation, that is [k'].

13 To synthesize glottalic pressure [k'], go carefully through the following steps.

(*i*) Tightly close the glottis and *keep it closed* (i.e. hold your breath) until the very end of the experiment (step v).

(*ii*) While keeping the glottis closed, bring the back of the tongue into firm contact with the roof of the mouth, making a [k]-closure—and hold that closure.

(*iii*) Slightly raise the larynx, compressing the air trapped between the glottal closure and the [k]-closure.

(*iv*) While maintaining glottal closure and high pressure of the trapped air, suddenly release the [k]-closure. The result should be a glottalic pressure [k'] with a short, sharp small explosion.

(*v*) Now, at last, open the glottis—which should have been held closed throughout the experiment.

Fig. 10 shows, diagrammatically, the sequence of events. Now go through the procedure several more times while looking at the diagram.

Having learned to produce a simple glottalic pressure [k'], try holding the breath for several seconds—keeping the glottis closed—and do a series of [k']s . . . [k'] [k'] [k'] on one stretch of glottal closure.

Finally, having acquired [k'], try making glottalic pressure [t'] and [p'] several times each.

In languages that use glottalic pressure stops, they are, of course, integrated into the stream of speech, and may be preceded or followed by vowel sounds. In the next experiment produce [k'] [t'] and [p'] with a vowel after them.

14 First make sure you can produce a glottalic pressure stop—if you are still uncertain about this, go back and look at Fig. 10 and repeat any of Exps. 11, 12, 13 that may be necessary.

Now, say [k'] and then when you finally open the glottis produce a vowel [a]—that is, say [k'] . . . [a], with a slight pause between them. Now reduce that pause little by little till it is as short as possible:

[k' . . . . . a] [k' . . . . a] [k' . . a] [k'a], and
[t' . . . . . a] [t' . . . . a] [t' . . a] [t'a], and
[p' . . . . . a] [p' . . . . a] [p' . . a] [p'a].

When you feel quite confident about the production of glottalic pressure stops, you might try producing some glottalic pressure fricatives. These are a little more difficult than stops because, to generate a fricative, such as [f] or [s], as we have seen, a stream of air must be forced through a narrow articulatory channel; but so little air is available for glottalic sounds (only what is trapped between the glottis and the oral articulatory channel) that the fricative channel must be very narrow indeed for the airflow to last long enough to generate a perceptible fricative hiss. However, since we are exploring all types of human speech-sounds it is worth while trying to produce glottalic pressure fricatives. Such sounds are used in several languages (for example, in the Caucasus), but more importantly, actually producing glottalic pressure fricatives illustrates certain principles rather well—such as the mechanism of fricatives and the nature and limitations of glottalic initiation.

15 Close the glottis, and while carefully keeping it tightly closed, form the articulation for [s]. Now, without opening the glottis, press upwards with the larynx (raise the larynx) and force an air-stream out through the [s]-articulation. You will find that it will last for only a very short time. To conserve the small amount of available air, and to keep the fricative sound of [s'] going for a longer time, tighten up the articulation as much as possible, so that the air is being forced through an extremely narrow channel. (Note that glottalic pressure fricatives, like glottalic pressure stops, are symbolized by an apostrophe placed after the appropriate letter, as in [s'] above.)

Now carry out the same experiment with [f']. Close the glottis and keep it tightly closed throughout the experiment. While keeping the glottis closed, form the articulation for [f']; now raise the larynx like a piston in the throat, compressing the air above it and squeezing it out through the lip–teeth articulatory channel. As with [s'] you will find that for [f'] too, you must make a particularly tight and narrow channel to keep the air flowing and the fricative hiss going for an appreciable time.

Having acquired a good [s'] and [f'] you can try adding a vowel, as with the glottalic pressure stops in Exp. 14.

So far, we have dealt only with glottalic *pressure* sounds; the stops [p'], [t'], [k'] and the fricatives [f'] and [s']. It is, of course, perfectly possible to initiate an air-stream by using glottalic *suction*. Probably the best way to do this, at first, is to alternate pressure and suction as in Experiment 16.

16 Tightly close the glottis, and keep it closed throughout the experiment. With glottis closed, produce a glottalic pressure [k']—that is, form a [k]-closure, press upwards with the larynx, and release the [k'] but *do not open the glottis*, until a second or two after the release of the [k']-stop.

Now, this time, immediately after releasing the glottalic pressure [k'], re-form the [k]-closure, and jerk the larynx *downwards* before releasing the [k]-closure. The result should be glottalic suction [k'↓]. Alternate a series of glottalic stops—pressure, suction, pressure, suction . . . keeping the glottis tightly closed throughout and alternately 'pressing up' and 'sucking down' with the larynx:

[p'] [p'↓] [p'] [p'↓] . . .
[t'] [t'↓] [t'] [t'↓] . . .

Finally, try the same experiment with glottalic pressure and suction fricatives:

[f'] [f'↓] [f'] [f'↓] . . .
[s'] [s'↓] [s'] [s'↓] . . .

5. Velaric initiation

There is one more type of initiation to be considered—one that does not use the air in the lungs, or the air trapped above the closed glottis, but only a very small quantity of air trapped in the mouth. Experiment 17 introduces this new type of initiation.

17 You are no doubt familiar with the clicking sound, expressive (in English[2]) of mild annoyance or regret, often represented in writing as 'tut tut' or, more accurately, as 'tsk tsk'. The phonetic symbol for this sound is [ǀ]. Produce a series of these sounds, rather slowly and introspectively: [ǀ], [ǀ], [ǀ] . . .

If you do this in a slow, but energetic, and thoughtful way you will notice a 'sucking' sensation located about the centre to front of the tongue, a moment before the tongue-tip breaks contact with the ridge behind the upper teeth.

Further careful observation reveals that the back of the tongue is being held up in the [k]-position, making a firm contact with the soft rear part of the roof of the mouth, which is known as the soft palate, or *velum*. Because of this tongue–velum contact, which is essential, this kind of initiation is called *velaric*—and the particular type you have just produced is *velaric suction* initiation since it involves a downward, 'sucking' movement of the centre of the tongue. Fig. 11 shows three steps in the production of a velaric suction stop [ǀ].

Having produced numerous examples of [ǀ], combine velaric suction initiation with a different articulation, namely the kind of 'clucking' sound which is used to urge on horses and which, on the analogy of 'tsk tsk' might be written 'tlk tlk'. This articulation starts with the tongue in the same position as for [ǀ], but after, or during, the 'sucking' motion of the tongue-centre the *sides* of the tongue (not the tip, which does not move) are suddenly pulled away from the molar teeth (on one or both sides) of the tongue. This sound is often called a 'lateral click' and the symbol for it is [ǁ].

Make a series of these lateral clicks, slowly, energetically, thoughtfully, and become aware of the mechanism of this velaric suction lateral sound [ǁ], [ǁ], (ǁ) . . .

Yet another type of velaric suction sound is produced by the same initiatory mechanism but is articulated at the lips. To make this sound, form the tongue–velum (k-type) closure as before, and at the same time close the lips. Now, while maintaining the k-type closure, perform the same sucking movement of the tongue as before and then release the lip-closure. The result is a 'kissing sound', symbolized by [ʘ].

The sounds you have just been experimenting with, [ǀ], [ǁ], and [ʘ], all have *velaric suction* initiation. We introduced the suction sounds first this time because, with velaric initiation the suction variety is much commoner and easier to produce than the pressure variety. Experiment 18 introduces *velaric pressure* sounds.

---

[2] In the Eastern Mediterranean and Middle East, this sound is often used as an accompaniment to a gesture (a slight backward toss of the head) meaning 'NO!'.

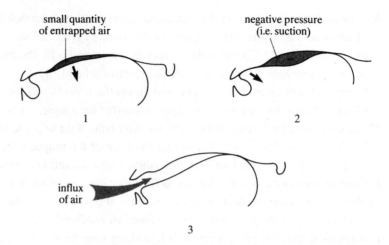

Fig. 11 Experiment 17: Three phases in the production of a velaric
suction stop (the click [ʘ])

18   Say a velaric suction [ʘ]. Now, immediately after the sucking movement of the
tongue and the release of the tongue-tip contact, *remake the contact* and
reverse the tongue-movement—that is, *press* instead of sucking—then release
the tongue-tip contact again. The result should be a velaric pressure sound,
for which there is no special symbol, so we shall represent it by [ʘ↑]. Continue
to alternate velaric suction [ʘ] and velaric [ʘ↑]: [ʘ] [ʘ↑] [ʘ] [ʘ↑] . . .

All this must be done without ever releasing the essential velaric (k-type)
initiatory closure. We will now demonstrate that velaric initiation, whether of
suction or pressure type, utilizes *only* the small amount of air trapped
between the tongue-centre and an articulatory closure further forward in the
mouth. To carry out this demonstration make a prolonged series of velaric
sounds, for example [ʘ], [ʘ], [ʘ], and while continuing to do this, breathe in and
out rather noisily through the nose. The experiment should be repeated with
hum substituted for breath. Make a series of [ʘ] sounds while uninterruptedly
humming through the nose. This proves that the velaric initiatory mechanism
is completely independent of the pulmonic air-stream—it uses *only* the air
trapped in the mouth in front of the velaric closure.

In this chapter we have done two things. First, we have established that there
are two basic components essential for the production of speech-sounds.
These are *initiation*—an activity that generates positive or negative pressure
in the vocal tract and thus initiates an air-stream—and *articulation*—an
activity that modulates the air-stream and thus generates a specific type of
sound. We shall study all possible types of articulation in a later chapter.

Secondly, we have discovered all the types of initiation normally used in speech. We have found that airflow can be initiated by the lungs (*pulmonic*), or the larynx, which contains the glottis (*glottalic*), and by the tongue, with a firm closure at the velum, or soft palate (*velaric*). The direction of the initiatory movement may be one that generates positive pressure and initiates an outgoing or *egressive* airflow (*pressure*), or one that generates negative pressure and initiates an inflowing, or *ingressive*, airflow (*suction*).

The terms *pressure* and *suction* refer to the immediate *result* of the initiatory movement, while *egressive* and *ingressive* refer to the *direction* of airflow through the mouth. The terms are virtually interchangeable. It is only with respect to voiced implosives (see pp. 47–49) that there might be some ambiguity, for in these, which are clearly 'suction' sounds, there is a slight *egressive* flow through the larynx, but an *ingressive* flow into the mouth.

6. Review of initiation types

The six types of initiation are summed up in Table 1.

The italicized names are those of initiation types that are regularly used in the languages of the world. Special names are sometimes given to stop-type articulations with these types of initiation, as follows:

Pulmonic pressure (egressive) stops: by far the commonest type, also known as *plosives*.
Glottalic pressure (egressive) stops: also known as *ejectives*, or as 'glottalized' stops, though this is a misleading name and should be avoided (misleading because the '-ized' form of the adjective suggests that the glottal component of the sound is merely a secondary articulation (cf. p. 101) rather than an essential feature of the initiation of the sound).

Table 1

Location of initiators	Direction	
	Compressive	Rarefactive
Lungs	*Pulmonic pressure*	Pulmonic suction
Closed glottis	*Glottalic pressure*	*Glottalic suction*
Tongue (with velar closure)	Velaric pressure	*Velaric suction*

Glottalic suction (ingressive) stops: particularly the voiced variety (described in the next chapter pp. 47–49) known as *implosives*.
Velaric suction (ingressive) stops: known as *clicks*.

Pulmonic pressure initiation is by far the commonest type of initiation in the languages of the world; in most languages it is the only type of initiation used, as in English. Even in those languages which use other types of initiation, pulmonic pressure is the most-used type.

Pulmonic suction initiation is not regularly used in any normal language. It can, however, occasionally be heard. Thus, in English the word *no* is sometimes pronounced on inhalation—i.e. with pulmonic suction. When *yes* is pronounced in approximately the same way only *ye-* is spoken on pulmonic suction, pulmonic pressure initiation being resumed on the *-s*. Pulmonic suction initiation is used occasionally to disguise the voice: I have heard Greek spoken with pulmonic suction initiation for precisely this purpose by disguised mummers on a feast-day in a village in Cyprus.

Glottalic pressure sounds (ejectives), though not normally used in English, are quite common in the languages of the world. They occur in many American Indian languages; for example the glottalic pressure [k'] in the Navaho words [k'ad] 'now', [k'ai] 'willow'. They also occur in all the languages of the Caucasus—the best known of which is Georgian, the language of the Republic of Georgia. They are found, too, in many African languages, including Hausa in Nigeria, and some varieties of Swahili in East Africa, and in various languages of the Far East.

The glottalic suction stops that were introduced in Experiment 16 are very rare in the languages of the world. But another type of glottalic suction stops—known as *voiced implosive*—is not uncommon in African languages, some American Indian languages, and some languages of South and South-east Asia. They will be described in the next chapter, in which we introduce a third important component in the production of many sounds.

Clicks are widespread as interjectional noises, marginal to language. As regular sounds, entering into the phonetic structure of words, they occur only in a few languages of southern Africa, namely Bushman, Hottentot, Zulu, Xosa. In the last language-name, the initial X represents a lateral click.

7. Initiator velocity, and initiator power (stress)

Before we leave the topic of initiation, we should take note of the fact that the effort or *power* exerted by any of the initiators can be varied over a wide range. The deflation of the lungs, for example, that generates pulmonic pressure initiation can take place either gently and slowly, or vigorously and rapidly. Experiment 19*i* and *ii* examines this difference.

19   Have a stop-watch, or any watch that shows seconds, available.

(*i*) Take in a deep breath so that your lungs are comfortably full. Form the articulation for a fricative, for example [s], and then start up a relatively slow and gentle initiation—that is, let the lungs slowly deflate without forcing at all, and note the starting time of the initiatory action. Continue the slow initiation as long as you can, noting the time when the flow ceases. The total duration of the flow is likely to be of the order of 5 to 7 seconds.

(*ii*) Now take in a similar breath—i.e. fill your lungs as before, form [s], and then perform an energetic *forceful* exhalation—a powerful initiator action that forces the air rapidly out of the lungs, timing as before. The chances are that the duration of the flow will be about half what it was the first time.

Since you started with the lungs about equally full, it is clear that the initiatory air-stream was being forced out about twice as fast the second time.

As you were carrying out Experiment 19 you would observe that the *sound* of [s] the second time (*ii*), generated by a faster airflow, was *louder* than the sound of the first [s]. You clearly had to use more energy to push the air out faster for the second [s]. What you were doing was propelling a stream of air through a narrow channel (the [s]-articulation) at (*i*) a low velocity and (*ii*) a high velocity. The articulatory channel was about the same size in each case, and hence offered about the same resistance to flow. To drive the air at a *high* velocity required more *power* than to drive it at a *low* velocity against the same resistance. So what you experienced in Experiment 19 was a difference of *initiator power*. In this case, the initiator was the lungs, but analogous variations in initiator power are possible with the other initiators. Thus, in glottalic pressure initiation it is possible to vary the speed and extent of the upward larynx movement. In the case of glottalic pressure stops (ejectives) like [k'] or [t'] the initiator is driving air against a total obstruction—the oral articulatory closure. As the larynx rises, the volume of the space between the closed glottis and the articulatory closure decreases and consequently the air pressure rises. The higher the larynx moves the higher the pressure, and, consequently, the greater the resistance to the initiatory movement, and—as a result—the greater the *power* required to raise the larynx.

20 Produce two glottalic egressive [k'] sounds—one with little initiatory power (*i*), the second with considerable initiator power (*ii*).

(*i*) Close the glottis (and carefully keep it closed throughout what follows); form a [k]-type articulatory closure; slightly raise the larynx, using little force, and release the [k]-closure, producing a weak ejective [k']—finally, open the glottis.

(*ii*) Close the glottis (and keep it closed throughout); form a [k]-type closure; strongly and energetically raise the larynx (generating rather high pressure behind the closure); release the [k]-closure producing a strong and rather noisy ejective [k']—finally, open the glottis.

Repeat this with other articulatory closures, i.e. with [t'] and [p'], noting in each case what it feels like and sounds like to initiate them first gently, and then vigorously—that is, with low initiator power and with high initiator power.

So the concept of differences in initiator power applies equally well to glottalic initiation and to pulmonic initiation. In Experiment 21 those who have acquired the ability to produce ejective fricatives (e.g. [s'] [f']) can see how they, too, can be produced with greater or lesser initiator power. If you still have difficulty with glottalic pressure fricatives, go back to Experiment 15.

21 (*i*) Close glottis and keep it closed throughout. Form the articulation for [s']. Slowly and gently raise the larynx, producing a glottalic pressure [s'] lasting for as long as you can continue to drive air out through the narrow articulatory channel—which, even at low velocity, will be only a second or less. Note the rather quiet hiss-noise of this [s'] produced with low initiator power.

(*ii*) Repeat the experiment, but this time with high initiator power, i.e. close glottis, form the [s']-articulation, energetically and rapidly raise the larynx driving the air out at a high velocity. Note that the hiss-sound of this [s'], produced with high initiator power, is much louder than that of the first, low-powered [s'].

Experiment in the same way with [f'].

It is easy to see that variations in initiator power can also be applied to velaric initiation. Without formal experimentation, pronounce a series of velaric suction sounds, for example, the 'tut-tut' click [ǀ], with greater or lesser energy, pulling down the tongue-centre with greater or less force, in creating the vacuum that precedes the release of the tongue articulation for [ǀ]. Here, again, we are dealing with an initiator moving at lower or higher velocity against a resistance, imposed, in this case, by the negative pressure (the partial vacuum generated by its own movement) and hence with different degrees of initiator power.

Initiator power, the degree of force exerted by an initiator in driving air against resistance, is the mechanical equivalent of what is called *stress* in phonetics. The term 'stress', however, is most commonly applied only to variations in *pulmonic pressure* initiation—although, as we have seen, exactly the same type of power-variation can occur with the other initiation types. A strongly stressed syllable (or, simply, a 'stressed syllable') is one produced with high pulmonic pressure initiator power. A weakly stressed syllable (or, simply, an 'unstressed syllable') is one produced with low pulmonic pressure initiator power.

Stress is one of the so-called *prosodic* features of speech, and will be discussed again in Chapter 9 where we will note some ambiguities in the term 'stress' as it is used in the description of languages.

Initiation is responsible, in part, for yet another feature of speech, namely, the *syllable*. This, too, we will take up in Chapter 9.

3

Phonation: A Third Basic Component

1. Voiceless and voiced fricatives

In Chapter 2, we established the existence of two basic components of speech production: *initiation* and *articulation*.

These essential components can be formally defined as follows:

Initiation: a bellows-like, or piston-like, movement of an organ, that generates positive or negative air pressure adjacent to it in the vocal tract and thus initiates an egressive (outgoing) or ingressive (ingoing) flow of air.

Articulation: an organic posture or movement—most commonly in the mouth—that modulates the initiatory airflow in such a way as to generate a sound of some specific type.

As we have pointed out, these two components are essential—without them no specific sound can be produced. In addition to these essential components, however, very many sounds have a *third* basic component that modulates their quality in certain ways. This third component of speech production is called *phonation*, and as usual we shall approach it experimentally.

22 Start by going back to the very first experiment—fill the lungs and then produce a prolonged [f f f f f . . .] sound. As we now know, this sound has two components—pulmonic pressure initiation, and an [f]-type articulation.

Now, instead of [f f f f f . . .], make a prolonged [v v v v v . . .]. That is a prolonged version of the initial sound of *Vera* or *vine*. Breathe in, and start it up, taking care to make a very vigorous and loud prolonged [v], thus: [v v v v v v . . .].

As you introspect about this you should observe that (*i*) the articulation of

[v] is exactly the same as that of [f]—lower lip against upper teeth, and (*ii*) the initiation of [v] is exactly the same as that of [f]—pulmonic pressure.

But there is an obvious difference in sound: the prolonged [f] is simply a long drawn out hissing sound: but the prolonged [v] is a long drawn out *buzzing* sound. If you listen carefully, you may observe that in [v] the hiss of [f] is still there, virtually unchanged, but that a *buzz* is added to it.

Carry out the same experiment with [s] and then with a prolonged, strong buzzing [z] as in *zero*: [s s s s s . . .] [z z z z z . . .].

Once again, as you introspect about what you are doing you will observe that the initiation and articulation of [z] are exactly the same as those of [s]. The only difference is that in [z] something is *added* that is not present in [s]— namely that same buzzing sound that was present in [v] but absent in [f]. To get a more dramatic impression of the difference between these pairs of sounds, put your hands tightly over your ears so that you cannot hear the sounds in the normal way, by air-conduction, but only 'inside your head' by bone-conduction.

Now, with the ears shut in this way first say [f f f f f] and [s s s s s], then [v v v v v] and [z z z z z]. You cannot fail to notice the strong buzzing sound that is added to [v] and [z], but absent in [f] and [s].

That strong buzzing sound that you hear with [v] and [z] is called *voice*, and we call [v] and [z] *voiced* sounds, while [f] and [s] are *voiceless*. Both *voiced* and *voiceless* are types of *phonation*: and the sound of voice is produced by the vibration of the *vocal cords* or (more descriptively) the *vocal folds*, inside the larynx—which, of course, is why the larynx is often called the *voice-box*.

23   Now alternate [f f f v v v f f f v v v f f f . . .] and [s s z z z s s z z . . .], that is, maintain the [f]- or [s]-type articulation firmly in place throughout, and keep the pulmonic pressure initiation going steadily throughout, but 'switch on' voice, then switch it off again, on again . . . and so on. In doing this, vigorously, but deliberately and introspectively, you will get the feeling that *phonation* (*voice* and *voicelessness*) constitutes a *third*, independently controllable component of sound-production. It is essential to acquire precise conscious control of this component—the ability to add or subtract *voice* to or from virtually any sound.

What you are doing when you alternate between voiceless and voiced phonation is changing the *set* of the glottis. The glottis, you will recall from Chapter 2, is the space between the vocal folds. In producing voiceless fricatives like [f] or [s] the glottis is wide open, so that the initiatory air-stream can flow through freely: when you 'switch on voice', you bring the vocal folds together, narrowing the glottis so that the air-stream sets the vocal folds rhythmically vibrating—rapidly opening and shutting and thus letting the air go through in a series of regularly recurring little puffs that we hear as the buzzing sound, or *tone*, of voice. Fig. 12 represents what was happening in Experiment 23—which it would be well to repeat while looking at the figure. Fig. 12 is similar to earlier figures (Figs. 3–6) in that it represents initiation, articulation, and the resultant sound—but it also includes *phonation*—indicating the open and vibrating states of the glottis. The noisy hiss-sound of the voiceless fricative is represented by the irregular scratchy line (as in Figs. 3–6) while the buzz or tone generated by the vibrating vocal folds is represented by a regularly recurring ('periodic' is the technical term) wave-form, with the irregular ('aperiodic') fricative hiss-noise superimposed upon it.

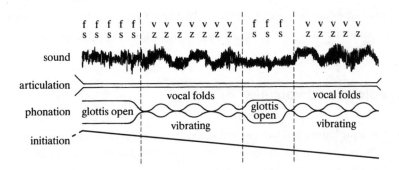

Fig. 12 Experiment 23: Voiceless and voiced fricatives

Both representations of the sound—the scratchy irregular hiss and the more regular wave with fricative hiss superimposed on it—are taken from instrumental recordings of the sound of actual voiceless and voiced fricatives.

To test your control of phonation—your control of the ability to produce voiceless or voiced sounds at will—experiment with various other articulations.

24 Isolate the *sh* sound at the beginning or end of such words as *shop* and *push*. The phonetic symbol for this voiceless fricative is [ʃ]. Say a prolonged [ʃ ʃ ʃ ʃ . . .] and, while rigidly maintaining the articulation and keeping the initiation going, suddenly switch on *voice*. In other words say [ʃ ʃ ʃ ʒ ʒ ʒ ʒ], the long [ʒ] being the symbol for the voiced counterpart of [ʃ].

Now alternate, changing nothing but the phonation: [ʃ ʃ ʒ ʒ ʃ ʃ ʒ ʒ ʃ ʃ . . .].

Next produce a voiceless fricative by bringing the back of your tongue close to the velum (the soft palate), at about the place of articulation of [k], but without actual closure. This is the sound of *ch* in Scots *Loch*, German *ach* (phonetic symbol [x]). If you are not familiar with these words the strong noisy voiceless fricative at the end of the expletive of disgust *yecch!* will do for the present.

Now say a prolonged [x]—and, while rigidly maintaining the articulatory posture of the tongue, suddenly switch on voice (the symbol for the voiced version of [x] is [ɣ]): [x x x x x ɣ ɣ ɣ ɣ . . .].

Now alternate [x x ɣ ɣ x x ɣ ɣ x x ɣ ɣ . . .]. Remember—in going from [x] to [ɣ] and back again, make absolutely no changes except in the phonation.

In Experiment 24 we derived voiced fricatives from voiceless ones. In 25 we discover some new or unfamiliar sounds by *devoicing*—replacing voice by voicelessness. The voiceless sounds we are about to discover have no specific symbols: they are represented by the symbols for the voiced sounds with a small circle beneath them [̥], reminiscent of the open glottis.

2. Voiced and voiceless *m n l r*

25 Say a prolonged [m] like the initial and final sounds of *mum*: [m m m m . . .].

Notice that in the articulation of [m] there is complete closure at the lips, but the soft palate is lowered so that air is flowing out through the nose. Note also that a normal [m] is voiced. You can detect this very clearly by closing your ears—as in Exp. 22—while saying [m m m . . .]. While carefully maintaining the articulation for [m] (the closed lips and lowered soft palate) and carefully and vigorously maintaining the initiation, suddenly 'switch off voice'—i.e. open the glottis: [m m m m m̥ m̥]. When they first try this experiment some people simply stop the initiation (i.e. stop breathing) when they change from voiced [m] to voiceless [m̥]. It is important not to do this. You must keep the initiator vigorously going throughout, so that when you switch from voiced [m] to voiceless [m] you can hear the air-stream flowing noisily, but voicelessly, out of the nose for a second or two: [m m m m m̥ m̥ m̥ m̥].

Try the same experiment with n: [n n n n̥ n̥ n̥].

Voiceless nasal consonants like [m̥] and [n̥] do not regularly occur in English, though they are perfectly normal sounds in some other languages, such as Burmese. There are, however, some exclamations or occasional utterances containing [m] used by English speakers. One of these is the exclamation [m̩m̩'m], with strong stress (marked by preceding ') on the last part—a kind of indignant *hm*. Another is the sequence ['mm̩m], stressed on the first or second [m], sometimes written as *mphm*, meaning 'yes'.

26   Now experiment with devoicing [l] and [r] sounds. Begin by isolating the [l] of *Lee* or *leaf*. Incidentally, we have up to now taken it for granted that the reader can isolate a sound from a word in which it is normally produced, but it may be helpful to say something about this. To isolate the [l] of these words, say the word normally several times; then several more times *lengthening* the initial sound, but taking care to keep it otherwise *exactly the same* as it was in the word as pronounced normally. Next, say this somewhat lengthened [l] but merely *imagine* the rest of the word.

Now say a prolonged [l], which you will clearly hear to be voiced, and, while rigidly maintaining the [l]-articulation and keeping the initiatory air-stream going suddenly switch off voice: [l l l l l̥ l̥ l̥].

Do this several times, and then pronounce voiceless [l] by itself. A voiceless [l] occurs in many types of English, after [p] and [k] in such words as *play* and *clay*. Experiment with these words and you will probably observe that this is so. If you say the words *pay* and *Kay* you will notice that there is a slight puff of breath, a brief moment of voicelessness, after the release of the stop before the voicing of the vowel begins: this is called *aspiration* and sounds with this puff of breath after them are *aspirated*. When an [l] follows the [p] or [k] the aspiration is carried over into the [l], which thus becomes partially voiceless [l̥ l]. Note that voiceless stops in the English of Scotland and the North of England are usually unaspirated: so the [l] of *play* and *clay* may be fully voiced in these varieties of English.

The best-known example of a language regularly using voiceless [l] is Welsh. This is the pronunciation of *ll* in Welsh, as in the place-name Llangollen. In fact, the Welsh *ll* is not strictly the voiceless counterpart of English *l*. The Welsh sound has a narrower articulatory channel, usually at only one side of the tongue. This unilateral Welsh [l̥] is a 'voiceless lateral fricative', for which there is a special symbol [ɬ]. See if, by squeezing your tongue out sideways into the cheeks, you can turn the rather weak [l̥] you have been making into a noisy fricative [ɬ], and then say [ɬangɔɬen] for Llangollen.

27   Experiment with one or more varieties of r-sound—a trilled [r], such as is commonly used in Italian and in the popular (but erroneous) conception of Scottish English, or an untrilled (fricative or approximant) *r* for which we may use the symbol [ɹ], such as is used in most types of English. For

convenience I will here use the symbol [r] for either or both of these. Say a prolonged [r]: [r r r r . . .], and note that it is voiced. Now do the same thing, but switch off voice (open the glottis) in the middle—carefully maintaining the articulation and initiation: [r r r r r r r̥ r̥ r̥ r̥ r̥ r̥].

Now alternate voiced and voiceless [r]: [r r r̥ r̥ r r r̥ r̥ r r r̥ r̥ r r r̥ r̥ r . . .], etc.

Note that in most types of English an [r] following aspirated [p] [t] [k] is partly voiceless; thus, *pray*, *tray*, and *cray* begin with [p r̥ r-], [t r̥ r-], [k r̥ r-].

3. Voiced and voiceless vowels

It is not only rather obviously *consonantal* sounds like [f], [s], [r], etc. that can be made voiced or voiceless; the same distinction also applies to *vowels*, as Experiment 28 shows.

28   Say the word *see*, then isolate and prolong the vowel [i], thus [s i i] [s i i i i] [i i i i i]. Note that this sound is voiced. Now start up a prolonged [i i i i i . . .]. Stop the initiation—stop breathing—but deliberately hold the articulation of the [i i] and introspect about it. You should feel that your tongue is bunched up in the front of your mouth, the sides of the tongue being pressed against the upper teeth from the molars at least as far forward as the canines.

Now that you are clear about what [i] feels like, start again: take a deep breath, start up a prolonged [i i i . . .] and while taking care to keep the initiation going and rigidly keeping the articulation in place, suddenly open the glottis, switch off voice, keeping everything else constant: [i i i i i i̥ i̥ i̥]. This sound [i] is very similar to the 'voiceless palatal fricative' [ç] used in such German words as ich [iç].

What are often called 'voiceless vowels' (although they may actually be whispered) occur in such languages as Cheyenne, Comanche, Malagasy and Portuguese.

4. The three components: Initiation, articulation, and phonation

It is now clear that there are three important components in the production of speech-sounds: *initiation, articulation*, and *phonation*. Just as we could break down, or analyse, and synthesize sounds by removing or adding the two basic components in Experiments 3–6, so we can do similar things with these *three* components. Thus we can start by silently forming an articulation—then add initiation, then add voice: or we can set the glottis for voice then add initiation: or we can start with a fully formed voiced sound, e.g. [z], then remove first voice then initiation or first articulation then voice . . . etc. Experiment 29 carries out several such operations.

29 Start by repeating Exp. 4 (the removal of articulation, keeping the initiatory air-stream going)—thus [f f f f h h h h] [s s s s h h h h]. Having reminded yourself of what it feels like to abolish articulation while keeping initiation going strongly, try the same experiment with a voiced fricative—[v v v]. This time, when you suddenly remove the articulation (if necessary, gripping the lower lip between finger and thumb and forcibly removing it from the upper teeth) carefully keep *both* initiation and phonation going. When the articulation is removed, but both the other components are still active, the result will not be the [h h h] that resulted in Exp. 4, but a vowel-like sound that we can represent as [ə ə ə], thus [v v v v ə ə ə].

Now carry out some further experiments, adding and subtracting components in various orders, e.g.:

Breathe in, then hold the breath, silently forming an [f]-articulation: hold the articulation for a few seconds, then start up pulmonic pressure *initiation*—immediately the fricative sound of [f] is heard. Keep initiation going, then suddenly switch on *voice* (phonation). Maintain voice [v] for a few seconds, then remove the articulation, leaving simply voice [ə], finally, relax the vocal folds, switching to simple voiceless and unarticulated breath [h].

The whole sequence may be represented as [(silent f f f) f f f v v v ə ə ə h h h]. Repeat the sequence, and then try some others, e.g. [v v v f f f h h h ə ə ə v v v] [h h h ə ə ə v v v f f f].

Carry out the same experiments with [s] and [z] and with [ʃ] and [ʒ] in place of [f] and [v].

If you carried out the sequence in Experiment 29 carefully and introspectively you should now have a clear idea, based on actual *experience*, of what it means to produce unarticulated voiceless initiation [h]; to add articulation [f]; to add voice [v]; to remove articulation leaving only initiation and phonation [ə], and so on. In short, you should have a solid understanding of the basic components of speech-production—*initiation*, *articulation*, and *phonation*—and how they may be combined in order to produce various types of sound.

5. The production of voiced stops

Up to this point we have experimented with voiceless and voiced fricatives, [f] and [v], [s] and [z], and [x] and [ɣ], etc., and a few other voiceless and voiced pairs, such as [m] and m̥], [l] and [l̥], [i] and [i̥]. We have not, however, experimented with voiced stops, that is, sounds like [b], [d], [g]. In order to do this we shall begin by superimposing the stops [p], [t], [k] on a voiceless pulmonic pressure air-stream.

30   (*i*) Superimpose [p] upon pulmonic pressure initiation, as in Exp. 7. Fill the lungs, start up the initiation then, while the air is flowing out [h h h], suddenly close the lips for a moment, [p], then release them. In doing this, try to keep the initiation going throughout—i.e. keep up the pulmonic pressure without any relaxation right through the moment when the lips are closed. If you do this, there will, of course, be a buildup of pressure behind the lips during the short period of their closure, and a consequent explosive release of air when the lip-closure is released—represented here by H: thus [h h h p H h h h]. Fig. 7 indicates what is happening. Do the same thing with [h h h t H h h h] [h h h k H h h h].

(*ii*) The next step is to see what happens when you carry out exactly the same operation, except that you substitute *voice* for the voicelessness of (*i*). This time, breathe in, start up initiation with the glottis set for *voice*, produce a prolonged [ə ə ə ə ə], but momentarily superimpose lip-closure upon the voiced air-stream, taking care to *keep the voice going throughout*: [ə ə ə b ə ə ə].

Here again, there will be a momentary buildup of pressure in the mouth behind the [b]-closure, and an explosive release into voice when the closure is broken. The important thing is to *contrive to keep the voice going* throughout: do not let it cease to sound during the period of lip-closure.

Listening to yourself (by normal air-conduction) while you repeatedly say [ə ə ə b ə ə ə] you will observe that the sound of voice which is quite loud during [ə ə ə], is somewhat muted during the moment when the lips are closed—but it must not cease during that time.

Now say [ə ə ə b ə ə] several times *with the ears closed*. Listening in this way, by bone-conduction, you will observe that the sound of voice suddenly gets *louder* during the moment of lip-closure. If this does not happen you are doing something wrong, probably allowing the voicing to stop during the articulatory closure of [b], thus turning it into a *voiceless* stop, a variety of [p].

Do the same thing with [ə ə ə d ə ə ə] [ə ə ə g ə ə], striving in every case to keep the voice going throughout—particularly during the stop.

If Experiment 30*ii* was carried out correctly, the sound produced in the middle of the stretch [ə ə ə . . . ə ə ə] should have been a fully voiced stop [b] [d] [g]. In each case, however, the stop was a very short one—that is, the closure was maintained for a very short period of time. In the next experiment, the duration of the stop will be increased, but voicing must continue throughout.

31 (*i*) Say [ə ə ə b ə ə ə], as before, with voicing going on continuously, right through the stop. Now try and *prolong* the period of closure while *keeping the voice going throughout*: [ə ə b ə ə] [ə ə b b ə ə] [ə ə b b b ə ə] (where [b] [b b] [b b b] represent *short* and then longer and longer [b]-articulations).

Check by closing your ears and listening by bone-conduction to see that voicing goes on *throughout* the stop.

Do the same with [ə ə d ə ə] [ə ə d d ə ə] [ə ə d d d ə ə] and [ə ə g ə ə] [ə ə g g ə ə] [ə ə g g g ə ə].

(*ii*) Now produce *initial* fully voiced [b]. As a guide to what to do, first say [v ə ə ə] with strongly voiced [v]. That is, take in a breath, form the [v]-articulation, get the glottis set for voice, then start up the glottalic pressure initiation. Voicing should start immediately and continue through the [v] and on into the [ə ə ə].

Now try it with [b]. Take a breath, form the [b]-articulation, get the glottis set for voice, and start up the initiation, saying [b ə ə ə], making absolutely sure that the voicing starts while the lips are still closed for the [b]. Do the same with [d ə ə] [g ə ə].

You may find it difficult to make fully voiced stops, that is, stops like [b] [d] [g], particularly the lengthened ones introduced in Experiment 31*i*. If you experiment assiduously with voiced stops, you will find that if you maintain a tight stop closure, as for [b], then no matter how hard you try you cannot keep the voicing going during the closure of the stop for more than a fraction of a second. You will find that the initiation, and the voicing, come to a stop very quickly. The reason for this becomes obvious if we look at the aerodynamics of a voiced stop.

Figure 13 shows a diagrammatic representation of the vocal tract, as a kind of bent tube, closed at the bottom by the lungs, which are contracting to force air up the windpipe. Some distance above the lungs is the larynx, within which are the vocal folds. When they are vibrating to produce voice,

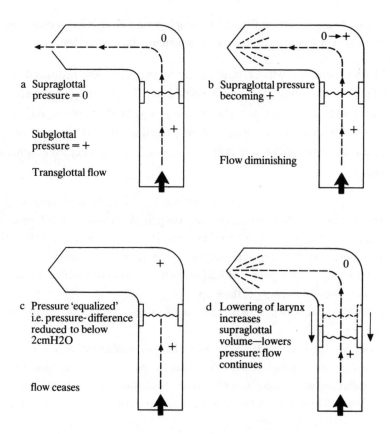

Fig. 13 Aerodynamics of a voiced stop

this is indicated by a wavy line. Above that, the tube bends into a horizontal position, to simulate the mouth, which can be closed by the lips, which are shown in Fig. 13a as separated to allow air to flow out of the mouth.

Figure 13a represents [ə ə ə], the lungs are contracting, raising the air pressure (+) below the glottis. The pressure above is pretty much atmospheric, represented by (0), so the air can easily flow from the high-pressure zone (+) below the glottis, up through the glottis, where it sets the folds vibrating as it passes through, into the low-pressure zone (0) above the glottis.

In Fig. 13b the lips have closed (for [b]), and as more and more air pours upwards into the mouth but cannot get out (because of the closed lips), the pressure above the glottis rises (0 → +), until, in Fig. 13c, it comes to equal—or nearly equal—pressure below the glottis. At this point, of course, flow through the glottis ceases, the vocal folds cease to vibrate, and voicing stops.

All this happens in a moment, and this is why it is difficult to maintain the voicing in a stop for more than a fraction of a second; difficult, but not impossible. Our study in Fig. 13 of the aerodynamics of a voiced stop suggests how voicing *can* be maintained for a longer period. We have to maintain the pressure-drop across the glottis for a longer time, and we can do this in one or both of two ways. One, we can increase the pulmonic initiatory activity, to increase the sub-glottal pressure; two, we can increase the volume of the cavity above the glottis so that the pressure will not build up there so quickly. The second, in fact, is the strategy that appears to be generally adopted in languages that demand full and somewhat prolonged voicing of stops. It is done by slightly *lowering the larynx* and possibly also enlarging the cavities above the glottis in other ways, such as expanding the pharynx (the space behind the mouth immediately above the larynx), and puffing out the cheeks (an expedient that is not available for [g], where the articulatory stricture is too far back, and scarcely available for [d]).

Figure 13 shows the larynx being lowered, so that the pressure above the larynx is again reduced to about zero, but gradually increasing $(0 \rightarrow +)$. The supraglottal pressure is low enough for flow through the glottis (and consequent voicing) to continue for a short time. In the next experiment, 32, we put this into practice.

32 While looking at Fig. 13 try once again to produce a [b] with lengthened closure—in fact [b b]—in [ə ə b b ə ə]. Proceed exactly as in Exp. 31*i* but this time, the moment the [b] closure is made, *start to lower the larynx*, and see how long you can keep voice going, while keeping the articulatory closure for [b] tightly in place. If you have forgotten how to lower your larynx go back to Exp. 12 in Chap. 2.

Now experiment with producing long [b], long [d].

We must remember that when we speak of a *voiced stop* (in a general phonetic context such as the present one) we mean a stop that has the vocal folds vibrating *during the entire closed phase* of the stop, just as a voiced fricative is one that has the vocal folds vibrating during the entire duration of the fricative stricture. Fig. 14 indicates, diagrammatically, the difference between voiceless and voiced fricatives and stops, flanked by a vowel-like [ə ə] sound.

It was necessary to emphasize that a voiced stop is one with voicing continuing throughout the closed phase especially for the benefit of readers in whose native language what are often *called* 'voiced stops' are partially or

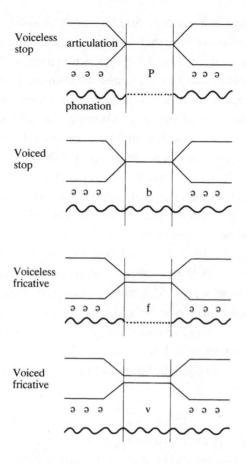

Fig. 14 Voiceless and voiced stop and fricative

completely voiceless. This is true, for example, of English, where in a word like *baby* the short medial [b] may be fully voiced, but in the initial [b] there may be no voicing at all during the closed phase, or the voicing may start only about one hundredth of a second (one centisecond, or 1 cs.) before the lip-closure is released. This contrasts with languages like French, where 'voiced stops' are truly, and fully, voiced, and in initial [b] the voicing may start as much as 10 cs. before the release of the closure. In English, final 'voiced stops', too, are generally only partly voiced. Thus, the final stops of such words as *ebb, Ed, egg,* may be almost completely voiceless, so that these words could be transcribed [e b̥] [e d̥] [e g̥], or [e b₀] [e d₀] [e g₀], where the 'voiceless diacritic' [₀] is offset a little to indicate that it is only the final part of the stop that is voiceless.

Readers can convince themselves of the near-voicelessness of English *b, d*, and *g* by saying such words as *bay day gay*, *bore door gore*, *buy die guy* and *ebb Ed egg*, *lab lad lag*, *dub dud dug*, with the ears covered in the manner described in Experiment 22 so that any voicing that is present during the closed phase of the stops is heard as a loud buzzing inside the head.

Readers whose native language is Chinese (Mandarin and most other major dialects) will find, by carrying out the same experiment, that the sounds represented by *b d g* in the Pinyin spelling system of their language are totally voiceless. They differ from *p t k* only in terms of *aspiration*, which we discuss below (p. 55).

Speakers of languages such as English and Chinese, which have no fully voiced stops initially and finally, should try to produce them as in Experiment 32.

6. Voiced implosives

If the larynx-lowering manœuvre carried out in Experiment 32 is performed in a particularly energetic manner, and if, at the same time, the pulmonic pressure is much reduced or entirely suppressed, then what started out as an attempt at a pulmonic pressure voiced stop may end up as a glottalic suction voiced stop, a *voiced implosive*.

Figure 15 shows an ideal voiced implosive. The initiatory movement that manipulates the air pressure in the vocal tract is the downward thrust of the

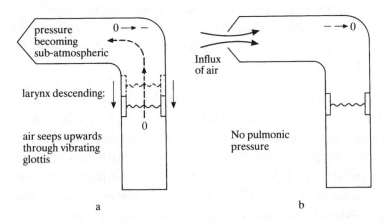

Fig. 15 Mechanism of voiced glottalic suction stop (voiced implosive)

larynx, with glottis set for voice. The downward larynx movement enlarges the space above the glottis, suddenly lowering the pressure there to below the atmospheric pressure. Since the lungs are inactive, there is little pressure below the larynx (0), but the pressure above the larynx is very low (−), and because the vocal folds are not tightly closed, but set for voice, a small amount of air seeps upward through the glottis into the vacuum above it, setting the vocal cords vibrating in the process. But this upward seepage of air, though enough to produce voice, is not sufficient to fill up the enlarged space above the glottis. Consequently, when the oral closure is suddenly released, the air pressure in the mouth is lower than atmospheric pressure, and as a result there is a momentary *influx* of air into the mouth.

This type of sound is called a *glottalic suction* stop (symbols ɓ, ɗ, ɠ) because the essential air-pressure change that initiates the sound is caused by the sudden downward movement of the larynx, and the effect of this is to generate negative pressure (suction) in the air trapped between the glottis and the oral closure.

Now that you understand the mechanism of voiced glottalic suction stops ('voiced implosives') you can experiment with producing them.

33 Close the lips and while keeping them closed, jerk the larynx downwards, trying to produce voice at the same time. Remember that the lungs do not participate in this type of initiation, so try to keep the chest fixated—the lungs inactive. If you suddenly open the lips just before the larynx has completed its downward movement you should observe a slight influx of air into the mouth.

It is sometimes helpful to think of 'sucking with the larynx' and to experiment with the production of *unreleased* voiced glottalic suction stops— i.e. unreleased [ɓ]. In doing this you make a sucking, gulping sound that generates a momentary buzz of voice in the larynx, but in which the lips are never actually opened.

A common error of people trying to produce [ɓ] [ɗ] [ɠ] is to turn these sounds into *pulmonic suction* sounds, that is, to try to produce them with inhalation—drawing air *downwards* through the larynx, instead of letting it seep *upwards* through the glottis as the larynx itself moves downward. Remember that, even though there is an influx of air from outside into the mouth on the release of [ɓ] [ɗ] [ɠ], there is *no inhalation*—no in-breathing— the lungs are not involved at all and the vacuum in the mouth is created solely by the downward movement of the larynx.

A good way to think of the difference between voiced pulmonic pressure stops [b] [d] [g] and voiced glottalic suction stops [ɓ] [ɗ] [ɠ] is as follows: in voiced pulmonic pressure stops we have a *moving column of air* passing upwards through a *static glottis*, while in voiced glottalic suction stops we have a *moving glottis* sliding downwards over a *static column of air*. As we know, this is not strictly accurate, since the larynx may move down a little in producing a (lengthened) voiced pulmonic pressure stop—but it is a very helpful way of visualizing the difference between the two types of sound: Fig. 16 illustrates the difference diagrammatically.

Voiced glottalic suction stops (voiced implosives) like [ɓ] [ɗ] [ɠ] occur in quite a number of languages in the Americas, in Africa, and in South and South-east Asia. But that is not why we ask the reader to experiment with them: we do this because experiments like 32 and 33 help the reader to get an experienced, internalized, understanding of some aspects of the aero-dynamics of speech, rather than a purely theoretical and intellectual knowledge.

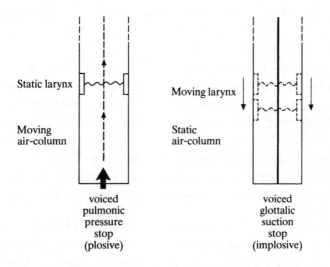

Static larynx

Moving
air-column

voiced
pulmonic
pressure
stop
(plosive)

Moving larynx

Static
air-column

voiced
glottalic
suction
stop
(implosive)

Fig. 16 Initiation of voiced plosives and voiced implosives

7. Principal phonation types

So far, in this chapter, we have considered only two types of phonation: *voiceless* (glottis wide open so that air passes through with minimal obstruction) and *voiced* (vocal folds brought together and thrown into vibration by the passage of air through the glottis). But these are only two of several different states of the glottis that are responsible for phonation.

In exploring states of the glottis we start with the vocal folds as widely separated as possible. This is the position of deep breathing. Even when the folds are as wide apart as possible the larynx still represents an orifice only about half as wide as the windpipe, or trachea, that extends below it to the lungs. Consequently, even the open glottis offers some resistance to air passing through, and in breathing in and out one can normally hear some sound generated by turbulent flow through the open glottis. Only if we slow down our breathing to a considerable extent is the sound of exhalation and inhalation abolished. From this wide-open position (the state of the glottis for breathing or for voiceless sounds) we can narrow the glottis, so that the orifice presents a much greater obstacle to the passage of air through it, and the flow thus becomes quite strongly turbulent, generating the 'hushing' sound that we call *whisper*.

34   Breathe in and out several times through the wide open glottis. As you will observe the flow of air through the glottis is turbulent and hence noisy, unless you slow it down considerably.

Now produce the sound of *whisper*—if necessary, begin by saying a few words to yourself in a whisper—then try to produce a prolonged unmodified whisper, a kind of [ə̦ ə̦ ə̦] where the little hook under the vowel symbol indicates whisper. This hook (a subscript comma) is not a currently used symbol of the IPA, but it was used in the early years of the Association, for example in *Aim and Principles of the IPA* (1904 and 1912).

Now alternate breath and whisper, at first in separate little bursts of breath and whisper [h h] [ə̦ ə̦] [h h] [ə̦ ə̦], and then in a continuum [h ə̦ ə̦ h ə̦ ə̦] . . . etc.

When you are quite sure that you can produce either breath or whisper at will, you can easily demonstrate that whisper involves a narrower channel through the glottis than breath does by means of Experiment 34A.

34A   Have a watch that shows seconds available, as in Exp. 19

Breathe in till the lungs are comfortably full, then allow the lungs to collapse by themselves, expelling the air as in normal exhaling. (This is *breath*, or voicelessness). You will probably find that the lungs empty quite quickly—in no more than 2 seconds.

Now breath in again till the lungs are comfortably full and this time when you allow them to collapse, don't just breathe out, but produce the sound of *whisper*. You will find that the whispered breath takes considerably longer to flow out—probably 5 to 7 seconds or more.

You used approximately the same quantity of air each time, but it obviously flowed out more slowly for whisper than for breath. This demonstrates that the glottal orifice is much narrower for whisper than for breath.

So, then, for breath (voicelessness) the glottis is wide open: for whisper it is considerably narrowed. A further narrowing of the glottis brings it into position for the production of voice, with which we have already experimented. Incidentally, if you carry out the same timing test with voice as you did with breath and whisper in Experiment 34A you will find that it takes still longer to empty the lungs: perhaps twice as long as it does for whisper. This is because the rapid opening and shutting of the vibrating glottis lets the air pass through only in a series of tiny puffs, and this naturally increases the time it takes for the full complement of air to flow out.

There is one more type of phonation to be considered. This is *creak*. It is a very low frequency 'creaking' or 'crackling' sound which—perhaps because it reminds some people of the sputtering noise of frying eggs or bacon—is sometimes called 'glottal fry'. Creak is produced with the glottis completely (but not very tightly) closed, except for a small segment near the front end of the vocal folds, which is vibrating rather slowly.

35 Produce a sustained vowel sound of the type [ə ə ə] or [a a a] on a very low pitch—about as low as you can reach. While keeping the sound going, try to lower the pitch still further till the tone of the voice degenerates into a cacophonous series of taps. At this point the frequency of the glottal vibration is so slow that you can perceive the individual little explosive bursts of air.

By trial and error, try to achieve a clear crackling noise with no admixture of the tone of voice. To do this, you may have to consciously tighten up your vocal folds, though not so much as to produce a glottal stop. This is *creak*.

We have now discovered four different types of phonation:

Voicelessness (or *breath*): with the glottis wide open, as in breathing or the production of voiceless sounds, such as [f, s, p, t, k].

Whisper: with a considerably narrowed glottis, so that the highly turbulent airflow through the glottis generates a strong 'hushing' noise: this is the phonation type of whispered speech, in which whisper is substituted for voiced sounds (while voiceless sounds remain voiceless).

Voice: the tone produced by the vibrating vocal folds: the phonation type of all *voiced* sounds, such as [v, z, m, l, i, a, u].

Creak: the crackling sound produced by keeping the vocal folds closed along most of their length, but allowing the air to escape in a low frequency series of bursts through a small vibrating segment near the front end of the glottis.

Figure 17 shows, purely diagrammatically, the state of the glottis as it might appear if you were looking down on it, for these four phonation types, and for complete glottal closure. The conventions used in Fig. 17 are mostly obvious, but note that the difference in the diagonal hatching in (c) and (d) is intended to suggest a difference in the frequency of vocal fold vibration—medium to high frequency for voice (c), and very low frequency for creak (d). Note that complete glottal closure is not a type of phonation. Phonation always involves a *flow* of air through the glottis. When the glottis is held in the closed position there is, of course, no flow. The functions of glottal closure are thus purely articulatory (for glottal stop [ʔ]) and initiatory (for glottalic pressure sounds and unphonated glottalic suction sounds). In the case of voiced implosives the glottis functions simultaneously as initiator and phonator.

There are various possible combinations of these types of phonation, the chief ones being *breathy voice, whispery voice* (also known as murmur), and *creaky voice*. Experiment 38 introduces these three combined phonation types.

36 *Breathy voice*: the glottis is rather widely open, but the rate of airflow is so high that the vocal folds are set 'flapping in the breeze' as the air rushes by. Exhale very strongly, contriving to produce some voice at the same time. Imagine that you are trying to blurt out a message when extremely out of breath, or speaking while sighing deeply.

Whispery voice or murmur: the vocal folds are vibrating to produce voice

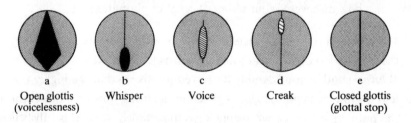

a	b	c	d	e
Open glottis (voicelessness)	Whisper	Voice	Creak	Closed glottis (glottal stop)

Fig. 17 States of the glottis

but at the same time there is a continuous escape of air generating the sound of whisper. Produce an energetic and prolonged strong whisper, and while it is going on add voice, to produce the mixture called 'whispery voice'. Producing voice with very relaxed vocal folds may help.

Creaky voice: proceed as in Exp. 35—start with low-pitched voice, then go still lower till some creak is heard mixed with voice—but in this case make no attempt to produce the pure creak that was the end result in Exp. 35.

Breathy voice, as we imply in 36, is the type of phonation we use when out of breath and panting. It is not otherwise used in English, although high-speed cinephotography of the larynx shows the glottis passing momentarily through a 'breathy voice' phase during the transition from voicelessness (breath) to voice in an initial [h], as in *happy*.

Whispery voice or 'murmur' is sometimes used in quiet, initimate, conversation in English, and is often associated with tenderness: it is, for example, the type of phonation used in saying 'I love you'. If you experiment with saying those words in a normal or tense voice, you will perceive the inappropriateness of this type of phonation! Whispery voice is used in some languages to distinguish words: thus in Hindi the sounds known as 'voiced aspirated stops' [bʰ] [dʰ] [ɖʰ] [gʰ] are produced with whispery voice which persists into the following vowel. In fact in some varieties of Hindi the most noticeable difference between such pairs of words as [bʰaˑt] and [baˑt] is simply that the vowel in [bʰaˑt] is pronounced with relaxed, whispery, voice, while the vowel of [baˑt] has rather tense voice.

Creak or creaky voice is a not uncommon phonation type of very low-pitched syllables in English, particularly in the British variety of English known as RP ('received pronunciation').

We can now provide a formal definition of *phonation*. *Phonation* is any of those phonetic activities of the larynx which have neither *initiatory* nor *articulatory* function.

8. Relationship of phonation to initiation

Since phonation (the various types of *voicelessness, whisper*, and *voice*) can occur only when there is an air-stream passing through the larynx, it follows that it can combine only with certain types of *initiation*.

Velaric initiation (e.g. velaric suction stops, or 'clicks') utilizes exclusively a small quantity of air trapped in the mouth. Consequently, clicks have no phonation. They may, however, be performed against a phonated background. Thus, as we saw in Chapter 2, it is possible to produce a series of clicks, say [ǁ], [ǃ], [ʘ], while uninterruptedly humming through the nose. The *hum* is a pulmonic pressure voiced sound. But the pulmonically initiated air-stream used for the hum passes out through the nose and is not at all used for the click. The latter is a velaric suction sound, and it is *unphonated*, because the air used in its production does not pass through the larynx, and thus has nothing to do with the production of voice. 'Voiced clicks' are sometimes referred to, but these can only be *unphonated* velaric suction sounds, performed against a *background* of pulmonically (or possibly glottalically) initiated voicing.

Glottalically initiated sounds, such as *glottalic pressure* [p'] [t'] [s'] and their inverse, *glottalic suction* counterparts, are *unphonated*, since in their production the glottis is tightly closed—no air is passing through to generate voiceless, whispered, or voiced phonation.

As we have seen, however, *glottalic suction* sounds *can* be phonated. In voiced glottalic suction stops (voiced implosives) the initiatory movement, is indeed glottalic. However, the glottis is not tightly closed, but is disposed for the production of voice, and as the larynx moves suddenly downwards a small quantity of air seeps upwards through the larynx, generating voice.

Pulmonic sounds, are, in principle, all phonated, i.e. voiced, voiceless, whispered, etc., with the exception of *glottal stop* [ʔ]. Glottal stop is, of course, *pulmonic*, since the pressure buildup below the glottis is initiated by the lungs. But since the glottis is tightly closed, forming the *articulation* of the sound, it cannot simultaneously be open to produce *voicelessness, whisper,* or *voice.* All other pulmonic sounds are phonated. But, it should be noted that there are constraints on the phonation of *pulmonic suction* sounds. If you try to produce a voiced vowel sound [ə ə ə . . .] on *inhalation*, i.e. with pulmonic suction initiation, you will find that it is virtually impossible. What is produced is a raucous croaking type of inverse voice. The shape of the glottis is such that it vibrates well under pressure from below, but not at all well under pressure from above. Consequently, a normal-sounding voice is not possible with pulmonic suction initiation.

When *voice* is produced, the vocal folds vibrate at a frequency determined by the tension of the vocal folds and/or the subglottal air-pressure. It is possible to vary the frequency of vocal fold vibration over a wide range, and consequently to produce the auditory effect of a wide range of *pitches.* All languages make some use of voice-pitch variation, and we shall study that in more detail in Chapter 9, 'Prosodic Features'.

9. Aspiration

One further important phenomenon connected with phonation is the time-relation between phonation changes (voiced-to-voiceless, and voiceless-to-voiced) and articulatory events.

For example, if we pronounce an initial stop consonant followed by a vowel, the voicing, which is essential for the vowel, may start simultaneously with the release of the stop-closure, or it may be delayed for a fraction of a second, or, again, the voicing may start *before* the stop-closure is released. Fig. 18 shows, diagrammatically, four different time-relations between the release of a stop and the onset of voicing.

In Fig. 18, the upper line represents the closed phase of an initial stop, for example, the lip-closure of a [p], followed by the sudden explosive opening of the lips. The lower lines represent the glottis either slightly open (as for whisper), wide open (as for breath), or vibrating.

In 18a the vocal folds begin vibrating at the moment when the lips separate. In 18b the wide-open glottis takes some time to close sufficiently for the vocal folds to start vibrating. Consequently, there is a period of voicelessness, a kind of [h]-sound, before the vocal folds begin to vibrate. In 18c the vocal folds begin to vibrate a moment *before* the lips separate, and in 18d

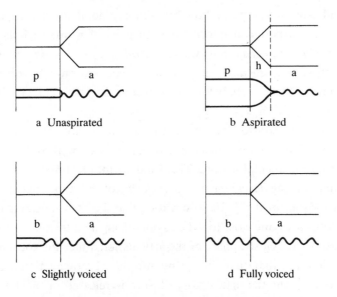

Fig. 18 Aspiration and voicing of stops

the vocal fold vibrations begin much earlier—as soon as the articulatory closure is formed.

It is clear that both 18a and 18b are *voiceless* stops: there is absolutely no vocal fold vibration during the articulatory closure. No. 18c is a *slightly voiced* stop—mostly voiceless, but with voicing just beginning before the release of the closure: initial [b] [d] [g] of English are often of this type. Finally, 18d is a *fully voiced* stop, with the vocal folds vibrating throughout the entire duration of the articulatory closure.

The difference between 18a and 18b is what chiefly concerns us at present. A stop in the production of which the vocal folds start vibrating to produce voice more or less simultaneously with the release of the articulatory closure (like 18a) is *unaspirated*. A stop in the production of which the vocal folds start vibrating only after a delay is *aspirated*, the voiceless puff of breath that intervenes between the release of the stop and the start of voicing is *aspiration*. In most types of English the voiceless stops [p] [t] [k] are aspirated when they occur before a stressed vowel as in *par*, *tar*, *car*. [pʰaˑ(r)] [tʰaˑ(r)] [kʰaˑ(r)], where (r) implies that in some dialects the [r] is pronounced, in others not. In varieties of English spoken in Scotland and the North of England, [p] [t] [k] are unaspirated. So, too, are the [p] [t] [k] after [s] in *spar*, *star*, *scar*, in virtually all types of English.

It is important to be quite clear about the distinction between unaspirated and aspirated stops, and the first thing to do, if you are a speaker of English, is to experiment informally with pairs of words such as *pie/spy*, *pan/span*, *pill/spill*, *tie/sty*, *tone/stone*, *till/still*, *key/ski*, *kin/skin*, *kill/skill*. If you say these energetically, but very slowly, you will probably observe the puff of breath that occurs before the vowel in the first member of each of these pairs.

In learning to control aspiration it is helpful to note that the delay in voicing, which is so evident in aspirated stops, is, as it were, only a *symptom* of a more fundamental feature. This fundamental feature is the width of the glottal opening *during the period of closure* of the stop articulation.

If you look again at Fig. 18a you will see that the lines indicating the state of the glottis are quite close together, symbolizing a glottis that is only open a little during the closed phase of the articulation. Since the vocal folds are already close together, they can spring into the vibrating action needed for voice the moment the articulatory closure is released. This state of the glottis has been appropriately named *prephonation* by Harris (1999). The area of glottal opening for prephonation is similar to that for whisper, though the location and shape of the narrow channel thus formed is different from that indicated in Fig. 17b, which represents only one type of whisper. In prephonation the channel extends forwards along the greater part of the glottis, as it may do in other forms of whisper.

The knowledge that *aspirated* stops are produced with a wide-open (breath-type) glottis, while *unaspirated* stops are produced with a narrowed glottis (of prephonation type, somewhat resembling whisper) suggests an experiment that will help to develop control of aspiration.

37   (*i*) Breathe in then begin a prolonged *voiceless* exhalation—a pulmonic pressure initiated air-stream flowing up through a wide-open glottis. Momentarily superimpose a [p] on the air-stream as in Exp. 7, thus [h h p H h h]. Note that in doing this your glottis is wide open throughout.

Repeat the experiment, but this time 'switch on' voice immediately after release of the stop, thus: [h h p H ə ə ə]. This should produce an aspirated [p]. Do the same with [t] and [k].

(*ii*) Breathe in as before, but now begin a prolonged *whispered* exhalation— a pulmonic pressure initiated air-stream flowing up through the glottis, generating the sound of whisper. Momentarily superimpose a [p] on this whispered air-stream, [ə̣ ə̣ p ə̣ ə̣] (where ə̣ represents a whispered ə).

Now repeat the experiment, but this time 'switch on' voice just as you release the stop. If you have indeed kept the glottis in the whisper configuration up to that point, voice should start immediately—with no delay. In other words, the result should be an *unaspirated* [p]. Do the same with [t] and [k].

You should now have a clear, experiential (not merely intellectual) knowledge of the difference between unaspirated [p] [t] [k] and aspirated [pʰ] [tʰ] [kʰ]. It is possible to produce exactly the same difference between two types of fricatives: unaspirated [f] [s] [ʃ] etc., and aspirated [fʰ] [sʰ] [ʃʰ]. In acquiring this distinction it is helpful, at first, to whisper the unaspirated ones, but make the aspirated ones very breathy. Aspirated fricatives are much rarer than aspirated stops in the world's languages, but they do exist. In some cases, for example Burmese [sʰ], the fricative itself has a much wider articulatory channel than that of the unaspirated [s].

The aspirated stops we have dealt with here are all voiceless. There is another type, known as 'voiced aspirated stops' or 'aspirated voiced stops', particularly common in the languages of northern India. In the production of these stops the phonation type is whispery voice: considerable pressure is built up during the closed phase, and on the release of the stop there is a burst of whispery voice before the vocal folds settle down to normal voicing for the vowel. These sounds are represented as [bʰ] [dʰ] [gʰ], etc., or [bʱ] [dʱ] [gʱ], in which the raised [ʱ] is the IPA symbol for 'voiced [h]', which is, in fact, a momentary burst of whispery voice. As we mentioned above, in North Indian languages, the entire vowel following [bʰ] [dʰ] etc. may be phonated with whispery voice.

In this chapter we have investigated, and experienced, the principal types of *phonation*, namely *voiceless* ('breath'), *whispered*, *voiced*, *creaky*, and the compound types *breathy voice*, *whispery voice* ('murmur'), and *creaky voice*.

We have investigated the special problems of voicing stop consonants, and the aerodynamic differences between *voiced pulmonic pressure* stops [b] [d] [g], and *voiced glottalic suction* stops ('voiced implosives') [ɓ] [ɗ] [ɠ].

We noted that the *pitch* phenomena of language depend upon the frequency of vibration of the vocal folds, and thus constitute a phonatory phenomenon.

And, finally, we have investigated the difference between *unaspirated* and *aspirated* stops.

4

Articulation: Stricture Types

1. Articulation: The 'final shaping' of sounds

We turn now to the third basic component of speech production—
articulation. As we have seen, *initiation* sets up an air-stream in the vocal
tract. For sounds with an air-stream flowing through the larynx, *phonation*
imparts a general modulation to the sound, making it voiceless, voiced,
whispered . . . etc. The important function of *articulation* is to impose upon
the (unphonated or phonated) air-stream a final 'shaping', as it were, so as
to generate a sound of specific type and quality.

For example, pulmonic pressure initiation impels a non-specific flow of
air up and out of the vocal tract. A close approximation of the articulating
organs forms a narrow channel through which the air-stream is squeezed,
becoming turbulent in the process. *Articulation* has thus 'shaped' the undif-
ferentiated air-stream into a sound of specific type, a fricative. Moreover,
the specific type of fricative depends on the location of the articulatory
channel: compare, for instance, [f] with [s] or [ʃ].

In vowel sounds like [i] [a] [u] (roughly as in *tea, tar, too*) the undifferenti-
ated initiatory air-stream has the general modulation of voice imposed
upon it by phonation, and this voice-modulated air-stream passes on, into
and through the mouth. But it is *articulation* that finally shapes the voiced
air-stream into the specific vowel sounds [i] [a] [u]. The particular oral
resonance frequencies that characterize each of these vowels are achieved
by placing the articulating organs in different positions.

In considering articulation we can think of the vocal tract from the larynx through the mouth to the lips, and through the nose to the nostrils, as a
kind of four-dimensional tube. We describe and classify articulations in
terms of these four dimensions: the *vertical, transverse,* and *longitudinal*
space dimensions, and *time*.

The *vertical* dimension is represented by the degree of closeness between the articulating organs, which, for the most part, approach each other 'vertically'. For example, lower lip against upper teeth, tongue against roof of mouth, etc.

In the transverse, or 'side-to-side', dimension we only have to distinguish between the *median* (or normal) and *lateral* location of the oral air-path: that is, whether the air-stream comes through the centre of the mouth, which is the commonest state of affairs, or is channelled along one (or both) side(s) of the mouth in *laterals* ([1]-sounds).

The longitudinal dimension, of course, represents the location of articulation at any point from the lips right back and down to the larynx.

Finally, *time* enters into the basic classification of articulations as a factor in separating off those types of articulation that are essentially *momentary gestures* from those that are essentially *maintainable postures*.

2. Maintainable stricture types: Stop, fricative, approximant, resonant, trill

We start with the vertical dimension, that is, with the different degrees or types of *stricture*. It is obvious that articulations can be formed with complete closure: we have seen this in [p] [t] [k]. On the other hand, the articulating organs may be far apart, as in an 'open' vowel like [a]. But clearly, intermediate positions are also possible, and we must now examine these.

38   Produce a prolonged and vigorous [v v v v] preferably while watching your mouth in a hand-mirror. We say 'vigorous' because this, like all phonetic experiments, must be done with firm, clearly felt, articulation, and powerful initiation. The aim after all, is to *feel* what the articulators are doing, and to hear the resultant sounds.

Note that this prolonged [v v v v] is markedly fricative. The hiss of turbulent airflow can be heard, superimposed upon and mingling with the resonant sound of voice. Note, also, that it is the *inner* part of the lower lip that is in contact with the edges of the upper teeth, and that the opening between the two lips is very small.

While keeping this prolonged [v v v v . . .] going, very slowly, deliberately, and introspectively slide the lower lip downwards, keeping it all the time in contact with the teeth but slowly widening the distance between the lips. If you do this correctly, very soon (i.e. when the lip has slid downwards only a millimetre or so) the hissing fricative noise fades out, leaving only the 'smooth' non-fricative sound of voice. The moment this transition from turbulent fricative noise to the smooth non-turbulent sound occurs, 'freeze' the lower lip in that position, i.e. keep it in contact with the upper teeth but move it no further. And observe the sound produced, noting how it differs from [v].

The sound [v] was clearly a *fricative*: but the sound you reached at the end of Experiment 38 was no longer a fricative, but an *approximant*. This is a sound with an articulatory channel very similar to that of a fricative, only a little wider. There is a special symbol [ʋ] for this particular approximant: *labiodental (lip-teeth) approximant* which is exactly the same as the labio-dental fricative [v], except that the channel is very slightly wider. But that tiny amount of extra width of the articulatory channel for the approximant is just enough to abolish the turbulence in the airflow and hence to abolish the fricative hiss. Experiment 39 continues the investigation of the difference between the articulatory strictures for *fricative* and *approximant*.

39 While initiating a strong voiced air-stream make a prolonged labiodental articulation, sliding the lower lip very slightly up and down so that you alternate between fricative [v] and approximant [ʋ], thus: [v ʋ v ʋ v ʋ v ʋ v ʋ . . .].

Now do exactly the same thing *silently*: i.e. *imagine* you are saying [v ʋ v ʋ v ʋ . . .] etc., but do not initiate an air-stream. In this way you can *feel* the difference between a fricative [v] and an approximant [ʋ]. Next, experiment with the difference between fricative and approximant at other places of articulation.

Make a vigorous and prolonged [z z z . . .]. As you do this you can feel the tongue pressing up against the ridge behind the upper teeth, leaving a very narrow central channel. (You can feel this better if you stop the initiation and hold a silent [z]-articulation.)

Now do with [z] exactly what you did with [v]—slowly, deliberately and introspectively relax the tongue allowing the articulation channel to widen a very, very little. Stop this channel-widening process the moment the turbulence and resultant hissing noise fades out, leaving only the 'smooth', non-fricative sound of voice.

This is an approximant articulated at exactly the same place as the fricative [z]. There is no special symbol for this approximant, but we can represent it by attaching the 'widening' diacritic mark [˕] to [z], thus [z̞]. Now alternate [z z̞ z z̞ . . .] slowly and deliberately, aloud and silently, getting once again the 'feel' of the distinction between a fricative and the corresponding approximant.

We have seen, then, that an approximant has an articulatory channel slightly wider than that of a fricative. When we start with a voiced fricative, like [v] or [z], and then very slightly open up the channel, we quickly reach the point where the hissing fricative sound disappears and all that is left is the smooth, non-turbulent sound of voice. But voice, of course, is still distinctly modulated by the articulatory stricture, which generates the sound of a quite specific approximant, according to the place of articulation.

We have determined by experimentation that a major difference between a voiced fricative and a voiced approximant is that in the fricative the airflow through the very narrow articulatory channel is *turbulent* (hence the fricative noise), while flow through the very slightly wider articulatory channel of the approximant is *non-turbulent* (hence, no fricative noise). We must now investigate the difference between *voiceless* fricatives and approximants.

40 Make a prolonged fricative [v v v . . .] but suddenly devoice it, while keeping the initiatory air-stream going with about the same effort as you started with, [v v v f f f]. When you switch off voice, i.e. open the glottis, you will experience a surge of increased rate of airflow, as the glottal resistance of voice is removed, and you will hear a strongly turbulent fricative sound.

Now do the same with the approximant [ʋ]—start it up and then devoice it [ʋ ʋ ʋ̥ ʋ̥]. Once again you will experience the surge of airflow as the glottal resistance is removed and you will hear a fricative sound: but the turbulent noise of the approximant is much less loud than that of the fricative.

The same experiment carried out with devoicing fricative [z] and approximant [ɹ] will yield a similar result.

What we learn from Experiment 40 is that the articulatory channel for a *fricative* is so narrow that the airflow through it is always turbulent, and hence noisy, whether it is voiced or voiceless. The articulatory channel for an approximant, however, is a little wider than that of a fricative, just to the extent that airflow through the channel is non-turbulent (hence no hiss-sound) when it is voiced, but it *is* turbulent and hence noisy (though not strongly so) when it is voiceless.

Before passing on from approximant to the next-wider degree of articulatory stricture we must look at two more examples of approximants and corresponding fricatives, specifically the approximants [i] and [l].

41 Say a prolonged [i i i i . . .], which is a vowel like the *ee* of *see*. Note that in [i i i . . .] there is no fricative noise: the airflow through the mouth is non-turbulent and the only audible sound is the resonant sound of *voice* (modulated articulatorily to produce the specific vowel [i]).

Now, while saying a prolonged [i] suddenly switch off voice; make no other change, i.e. hold the tongue in the same articulatory posture throughout, but suddenly open the glottis, thus: [i i i i̞ i̞ i̞].

As soon as you devoice [i] the hissing noise of turbulent airflow can be heard. So, the vowel [i] has smooth, non-turbulent flow when voiced, noisy turbulent flow when voiceless. In other words, [i] is a typical approximant.

Say a long [i i i . . .] again, and this time, as you are saying it, deliberately tense your tongue and force it upwards into the palate. As you narrow the articulatory channel in this way, the airflow becomes turbulent and fricative noise begins to be heard. The vowel [i], which is a 'voiced dorso-palatal approximant', has now been changed into a voiced dorso-palatal fricative, symbol [j]. To further familiarize yourself with the difference between an approximant and a fricative, alternate [i] and [j]: [i j i j i j i j . . .], aloud and silently. Now devoice the fricative [j] and you have the voiceless dorso-palatal fricative [ç], the sound of *ch* in German *ich*.

Other vowels, of the type we describe as close (in Chapter 7), are also approximants: you can experiment with the *oo*-vowel [u] of *too*, for example. The next experiment is concerned with [l].

42 Make a prolonged [l]-sound, like the initial [l] of English *leaf*: [l l l l l . . .]. Clearly, the airflow is non-turbulent, since there is no hissing, fricative-like sound.

Now, devoice [l], thus: [l l l l̞ l̞ l̞]. When the glottis is opened for [l] some degree of noisy hiss is heard—the flow has become turbulent. So [l] clearly fulfils the conditions for an *approximant*: it has non-turbulent airflow when voiced but (weakly) turbulent flow when voiceless. The sound [l] is a lateral approximant.

Just as the approximant [i] was converted into a fricative, so the lateral approximant [l] can be converted into a lateral fricative. Make a prolonged [l], [l l l . . .] and while doing this expand the tongue—strive to push the sides of the tongue out sideways, so that they squeeze between the molar teeth. With a little trial and error you can narrow the lateral channels of [l] so much that a lateral fricative type hiss begins to be heard along with the sound of voice. The symbol for this voiced lateral fricative is [ɮ]. Once you can produce [ɮ] devoice it, to produce the voiceless lateral fricative [ɬ].

Alternate lateral approximant and lateral fricative, voiced [l ɮ l ɮ l ɮ l ɮ . . .] and voiceless [l̥ ɬ l̥ ɬ . . .].

There is one further degree of stricture beyond approximant. Experiment 43 is designed for the discovery of this still more open type of stricture.

43 The vowel [i] was clearly shown, by the test of devoicing, to be an approximant (no turbulence when voiced, turbulent flow when voiceless).

Start from [i] and open up your mouth, dropping the jaw and lowering your tongue, till you reach a vowel of the type [ɛ] as in *bed*, or the [æ] of *bad*.

Produce a prolonged [æ]: [æ æ æ . . .]. Note that in the production of this vowel, just as for [i], there is no noisy turbulent airflow. All you can hear is the 'smooth' sound of voice, modulated by the mouth-shape to produce the sound of [æ].

Now, while making a prolonged [æ], suddenly devoice it: [æ æ æ̥]. The result is quite different from what happened with [i]. On devoicing [æ] you can hear no hiss of turbulent airflow through the mouth as you could with [i̥]: only a faint 'hushing' noise of air passing through the glottis. That is to say, it has no 'local turbulence'.

Compare the effects of devoicing [i] and devoicing [æ] several times: [i i i i i̥ i̥ i̥] [æ æ æ̥ æ̥ æ̥] [i i i i̥ i̥ i̥] [æ æ æ̥ æ̥] . . . etc.

The result of this experiment is clear. Airflow through the oral articulatory channel for [i] is non-turbulent when voiced, but turbulent when voiceless. For [æ] it is non-turbulent when voiced, *and also* non-turbulent when voiceless.

In Experiment 43 we have demonstrated that [i] is a typical approximant, but [æ] is clearly something different. We call this latter type of sound, which never has noisy local turbulence, a *resonant*.

We shall, in fact, have little occasion to use the term resonant because the only sounds with this very wide type of stricture are vowels like [ɛ] and [æ], and, as we shall see in Chapter 7, we normally use a different terminology in the description of vowels.

We can sum up what we have discovered so far about different degrees of articulatory stricture—different stricture types—as shown in Table 2. As we have seen, the criterion for distinguishing one of these stricture types from another is an aerodynamic and acoustic one—the presence or absence of turbulent airflow through the oral articulatory channel (local turbulence) and resultant hiss noise. (+ means presence and – means absence of local turbulence.)

Table 2

Stricture type	Turbulent flow when	
	voiced	voiceless
Fricative	+	+
Approximant	–	+
Resonant	–	–

There are three other stricture types to be considered: *trill, tap* (and *flap*), and *semivowel*.

Trill involves neither the complete and maintained closure of a stop, nor the maintained openness of the three stricture types in the table we have just seen, but, rather, an alternation between them. In trill one flexible organ repeatedly taps against another under the influence of a powerful air-stream. Approaching this stricture-type experimentally we start in Experiment 44 with the easiest type of trill, a bilabial (two-lip) one.

44 Place the upper and lower lips lightly together, in a somewhat 'pouting' posture—that is, kept perfectly flat (not rounded) but pushed forward so that it is the *inner* parts of lips that make contact. Now start up a powerful pulmonic pressure initiation ('blow hard') and, perhaps after a little adjustment of lip-tension and initiatory pressure, the lips will start flapping regularly, periodically, against each other.

This is a voiceless pulmonic pressure bilabial trill, and it resembles a sound made by horses (and *to* horses by horse-drivers in the days when such people were common). While doing a prolonged voiceless bilabial trill, switch on voice.

A voiced bilabial trill is sometimes used as part of a gesture expressing coldness, written *brrr!* Voiced bilabial trill is a regular sound of a few languages, such as Nias, the language of an island off the west coast of Sumatra. Bilabial trill is represented by a small capital [ʙ].

Experiments with bilabial trill will have shown you the general principle of trill-production. There are, however, two other types of trill that are more commonly used in languages, namely the *apico-alveolar* trill [r], produced by allowing the tip (apex) of the tongue to flap against the ridge behind the upper teeth (alveolar ridge), and the *uvular* trill [ʀ], produced by letting the uvula (the pendulous rear extremity of the roof of the mouth) vibrate in a longitudinal groove formed in the back of the tongue.

45 Raise the tip of the tongue slightly and let it rest loosely against the extreme
back of the ridge behind the upper teeth. Now start up a powerful pulmonic
pressure initiatory air-stream (voiceless) i.e. blow hard.

By trial and error adjustments of the precise position and tension of the
tongue, and of the initiatory pressure, you may be able to start the tongue-tip
regularly, periodically, flapping against the alveolar ridge. This is [r̥]. Having
acquired the voiceless [r̥] produce a prolonged [r̥ r̥ r̥ . . .] and switch on voice in
the middle of it [r̥ r̥ r̥ r r r]. Incidentally, in experimenting with trills it is often
best to start with *voiceless* ones, since it is easier to set organs trilling with the
more powerful voiceless air-stream than with the voiced one.

Uvular [ʀ] can be developed from *gargling*: most people are familiar with
the technique of gargling with disinfectant, salt water, etc. To develop uvular
[ʀ], take a little water into the mouth, throw the head back and gargle. Then
reduce the amount of water, till finally you can do it merely with a little saliva
at the back of the mouth.

For some reason most people practise gargling with a *voiced* air-stream,
but this is quite unnecessary. It is probably better, in making the transition
from a gargle to a uvular trill, to use a *voiceless* airstream first, producing [ʀ̥].

The apico-alveolar trill [r] is a fairly common sound in languages: it is a
typical Italian *r*, or the Castilian Spanish *rr* (note that in many Latin
American forms of Spanish *rr* represents quite a different sound): it is also
a type of *r* traditionally used by stage Scotsmen (real Scots rarely use a
strongly trilled r).

The uvular [ʀ] is one form of N. German *r*, it is also a type of *r* often used
in modern Israeli Hebrew, and occasionally in French—though it must be
noted that in these languages *r* is quite often a uvular fricative, or even a
uvular approximant. This is particularly true of French.

All the articulatory stricture types dealt with so far—*stop, fricative,
approximant, resonant,* and *trill*—have one thing in common. This common
feature is the fact that all of these stricture types are *maintainable* articulations. The closure of a stop (which is, of course, the one essential phase) can
be held for an indefinite period of time. The articulatory strictures of fricatives, approximants, and resonants can also be maintained indefinitely. A
trill, too, is an articulatory posture which can be maintained for an indefinite time: the vibratory movement characterizing a trill is not an active performance of the articulator, but simply a passive response to the air-stream,
which sets the articulator 'flapping in the breeze'. So then, all these stricture
types are essentially *maintainable*—a stop or a fricative, for instance can be

quite short, but they can also be very long, i.e. can be maintained for a long time.

3. Essentially momentary stricture types: Tap, flap, semivowel

The remaining two articulatory stricture types are, by contrast, character-ized by being essentially *momentary*. *Tap* and *flap* both involve an essen-tially momentary contact between articulators. In a *tap* one articulator starts out towards another, makes momentary contact and immediately withdraws: the whole event is a momentary flicking movement. One of the best-known *taps* is the flicking movement of the tip of the tongue against the teeth-ridge [ɾ], which often represents a *t* or *d* between vowels in Ameri-can English, as in *latter* or *ladder* [læɾɚ], or an *r* between vowels in some types of British English, as in very [vɛɾɪ]. This type of apical (tongue-tip) tap is also the single *r* of Spanish *pero* [peɾo].

A *flap* typically differs from a tap in that the momentary contact occurs, not with a 'flicking' motion, but as one articulator momentarily strikes another *in passing*. A typical example is the 'retroflex flap' [ɽ]—a sound that occurs in Hindi in such words as [gʰoɽa] 'horse'. To produce this retroflex flap curl the tip of the tongue up and back (this is 'retroflexion') then let it shoot forward so that it momentarily flaps against the extreme back of the teeth ridge before it flaps down on to the floor of the mouth. Thus the *tap/flap* stricture type involves an essentially momentary contact between articulators: it is impossible to maintain the contact in the way that one can for stops.

The other essentially momentary articulatory stricture is *semivowel*. A semivowel is a momentary approximant. Thus the semivowel occurring at the beginning of the English words *word, wall* or in the middle of the words *away, aware* (phonetic symbol [w]) is essentially a momentary or ultra-short [u] vowel. The semivowel occurring at the beginning of *yard, you* or in the middle of *Maya* (written *y* in English, but [j] in IPA) is an ultra-short [i] vowel.

In Experiment 46 we develop semivowels from the corresponding vowels:

46 The vowel [i], you will recall, is a typical approximant, and the same is true of [u]. The semivowels are similar approximants, except that they are ultra-short.

Take in a deep breath, and then start saying a very prolonged vowel, starting as a prolonged [a] (like the vowel in *calm*), then suddenly changing to a prolonged [i] (like the *ee* of see), then changing back to a prolonged [a], thus: [a a a a a i i i i i a a a a a]. Produce this sequence several times, then start systematically *shortening* the [i], thus:

[a a a a a i i i i i a a a a a]
[a a a a a i i i i a a a a]
[a a a a a i i i a a a a]
[a a a a a i i a a a]
[a a a a a i a a a]
= [a a a a a j a a a]

As you arrive at the last sequence, with a *very* short [i], you will observe that the [i] no longer sounds like a real vowel, but has turned into something that sounds like English *y* (IPA [j]).

This demonstrates that the semivowel [j] is, in effect, an ultra-short [i].

Carry out the same experiment with [u] and note how it finally turns into the semivowel [w].

[a a a a a u u u u u a a a]
[a a a a a u u u a a a]
[a a a a a u u a a a]
[a a a a a u a a a]
= [a a a a a w a a a]

Experiment 46 shows how a semivowel is the same as an approximant vowel, except that it is momentary. As soon as you *prolong* the approximant stricture of [j] or [w], it turns back into a vowel. Vowels are *maintainable* sounds. Semivowels are *momentary*. Another way of describing the difference is to say that a vowel has three phases: an *approach* (or 'on-glide'), when the articulators are going into position, a *hold* when the articulators remain in position for an appreciable time, and a *release* (or 'off-glide') when the articulators move away from the position they took up during the 'hold'. A semivowel, on the other hand, has only one or two phases—it completely lacks the *hold* phase. An initial semivowel, like the *y* [j] in *yes* has no audible approach, no hold, but only a rapid release, or off-glide from the [i] position. A medial semivowel, like the [w] in *away*, has an approach (on-glide) followed immediately by a release (off-glide) with no intervening hold. The articulators go from a neutral or relaxed position into the position for [w], which they immediately leave again.

We can now sum up the various types of articulatory stricture as shown in Fig. 19. In this figure, the movement of one articulator up to another is depicted in a self-evident way, and, where appropriate, the type of airflow through the articulatory channel is conventionally represented as follows:

————— voiceless, non-turbulent
⸺⸺⸺ voiceless, with turbulence (hence hiss-noise)
⌇⌇⌇ voiced, non-turbulent
⌇⌇⌇ voiced, with turbulence (hence hiss superimposed on the sound of voice).

So far we have covered the 'vertical' dimension of articulation—the degree or type of articulatory stricture, and the 'time' dimension, in which we must distinguish between those articulation types which are maintainable for an indefinite period of time and those which are essentially, obligatorily, momentary, non-prolongable.

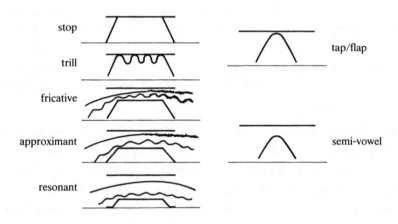

Fig. 19 Major stricture types

4. The transverse dimension: Median and lateral articulation

We now turn to the *transverse* dimension of articulation—the location of the oral air-path, that is, the distinction between a *median* or central and a *lateral* articulation channel.

The vast majority of speech-sounds have a median articulation channel, but a few have a complete obstruction in the median or central part of the mouth leaving open a channel, or channels, along one or both sides of the tongue. We have, in fact, already referred to the characteristic lateral articulation of [l]-sounds, but in Experiment 47 we approach the distinction between median and lateral articulation experimentally.

47 Say a prolonged [s s s s s . . .]. Now reverse the air-stream—i.e. produce a pulmonic suction ↓ [s s s . . .]. As you do this you should be aware of cold air passing into the mouth over the tip and central part of the tongue, while the sides of the tongue make contact with the teeth ridge and the upper side teeth. In other words, [s] has a *median* articulation channel, which can be most clearly felt when cold air flows in from outside along the centre-line of the tongue.

Now say a prolonged [l] [l l l . . .] and devoice it: [l l l l l l̥ . . .]. While saying [l̥ l̥ l̥ . . .] reverse the air-stream. As you say this pulmonic suction voiceless ↓ [l̥ l̥ l̥ . . .] you can feel cold air entering the mouth at the *sides* rather than the centre and flowing past the upper side teeth. Clearly, [l] has a *lateral* articulation channel.

If you *silently* alternate between the articulatory postures for [s] and [l] you can feel the difference between a median and lateral articulation. As you pass from silent [s] to silent [l] you can feel (*i*) the tip of the tongue coming up to make contact with the teeth-ridge, (*ii*) the side(s) of the tongue breaking away from the upper side or back teeth to open up the lateral channel(s).

As we have already discovered, the lateral [l] is a lateral approximant: by swelling out the tongue sideways, squeezing the sides of the tongue between the teeth, one can convert lateral approximant [l] into voiced lateral fricative [lʒ]: devoicing then converts [lʒ] to the voiceless lateral fricative [ɬ].

It is obvious that the closure phase of a *stop* can be neither median nor lateral, since the closure blocks up the entire width of the mouth: we don't refer to 'median stops'. However, a stop can be *approached* or *released* either medially or laterally.

48 (*i*) Say the word *felt* silently. Say it again, silently, prolonging the [l]—[f e l l l l t] (silent). Finally isolate the last part, silently—[l l l l l t] (silent). As you do this you can feel the tongue-tip in position for silent [l], then suddenly swelling out sideways to make the necessary complete closure for silent [t]. This is a stop, [t] with lateral approach. Compare this, silently, with the normal, medial, approach in *hat*. Silently alternate [.. æ æ t] [.. l l t].

(*ii*) Say the word *battle* silently. Say it again, and then cut off first the *b*, saying silent *attle* [æ t l], then cut off the [æ] leaving only silent [t l]. Silently prolong the final [l], saying [t l l l l] (silent). This is a stop with lateral release. Compare it, silently, with the normal central release of *at* [æ tʰ].

The most characteristic part of a stop is, of course, the *hold*—the actual period of closure during which pressure builds up behind the stop. This essential part of the stop, as we see from Experiment 48, is always a total blockage of the oral air-passage.

Figure 20 suggests the combination of some major stricture types with *median* or *lateral* air-path. For the reason just explained, *stop* is shown as a single complete closure, which is neither median nor lateral.

To sum up, then, in this chapter we have looked at some aspects of articulation, the component of speech-production that is responsible for the 'final shaping' of a specific type of sound. We have discovered the following types of *articulatory stricture: maintainable* (prolongable)—*stop, trill, fricative, approximant, resonant,* and *momentary* (non-prolongable)—*tap/flap* and *semi-vowel.* It is sometimes useful to group some of these stricture types under the cover terms *obstruent* (those which involve a major obstruction to airflow, namely stop, fricative, and trill) and *non-obstruent* (all the rest).

In addition, we have looked at the two different oral air-paths: *median* or central (by far the commonest path, in which the air flows out along the medial line of the mouth), and *lateral* (in which the mouth-passage is blocked in the centre so that air flows out only along the side(s) of the tongue—the air-path of [l]-type sounds).

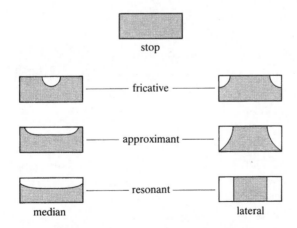

Fig. 20 Major stricture types in the transverse dimension

5

Articulation: Locations

In the last chapter we looked at various articulatory *stricture types*, representing what we called the 'vertical' and 'time' (prolongable/non-prolongable) dimensions of articulation, and at the location of the *oral air-path*, representing the 'transverse' dimension of articulation (median/ lateral).

Now we turn to the very important quasi-longitudinal dimension of articulation, namely, the *location* of articulatory strictures within the vocal tract. For the purpose of describing articulatory locations we divide the vocal tract into three areas: *nasal*, *oral*, and *pharyngeo-laryngeal*. These areas are indicated in Fig. 21.

There is a clear natural division between the *nasal* area and the others, constituted by the orifice at the back of the nose, which can be closed by raising the velum or soft palate, as shown by a broken line in Fig. 21. For phonetic purposes, the oral area consists of the mouth cavity, bounded by the whole of the under surface of the roof of the mouth, back to the uvula, and by the whole of the surface of the tongue back to the tip of the epiglottis. The pharyngeo-laryngeal area consists of the pharynx, the space behind the mouth and down to the larynx, and the larynx itself.

1. The nasal area

The *nasal area* consists of the nasal cavity, which is for the most part a complex but immobile chamber coated with mucous membrane which may swell pathologically, as when we have a cold, but is not capable of voluntary movement. Some voluntary control, and hence some variety of articulation, is possible only at the two ends of the nasal cavity, the nostrils and the pharyngeo-nasal orifice—the 'nasal port', as it is sometimes called.

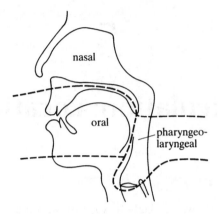

Fig. 21 The major articulatory areas

The nostrils can be narrowed, or widely opened ('flared'), and can thus modulate airflow out of the nose, but this potentiality is not known to be exploited for articulation in any language. It may be noted in passing, however, that when you devoice a nasal sound such as [m] or [n] you can hear a slight hiss-noise of turbulent airflow through the nostrils. Since these nasal sounds are quite free of turbulence when voiced, the airflow becoming turbulent when voiceless, they are typical approximants, and might well be called 'nostril' (or, better, using the latinate term) 'narial' approximants. However, we do not, in fact, use the term 'narial approximant'. All sounds articulated with the velum lowered (the 'nasal port' open) so that air flows through the nose are simply called *nasal* or *nasalized*.

In *nasals*, such as [m] [n] [ŋ] as in *mum, nun,* and the final sound of *lung,* the velum or soft palate is lowered, but there is a complete closure in the mouth (at the lips for [m], between tongue-tip and teeth or teeth-ridge for [n], between tongue-back and soft palate (velum) for [ŋ]). Consequently all the air used in their production is shunted through the nose.

In *nasalized* sounds, the nasal port is open (exactly as for nasals), but at the same time the passageway through the mouth is also open, so that the air flows out through both mouth and nose. Typical nasalized sounds are the nasalized vowels of French, as in *un bon vin blanc* [œ̃ bõ ṽɛ̃ blã]. These are sometimes called, simply, 'nasal' vowels—but it is clear that they differ from the nasal consonants [m] [n] etc. as indicated above. Experiment 49 explores the differences between *nasal* consonants, *nasalized vowels*, and purely *oral vowels*.

49 Say a prolonged [m m m . . .] and note how air is flowing out of the nose. If
you hold your hand just below the nostrils you can faintly feel the warm air
gently flowing out. If you suddenly devoice [m] the nasal airflow becomes
much more obvious: [m m m m̥ m̥].

To get the feel of raising and lowering the velum—closing and opening the
nasal port—say a prolonged [m] punctuated by inserted [b] stops. Keep the
lips tightly closed throughout the entire experiment merely flipping the nasal
port momentarily shut for each [b] then opening it again for the nasal [m]:
[m m b m b m b m b m b m . . .].

Do the same with [n] and [ŋ] (the nasal heard at the end of *long*): [n d n d n
d n d n d n . . .] [ŋ g ŋ g ŋ g ŋ g ŋ g ŋ g ŋ . . .]. You may be able to feel the nasal
port opening and closing more clearly if you repeat the experiment with
voiceless nasals: [m̥ p m̥ p m̥ p m̥ p m̥ . . .], etc.

Finally, do the same sequence of experiments completely silently—that is,
with no initiatory air-stream. In this silent experiment you can feel, even
more clearly, the proprioceptive sensation of opening and closing the nasal
port: [m̥ p m̥ p m̥ p m̥ . . .] (silent), etc.

As a result of Experiment 49 you should find it possible to lower and
raise the velum—to open and close the nasal port—at will. The next
experiment concerns *nasalized vowels* and the difference between them and
purely oral vowels.

50 Produce a prolonged vowel of the [ε]-type something like the vowel of English *bed* or *bad*. While this prolonged [ε ε ε . . .] is going on, relax the velum,
let it drop down to open the nasal port while carefully keeping the [ε] going:
or simply 'think nasal', i.e. while keeping the [ε] going, think about the sensation of making a nasal sound. In other words, contrive to get air to flow out
of *both* mouth and nose, converting [ε] to the corresponding nasalized vowel
[ε̃], thus: [ε ε ε ε ε̃ ε̃ ε̃ ε̃]. Having done this once or twice, alternate: [ε ε̃ ε ε̃ ε ε̃ ε ε̃].
Now do the same with some other vowels, e.g. [i] as in *see* [i ĩ i ĩ . . .], [ɔ] as in
saw [ɔ ɔ̃ ɔ ɔ̃ . . .], [ɑ] as in *pa* [ɑ ɑ̃ ɑ ɑ̃ . . .]. If you hold the back of your hand,
or a finger, very close to your nostrils you should feel warm air coming out
of your nose for [ε̃] [ĩ] [ɔ̃], etc., but *not* for [ε] [i] [ɔ].

Some people nasalize very open vowels, like [ɑ] all the time, saying [pɑ̃] [spɑ̃]
[kɑ̃(r)], etc. for *pa spa car*. Test for this as just described. If you do nasalize
these vowels experiment with 'thinking oral' (i.e. imagining the sensation of
closed nasal port, as for a purely oral sound) while saying [ɑ]: or go back to
alternating [i ĩ i ĩ . . .], then try to get the same sensations into [ɑ ɑ̃ ɑ ɑ̃ . . .], etc.

2. The oral area: Upper and lower articulators

We turn now to the *oral area*. In purely oral sounds (that is, in the majority of all speech-sounds) the velum is raised, closing the entrance to the nose, and the air flows solely through the mouth. Articulations in the oral area are carried out by the juxtaposition of lower and upper articulators. The *lower articulators* are those attached to the lower jaw—the lower lip, lower teeth, and tongue. The *upper articulators* are the upper lip, the upper teeth, and the whole of the roof of the mouth. We will examine all of these in some detail, and get to know them by feel, tactilely and proprioceptively, but first the reader should examine what he can see of his mouth in the mirror.

Open the mouth very wide and compare what the mirror shows with Fig. 22. The lips and the upper and lower teeth are obvious. The floor of the mouth is mostly occupied by the tongue, which can be put into many different shapes and positions. Some people, but apparently not all, are capable of forming such a deep groove in the centre of the tongue that they can see the tip of the epiglottis, like a little yellow and red-streaked second tongue at the very back of the mouth. The tip of the epiglottis is shown in Fig. 22, but don't be surprised if you can't see it.

Looking at the roof of the mouth, one can see the back of the soft palate, or velum, terminating in the uvula, and, at the extreme back of the mouth, the back wall of the pharynx.

We now consider the upper and lower articulators and the *zones* where articulation can take place within the mouth. It will be useful to have a

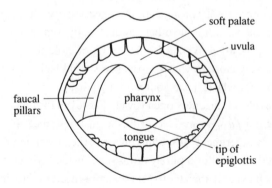

Fig. 22 Some features of the oral cavity

quick look at Figs. 23, 24, and 25 before we carefully work through various articulations.

Figure 23 shows how the upper articulatory area is subdivided, first into the natural distinction between a *labial* and a *tectal* division, the latter embracing the entire roof of the mouth (from Latin *tectum* 'roof') from the upper teeth back to the uvula.

The labial division includes an outer (exo-) and an inner (endo-) part of the lips. The tectal division breaks down naturally into two regions: a *dentalveolar* region, which includes the upper teeth and the teeth-ridge or alveolar ridge, and a *domal* region, which covers the whole remaining 'domed' part of the roof of the mouth.

Each of these two regions (dentalveolar and domal) breaks down naturally into two *zones*. The dentalveolar region includes the *dental* zone, consisting of the upper teeth, and an *alveolar* zone, consisting of the whole alveolar ridge. The domal region breaks down into the hard palate (*palatal* zone) and the soft palate, or velum (*velar* zone). You can feel the division between these zones if you run your finger back over the roof of your mouth. You will observe that the front part is quite hard and unyielding, but when the finger reaches the end of the palatal and the beginning of the velar zone, the roof of the mouth feels quite soft.

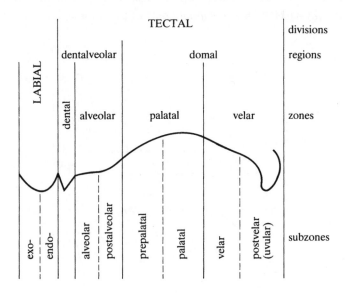

Fig. 23 Upper articulatory locations

For the present it is not necessary to study Fig. 23 in detail, or to memor-
ize the terminology introduced in it. Use it for reference when we systematically work backwards through the mouth feeling out every zone and
subzone and becoming completely familiar with them through the tactile
and proprioceptive sensations.

Figures 24 and 25 summarize the lower articulatory area. Fig. 24 shows
subdivisions of the tongue. The reader should examine the tongue in a
mirror. Note its position of rest, look at its shape when protruded, when the
tip is raised, and turned back, when it is placed in position for [t], for [k],
and so on. There are no visible divisions on the tongue surface, but it should
not be difficult to identify the tip or *apex*, and the *rim*. The *blade* (Latin
lamina) is that part of the upper surface of the tongue, extending about 1.0
to 1.5 cm. back from the apex, that usually lies just under the alveolar ridge
when the tongue is at rest, and its rim touching the backs of the lower teeth.
The remainder of the upper surface of the tongue is the *dorsum*. The front
part of the dorsum (anterodorsum) practically always articulates against
the roof of the mouth in the palatal zone, while the posterodorsum articulates in the velar zone. It is thus seldom necessary to specify antero- or
postero-dorsum in describing sounds.

Returning to the front end of the tongue, if you turn the apex up and
somewhat back a certain amount of the underside of the tongue becomes
visible. This underside of the tongue, lying largely beneath the blade, is
called the 'underblade' or *sublaminal* part of the tongue.

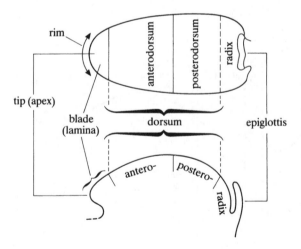

Fig. 24 Subdivisions of the tongue

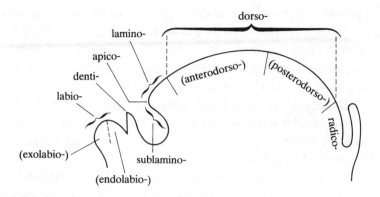

Fig. 25 Lower articulatory locations

In naming the lower articulators we use latinate prefixes, *labio-apico-*, etc. attached to the names of the upper articulatory zones or subzones. Thus, juxtaposition of lower lip and upper teeth is *labiodental*; juxtaposition of tongue surface and soft palate is *dorsovelar*, and so on.

Figure 25 shows the prefixes used in naming the lower articulators. Those in parentheses (exolabio-, endolabio-, anterodorso-, posterodorso-) are not very commonly used, but the first two are sometimes useful and will be referred to further below.

We are now in a position to start working experimentally through the various articulatory locations.

3. Labial articulations: Bilabial and labiodental

51   *labio-labial* or *bilabial*. The bilabial stops [p] and [b] need no introduction, but now close the lips as for [p], start up pulmonic pressure and allow the lips to separate very slightly so that a turbulent air-stream escapes through this narrow channel, generating a *voiceless bilabial fricative* [ɸ]. Produce a long [ɸ ɸ ɸ . . .], then voice it [ɸ ɸ ɸ β β β β] taking care to maintain turbulent flow. This is a *voiced bilabial fricative* [β].

Now make a long voiced bilabial fricative, i.e. force a prolonged voiced air-stream somewhat noisily through a very narrow aperture between the lips: [β β β . . .]. Do this again, but this time, while carefully keeping the voiced air-stream going and maintaining essentially the same bilabial stricture, slowly and carefully open up the channel between the lips very very slightly. The fricative noise should disappear: fricative [β] has been converted into the approximant [β̞] there being no special symbol for a bilabial approximant, we represent it by the symbol for the bilabial fricative plus the diacritic [̞] meaning 'more open'.

Now experiment with saying the voiceless and voiced bilabial fricatives [ɸ] and [β] and the voiced bilabial approximant [β̞] between vowels: [a ɸ a] [ɛ ɸ ɛ], [a β a] [ɛ β ɛ], [a β̞ a] [ɛ β̞ E], etc. Some textbooks say that, in Spanish, *b* between vowels as in *haber* and *beber* is a bilabial fricative. More commonly, however, this Spanish medial *b* (like Spanish medial *d* and *g*) is an *approximant*, not a fricative, thus: [a'β̞er] [beβ̞er].

The voiceless bilabial fricative [ɸ] is a common pronunciation of Japanese *h* before *u*, as in Mt. Fuji = *hudi* [ɸɯdʑi] (the exact values of the symbols [ɯ] and [dʑ] will be given later).

Other bilabial sounds are the nasal [m], and the bilabial trill. We might also mention the semivowel [w] as in English *we* and *wait*. The articulation of [w] obviously involves the lips, but it is not a pure bilabial. In the first place, it requires some degree of *rounding* of the lips. Secondly, in addition to the bilabial articulation [w] also has a dorso-velar component: the back of the tongue is raised up towards the velum. It is thus a *co-articulated* sound and will be referred to again below, under co-articulation.

In Chapter 2 we discovered experimentally that the articulation of the fricatives [f] and [v] requires the juxtaposition of the lower lip and upper teeth, and in Chapter 4 we discovered the corresponding labiodental approximant [ʋ].

Now we must carefully contrast *bilabial* [ɸ] [β] and [β̞] with *labiodental* [f] [v] and [ʋ].

52 *bilabial* and *labiodental*: Alternate aloud and then, more importantly, *silently*, between bilabial [ɸ] and labiodental [f]: [ɸ f ɸ f ɸ f ɸ f ɸ f . . .], and now between bilabial [β] and labiodental [v], [β v β v β v β v . . .]. and now between bilabial [β̞] and labiodental [ʋ], [β̞ ʋ β̞ ʋ β̞ ʋ . . .].

You must by now be very clear about the distinction between *bilabial* and *labiodental* articulation. Before leaving bilabial and labiodental articulations (for both of which the general cover term *labial* can often be used) we must take note of the distinction between *outer* (*exo-*) and *inner* (*endo-*) labial articulations.

53 Observe that it is possible to make the labial closure for [p] and [b] in two different ways. (*i*) Tense the lips somewhat, adopting a kind of severe, tight-lipped, posture so that the parts of the lips that come together are near their outer edges, and what you see in the mirror is a very thin line of lip. This type of bilabial articulation, bringing together the outer surfaces of the lips is *exolabial* (bi-exolabial, to be precise).

(*ii*) Let the lips relax and push them forward somewhat, while keeping them flat (not rounded) and let the soft inner surfaces of the lips come together. Now you can see relatively thick lips in the mirror. This type of bilabial articulation, juxtaposing the inner surfaces of the lips is *endolabial* (bi-endolabial, to be precise).

In those few languages that have a bilabial trill it is of a lax endolabial type. There is also a linguistically relevant contrast between bi-exolabial and bi-endolabial [p] and [b] in at least some varieties of Irish Gaelic.

The [f] and [v] of English (and of French, Russian, etc.) are usually *endolabio-dental*, and this is an important point to note in teaching these sounds to speakers of languages (such as Japanese) with no labiodentals. Learners must be explicitly told to place the *inner* part of the lower lip against the edges and *outer* surface of the upper teeth (otherwise they are liable to place the outer surface of the lower lip against the inner surface of the upper teeth, with bizarre results).

It is difficult to produce an airtight closure between the lip and the teeth, since the air tends to escape through the interstices between the teeth. Probably for this reason labiodental stops apparently do not occur in languages and the IPA provides no symbols for them, though it does provide a symbol, [ɱ], for labiodental nasal. This occurs as a variant, or *allophone* (see Chapter 10) of [m] in such English words as *triumph* and *nymph*. It is probably realized most frequently as a nasalized approximant rather than the usual type of nasal, which requires an airtight oral closure.

Passing further into the mouth we must take note briefly of articulations that involve the lower teeth, that is *denti-labial* and *denti-dental* (or *bidental*).

54 Silently bring the *lower teeth* into contact with the *upper lip* and then start up voiceless pulmonic pressure initiation. The result is a kind of [f]-like fricative, but a *dentilabial* one, not a labiodental one. There is no phonetic symbol for this dentilabial fricative, which is not known to occur regularly in any language. Note, however, that in the phonetic literature (particularly in French) one sometimes finds the term 'dentilabial' meaning what is properly called *labiodental*, used by persons who do not adhere to the convention that we strictly follow, namely, that the prefix (e.g. *labio-*) always refers to the *lower*

articulator, while the rest of the term (e.g. -*dental*) always refers to the *upper* articulator.

Bidental articulation hardly warrants a special experimental approach: you simply bring the upper and lower teeth together ('clench the teeth') and blow noisily through them. This is a *bidental fricative*—a sound that is practically unknown in languages though it does occur (as a variant of the dorso-velar fricative [x]) in one sub-dialect of the Shapsug dialect of Adyghe (Circassian) of the north-west Caucasus.

4. Dentalveolar articulations

We come now to a part of the mouth where we must spend a good deal of time, since a considerable variety of articulations can be produced there. This is the *dentalveolar* region.

Both the tip, or *apex*, and the *blade* of the tongue can articulate in various ways against the upper teeth, and against the front and back subzones of the teeth ridge—the *alveolar ridge*. We thus have the possibility of both *apico-* and *lamino-* articulations against the *dental* zone, and against two parts (front and back) of the *alveolar* zone. These are what we must now explore.

55 Silently place the apex and rim of the tongue against the backs of the upper teeth. Slowly and introspectively draw the tongue backwards, feeling the alveolar ridge, just behind the upper teeth. As the tongue slides very slowly backwards over the surface of the alveolar ridge you should get an impression of the shape of the ridge. Immediately behind the teeth it is relatively flat, then, as the tongue slowly slides further back, you can feel that the ridge is no longer flat and more or less horizontal, but is beginning to curve upwards. If you keep on sliding the tongue-tip slowly backwards you will feel it passing the most 'ridge-like'—the most convex—part of the alveolar ridge, and then moving on to the more concave arching front part of the hard palate. You have now gone beyond the alveolar ridge and have entered the front-palatal, or *prepalatal*, subzone of the hard palate.

Repeat this investigation several times until you are quite familiar with the shape of the alveolar ridge, as felt by your tongue.

Some people have a more prominent alveolar ridge than others. Fig. 26 shows, schematically, two extremes of this kind. If you run your tongue

Fig. 26 Two extreme types of alveolar ridge

over your alveolar ridge, as you look at Fig. 26 you will be able to estimate the degree of prominence of your own alveolar ridge. The front edge of the alveolar ridge is at the place where the upper teeth recede into the gums, but there is no sharp division between the rear end of the alveolar ridge and the beginning of the hard palate. The alveolar ridge may be taken to end beyond its most convex part, at the point where the convexity of the ridge gives way to the concavity of the hard palate. Thus, as you can feel with your tongue, the alveolar ridge may be considered to have two parts—a rather flat front part, and a curved, convex, back part. These two parts of the alveolar ridge are what we call the *alveolar* subzone (the front part), and the *postalveolar* subzone (the back part, which might more appropriately be called the 'posterior alveolar' subzone).

We can now begin, in Experiment 56, to experiment with articulations in the dentalveolar zone, articulations made with the tip (apex) of the tongue as the lower articulator. Look at Fig. 27 while carrying out Experiment 56.

56   Silently place the tip (and rim) of the tongue against the backs of the upper teeth and make a *stop* in this position. This is *apico-dental* [t̪], the small tooth-like diacritic mark under the [t̪] means that it is *dental* rather than *alveolar*. (Fig. 27a.) In fact Fig. 27a represents a rather uncommon variety of dental stop articulation. More often than not in languages that have dental stops, the blade of the tongue simultaneously makes contact with the alveolar ridge behind the teeth.

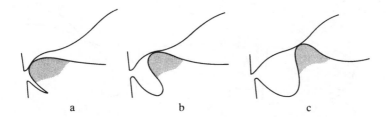

a   b   c

Fig. 27 Apico-dentalveolar stop articulations

Now, very slowly, carefully, and introspectively draw the tip of the tongue backwards. As soon as the tongue-tip is completely free of the teeth, but is still in contact with the relatively flat part of the alveolar ridge, hold that position, and then make a voiceless stop from there. This is *apico-alveolar* [t]. (Fig. 27b.)

After producing two or three apico-alveolar [t]s, and being quite clear about the tactile and proprioceptive differences between alveolar [t] and dental [t̪], slide the tongue-tip very slowly back, keeping contact with the ridge till you can feel it touching the extreme back of the ridge, at its most convex point, just before it begins to merge with the concave palate.

Make a voiceless stop from this point. This is an apico-postalveolar [t̠], the subscript line (minus sign) means that it is retracted from the alveolar position. (Fig. 27c.)

You should now have acquired a clear understanding of the *dental, alveolar* and *postalveolar* places of articulation. The three stops pronounced in Experiment 56 were all *apical*. But it is possible to articulate stops at these same locations using the *blade* of the tongue, that is, the part of the upper surface of the tongue lying immediately behind the tip, and extending back from the tip along the centre-line about 1 to 1.5 cm. Articulations made with the blade are called *laminal*, or, in the prefixed form, *lamino-*. (See Fig. 28.)

57   Place the tip of the tongue lightly against the backs of the *lower* teeth, or better, the lower gums. Keep it anchored there, out of the way, while you silently bring the *blade* of the tongue into contact with the backs of the upper teeth. This is a *lamino-dental* contact, and you can make a lamino-dental [t̪] at this location (Fig. 28a).

Now while keeping the tongue-tip anchored to the lower teeth, and thus out of the way, silently bring the blade into contact with the alveolar ridge. Perhaps the best way to do this is to start from the lamino-dental position

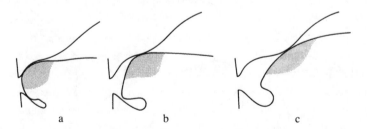

a   b   c

Fig. 28 Lamino-dentalveolar stop articulations

(blade against backs of upper teeth) and slide the blade back very slightly till it is just clear of the upper teeth. This is *lamino-alveolar*, and you can make a lamino-alveolar stop [t] at this location. If you carefully compare *apico*-alveolar [t] with *lamino*-alveolar [t] you may notice that the release sound—the little burst of noise—heard as the tongue breaks away from the ridge, tends to be less clean-cut, a little more 'sloppy' in the case of the *laminal* [t]. In fact, it may sound a little like [ts] rather than simple [t]. (Fig. 28b.)

Now, in order to shift back to make a *lamino-postalveolar* stop articulation you will probably have to remove the tongue-tip from the lower teeth. Nevertheless, you must contrive to make contact between the *blade* (not the apex) and the postalveolar subzone—the most convex part of the ridge. (Fig. 28c.) Make a lamino-postalveolar stop from this place of articulation [t̠]. You may find that the articulatory location of this lamino-postalveolar stop is about that of the starting point (the *stop* segment) of the English *affricate* [tʃ] as in *church*. (On affricates see Chap. 6.)

You will have observed that the IPA supplies no special symbols or diacritics for the laminal [t]s. This is not a serious disadvantage, since distinction between apical and laminal [t]-sounds is rare in languages.

Now we must experiment with a series of *fricatives* in the dentalveolar region.

58   Silently raise the point of the tongue, and let its apex and rim just touch the cutting edges of the upper teeth. Holding this articulation start up pulmonic pressure initiation, and resultant egressive air-stream, and the result should be an *apico-dental fricative* [θ], exactly or very nearly the English *th* of *thin*. Note that typically the English [θ] is a rather wide channel fricative, the blade of the tongue is relaxed and rather flat, and the rim of the tongue either touches or is just *behind* the edges of the upper teeth—the tongue does not normally protrude between the teeth for this sound. (Fig. 29a.)

Now silently retract the tongue-tip a very little and turn it up a little so that the edges of the tongue-rim make contact with the alveolar ridge, leaving a very narrow central channel. This is the position for an *apico-alveolar fricative*: if you now produce an egressive air-stream you will hear a rather 'whistling' kind of [s]-sound. (Fig. 29b.) Retracting the tongue-tip still further, till it is at the maximally convex extreme back of the alveolar ridge you can feel an *apico-postalveolar fricative* type of articulation. An egressive air-stream will now generate a [ʃ]-sound, like a kind of *sh* as in English *shop*, but by no means the commonest variety of this (which is laminal): the *sch* sound of North German, and the Russian sh ш are rather typically of this apico-postalveolar type. (Fig. 29c.)

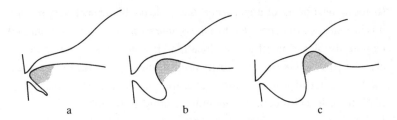

Fig. 29 Apico-dentalveolar fricative articulations

The main things achieved in 58 will be a further familiarity with the three major dentalveolar zones of articulation: dental, alveolar, and postalveolar. Experiment 59 investigates laminal articulation at two of these locations.

59 Let the apex and rim of the tongue lie lightly against the backs of the lower teeth. Press the sides of the tongue-blade up against the alveolar ridge, leaving a very narrow channel in the centre. An egressive air-stream through this narrow channel generates a typical *lamino-alveolar* [s]-type *fricative*. (Fig. 30a.)

Now retract the tongue a little detaching the tip from the lower teeth, and form a narrow articulatory channel between the blade and the most convex back part of the ridge—a *lamino-postalveolar fricative*, a kind of [ʃ]. (Fig. 30b.)

Silently, and slowly, alternate [s]/[ʃ] till you are sure you can feel the difference between them.

We have now covered the major types of stop and fricative articulation in the *dentalveolar* region. You can use the knowledge acquired from Experiments 58–9 to make a silent, introspective, analysis of some sounds of your own language: for example, are your [t] [d] [n] [l] *apical*, or *laminal*, *dental*, or *alveolar*? And if your language has a *trilled* or *tapped* [r] or [ɾ] where is it articulated? If you have [s]—and/or [ʃ]-sounds—in your language, are they

Fig. 30 Lamino-dentalveolar fricative articulations

apico- or *lamino-*, *dental, alveolar*, or *postalveolar*, etc.? If your native language is Polish, what are the articulatory differences between *s, sz, ś*? If your language is Russian, how does the primary articulation of [t] and [d] in [tot] 'that', [da] 'yes' compare with that of palatalized [tʲ] in [tʲotʲə] 'aunt' and [dʲadʲə] 'uncle'? (On palatalization see Chapter 6.) If your language is Arabic compare the dentalveolar articulations of plain [t] and [s] as in [tiːn] 'fig', [siːn] 'the letter s', and of 'emphatic' [ṭ] and [ṣ] as in [ṭiːn] 'mud' and [ṣiːn] 'China'. You may find the dentalveolar articulations much the same, the difference between the plain and emphatic consonants depending chiefly on the back of the tongue (see Chap. 6 Sect. 2).

If your language is English, silently compare the [t] and [d]-sounds in (*a*) *eight wide*, (*b*) *eighth width*, (*c*) *try dry*. Can you observe differences between them? And if you use a *tap* in the middle of *better* (American), or in the middle of *very* (British) is it *apico-* or *lamino-*, *dental, alveolar*, or *postalveolar*? How do you articulate the *r* in *red*? In British types of English it is likely to be a variety of *apico-postalveolar approximant* (or, more rarely, *fricative*) [ɹ]. In American types of English you may find that the tongue-tip is rather far behind the postalveolar location and that the whole body of the tongue is bunched up, coming rather near the velar articulatory zone. There is a considerable amount of variation—both regional and personal—in the pronunciation of English *r*s, so your own *r* may not exactly correspond to any described here. By silently isolating your *r* and introspecting about it see if you can discover how it is articulated.

We can now review the principal types of dentalveolar articulation and the IPA symbols used to represent them:

stops: (apico- or lamino-) dental [t̪] [d̪], alveolar [t] [d], post-alveolar [ṭ] [ḍ].
fricatives: *apico-dental* (wide channel), [θ] [ð]
  alveolar (normally *lamino-*), [s] [z]
  postalveolar (*apico-* or *lamino-*), [ʃ] [ʒ]
approximants: no special symbols, except for apico-postalveolar [ɹ], which is most commonly approximant, but may also be fricative. There is not much difference between the fricative apico-postalveolar [ʒ], as in Polish [ʒɨw] Russian [ʒɨɫ] '(he) lived' and the apico-postalveolar fricative [ɹ] (as often in British English *dry* [d̠ɹai]): but there is some difference. In [ɹ], but not in [ʒ], there is a slight spoon-shaped hollow in the centre of the tongue, just behind the blade, which is absent in [ʒ].

Approximants of other dentalveolar types can be represented by using the 'opening' diacritic: thus [ð̞] [z̞] represent apico-dental and lamino-alveolar approximants.

trill and *tap*: [r] and [ɾ].

lateral approximants: (dental, alveolar, or postalveolar) [l].

lateral fricatives: (dental, alveolar, or postalveolar) [ɬ], [ɮ].

nasals: (dental, alveolar, or postalveolar) [n].

5. Retroflex and palatal articulations

Having explored the dentalveolar region of articulation we now proceed further back into the mouth.

First, immediately behind the postalveolar subzone we come to *sublamino-prepalatal* articulation, otherwise known as *retroflex*.

60 Silently place the tip of the tongue against the postalveolar part of the alveolar ridge. Now slide it back beyond the postalveolar subzone, to where the hard palate ceases to be convex. As your tongue enters this concave zone it is pointing almost straight up, and the *underblade*, or sublamina, begins to make contact with the prepalatal arch. This is *sublamino-prepalatal* articulation, or, since the apex of the tongue is virtually curled backwards, *retroflex*.

Produce a series of retroflex sounds from this place of articulation:

stops [ʈ] [ɖ], fricatives [ʂ] [ʐ], approximant [ɻ], lateral approximant [ɭ] and nasal [ɳ]. (See Fig. 31a.)

There is also a *flap* articulated in the retroflex zone, symbol [ɽ]. To produce this, start with the tongue-tip curled well back, then let it shoot forwards and downwards, lightly striking the prepalatal arch, just behind the alveolar ridge, on the way down. (See Fig. 31b.)

Retroflex consonants are particularly characteristic of languages of India. They are often quite strongly retroflex in the Dravidian languages, but tend to be somewhat less so in the Indic languages of northern India. In Hindi, for example, [ʈ] and [ɖ], as in [ʈiːn] 'tin' and [ɖoːl] 'bucket', may not be much further back than apico-postalveolar [t̠] [d̠]. However, they contrast with apico-dental stops [t̪] [d̪] as in [t̪iːn] 'three' [d̪oː] 'two', and the more retracted stops are normally called 'retroflex' and written [ʈ] and [ɖ]. Hindi [ɽ], however, occurring in such words as [gʰoɽa] 'horse' [ləɽka] 'boy', is a truly retroflex flap.

Next, we must examine dorsal articulations in the *prepalatal* zone—that

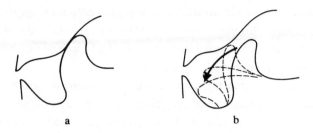

a   b

Fig. 31 Retroflex articulations: (a) stop (b) flap

is non-retroflex articulations involving juxtaposition of the dorsal surface of the tongue and the hard palate. The hard palate is divided into a front half—the upward-backwards sloping *prepalatal* arch—and a rear half—the high vault of the hard palate back to the line of division between the hard and soft palate: this is the *palatal* subzone proper (see Fig. 22). We start with *dorso-palatal* (not prepalatal) articulation (see Fig. 32).

61   Silently form and hold the articulation for a vowel [i] as in *see*. Introspecting about the tactile and proprioceptive sensations of silent [i] note how the tongue is bunched up in the front of the mouth. The vowel [i], of course, is a *dorso-palatal approximant.*

   Now push the central part of the tongue upwards, narrowing the articulation channel of silent [i] until it disappears altogether as the centre of the tongue makes contact with the highest part of the hard palate. (See Fig. 31.)

   From this position make a voiceless dorso-palatal stop [c] and a voiced dorso-palatal stop [ɟ].

   Form and hold the stop of [c], i.e. hold the tongue dorsum in firm contact with the hard palate, but nothing else: there must be absolutely no contact between the anterodorsum and the prepalatal subzone, or between the blade and the postalveolar subzone. Now, release the centre of the tongue very slightly, so that you form a very narrow dorso-palatal articulation channel:

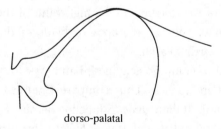

dorso-palatal

Fig. 32 Dorso-palatal articulation

initiate an egressive air-stream which ought to become strongly turbulent as it flows through this narrow channel, forming a dorso-palatal voiceless fricative [ç]. We already reached a sound very much like [ç] by devoicing [i] in Exp. 29. This [ç] is the sound of *ch* in German *ich*.

Now add voice, but be sure that you have a really narrow fricative type channel, so that when you voice [ç] it becomes a voiced dorso-palatal fricative [ʝ], and not the approximant [i]. The symbol [ʝ] is useful, in order to distinguish between the *fricative* [ʝ] and the *approximant* or *semivowel* [j]— exemplified by the *y* in English *yes*.

Since it is normally the dorsal part of the tongue (and, specifically, the anterodorsal part) that articulates against the hard palate, we commonly drop the prefix and talk simply of *palatal* articulation. The palatal stops [c] and [ɟ] are not very common in languages, but they are sometimes exemplified by the *ty* and *gy* of Hungarian ['faːcol] 'veil' and ['mɑɟɑr] 'Hungarian' though they are perhaps more often pronounced as prepalatal affricates [cɕ] [dʑ]. In addition to the palatal stops [c] and [ɟ], the fricatives [ç] and [ʝ], the approximant [i], and the semivowel [j] we can have a palatal nasal [ɲ] and lateral [ʎ].

The palatal nasal [ɲ] is traditionally said to be the pronunciation of the French *gn* in *campagne*, the Italian *gn* in *ogni*, the Spanish *ñ* in *mañana*. However, in these languages the [ɲ] is not always pronounced as a genuine palatal nasal. It may, instead, be pronounced as an apico-alveolar, lamino-postalveolar, or lamino-prepalatal nasal followed by a palatal semivowel [nj].

Palatal [ʎ] is traditionally said to be the pronunciation of Italian *gl* in *egli*, Castilian Spanish *ll* in *pollo*. Again, however, it is not always pronounced as a genuine palatal [ʎ] in these languages, but rather as [lj]. In Latin-American varieties of Spanish *ll* is commonly pronounced as [ʎ], but sometimes as a semivowel [j] or a fricative [ʒ].

As a matter of principle, the student of phonetics should experiment with producing *genuine* dorso-palatal [ɲ] and [ʎ], with contact only between the dorsal surface of the tongue and the high vault of the hard palate, but absolutely no contact between the apex or blade of the tongue and the alveolar ridge or prepalatal arch.

It may be useful to compare genuine [ɲ] and [ʎ] with the sequences [nj] and [lj] that occur in English. Thus compare English *onion* [ʌnjən] with French *agneau* [aɲo], Italian *agnello* [aɲɛllo] 'lamb', Spanish *año* [aɲo] 'year'; English *billiards* [biljə(r)dz], Italian *bigletto* [biʎɛtto] 'ticket', Spanish *billar* [biʎar] 'billards', etc.

Before leaving the palatal zone we must mention the possibility of articulation in the front part of the zone—the *prepalatal* subzone. Experiment 62 introduces this subzone.

62 Produce a voiceless palatal fricative [ç]—if necessary, develop it from [i] by devoicing and narrowing the channel somewhat. Now, while maintaining a prolonged [ç ç . . .], raise the apex and blade of the tongue somewhat so that the anterodorsal surface of the tongue comes close to the prepalatal arch, doing, in fact, what you were explicitly told *not* to do in producing genuine palatal [ç].

Once you get some kind of dorso- or lamino-prepalatal fricative noise into the sound, try to slacken off the prepalatal constriction somewhat. The result should be a lamino-prepalatal fricative [ɕ] or voiced [ʑ]. The same result can be arrived at by starting with a lamino-postalveolar type of [ʃ] and then contriving to get more palatal constriction into it: saying lamino-postalveolar [ʃ] while 'thinking [ç] or [i]'.

This kind of lamino- or dorso-prepalatal fricative is the Polish ś, which is sometimes called, quite reasonably, a 'palatalized [ʃ]'.

One can also articulate a *stop* in the prepalatal subzone, or an *affricate* (stop released into homorganic fricative—see Chap. 6) which may be represented as [cɕ] [ɟʑ] or [tɕ] [dʑ].

Figure 33 indicates the different tongue-positions for an *apico-postalveolar* [ʃ] (33a), a *lamino-postalveolar* [ʃ] (33b), a *lamino-prepalatal* [ɕ]

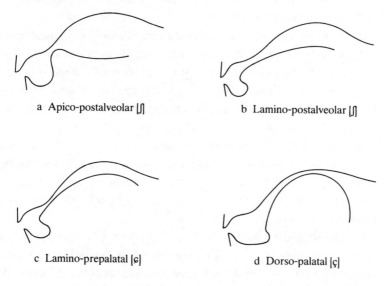

a Apico-postalveolar [ʃ]

b Lamino-postalveolar [ʃ]

c Lamino-prepalatal [ɕ]

d Dorso-palatal [ç]

Fig. 33 Some postalveolar and (pre)palatal articulations

(33c), and a *dorso-palatal* [ç] (33d). It may be useful for the reader to produce these four types of fricative, silently and aloud, while looking at the figure. It should be noted that in the older terminology of the IPA apico- or lamino-postalveolar fricatives of the type [ʃ] and [ʒ] are called 'palato-alveolar', while lamino- or dorso-prepalatal fricatives of the type [ɕ] and [ʑ] are still called 'alveolo-palatal'. This terminology is not recommended, since it is inconsistent with the strict principle of using the prefixed term to designate the *lower* articulator (as in *labio*-dental, *apico*-alveolar).

6. Velar and uvular articulations

We go on now to *dorso-velar* articulation—that is, articulation between the back of the tongue and the soft palate. This is the place of articulation of typical [k] and [g] sounds. So in 63 we begin with those.

63   Form the articulation for a [k] as in English *car*; hold it silently for a moment, then silently release it. Repeat this several times, introspecting about what it feels like. Contrast this *dorso-velar stop* [k] with a *dorso-palatal stop* [c]. Note how the body of the tongue is thrust well forward for [c], so that contact can be made with the highest part of the hard palate. For [k], however, the body of the tongue, though clearly further back than for [c], doesn't feel particularly strongly drawn back.

Once you are satisfied you can feel the midvelar (mid-soft palate) contact for [k] hold the tongue in that [k]-position and, while taking care not to shift the tongue either forward or back, open up a very small channel between the tongue and the soft palate. If you propel an egressive air-stream (i.e. blow) through that narrow dorso-velar channel you should hear the sound of the *voiceless dorso-velar fricative* [x]. Make sure it *is* velar. Some people tend to let the tongue slip back and make a *uvular* fricative [χ]. We will come to that in Exp. 65, but for the moment what is required is a purely dorso-velar [x].

Make a prolonged [x x x x x . . .], then do it again, switching on *voice*, but making no other change: [x x x ɣ ɣ ɣ . . .], where [ɣ] is the symbol for a voiced dorso-velar fricative.

Starting from the voiced velar fricative [ɣ] develop a velar approximant [ɰ]. Say a prolonged [ɣ ɣ ɣ . . .], noting that it is truly fricative, i.e. there is a fricative hiss-noise superimposed upon the smooth sound of voice. Now while saying prolonged [ɣ ɣ ɣ . . .], very slowly, and very slightly, open up the articulatory channel, just to the point where the hiss-noise of turbulent air-flow ceases: [ɣ ɣ ɣ ɰ ɰ]. This is the velar approximant, [ɰ].

Now that you are clear about *dorso-velar* (or simply *velar*, as we often call it) articulation you can note that there is also a velar nasal [ŋ]. This is the nasal that occurs at the end of *lung* [lʌŋ] in English. Note that [ŋ] never occurs at the beginning of a syllable in English. However, if you isolate [ŋ] you will find it quite easy to put a vowel after it, and say [ŋa] [ŋi], etc.

In English, and many other languages (it is very noticeable in French, for example), [k] and [g] are purely velar only before such vowels as [ɑ] and [u], as in English *car*, *guard*, and *cool*, *goo*. Before front, or palatal, vowels like [i] as in *key*, *geese*, however, the articulation of [k] [g] is shifted forward a little. If you articulate these words silently, then isolate the [k]/[g] of each and compare the ones that occur before [i] with the others, the forward shift of tongue-position before [i] will be obvious. But note that even though the tongue is somewhat advanced in *key* and *geese*, it does not go nearly as far forward as the palatal position of [c] and [ɟ]. Before [i] the English velar stops are somewhat 'fronted' (i.e. slightly advanced from the fully velar location that they have in such a word as *car*), but they are not fully palatalized, and certainly do not become palatals.

The next, and the last, articulatory location in the oral area is *dorso-uvular*, or simply *uvular*. We investigate sounds made at this location in Experiment 64.

64 Make a [k]-closure and then, silently, or almost silently, make a prolonged series of faint [k]-type sounds [kʰ kʰ kʰ . . .], etc. while slowly sliding the tongue back and down as far as you can. You will end up making a stop at the very furthest back part of the soft palate. The extreme back of the tongue is in contact with the uvula and the extreme back of the velum (soft palate). If you let a little pressure build up behind this extreme back closure, then release the closure, you will hear a *uvular stop* [q]. If you repeat this experiment—a series of faint stops of the [kʰ kʰ kʰ . . .] type steadily moving back from the *velar* to the *uvular* positions—you will observe that the sound of the little burst of noise occurring on the release of each stop goes down in pitch by about an octave over the whole range.

Another observation you may make is that the release of velar [k] is relatively 'clean', while that of [q] is more 'sloppy'. This is because the convex tongue-surface can break away from the whole contact-area of the concave velar surface almost instantaneously but separation from the more flexible and irregular surface of the extreme back of the velum, including the uvula, is less instantaneous, less clean-cut.

Having produced the voiceless uvular stop [q] (not a difficult sound) and having repeated it several times, you might try to produce the corresponding voiced sound—the voiced uvular stop [ɢ]. This is much more difficult, because the tongue is so far back in the articulation of a uvular, that the space between the oral closure and the glottis is very small: consequently as the air used in generating voice flows upwards through the glottis the essential pressure-difference across the glottis is abolished almost immediately, and voicing ceases.

Other uvular articulations are the fricatives [χ] and [ʁ], the approximant [ʁ], the nasal [N], and the trill [R]. They are investigated in Experiment 65.

65   Form the closure for a uvular stop [q] and hold it. Now, while holding that uvular articulation posture, open up a small central channel, and propel an egressive air-stream through it. The result should be the *voiceless uvular fricative* [χ].

Another way of approaching [χ] is to start with a velar [x] and then move progressively backwards, as you did with [k . . . q] in Exp. 64. In this case, make a velar fricative [x], and while keeping the fricative noise going, slowly slide your tongue back and down, till you have arrived as far back as you can go, at [χ]. Once again, notice as you do this that the pitch of the fricative hiss goes down by nearly an octave.

Having produced [χ], prolong it and then switch on voice [χ χ χ χ ʁ ʁ ʁ ʁ]. The result is the *voiced uvular fricative* [ʁ]. If you now make a prolonged [ʁ] then, while keeping the voice going and the same general tongue-posture, very slightly widen the articulatory channel and you will convert the uvular fricative [ʁ] to the *uvular approximant* [ʁ].

The uvular nasal [N] should give no trouble, since it can easily be reached, like [q] and [χ], by sliding back from the corresponding velar, [ŋ]. There remains the uvular trill [R]. If you can *gargle*, and most people can, then you can produce a uvular trill. It is only necessary to reduce the amount of water used in gargling, finally using only saliva, to pass from gargle to [R]. In addition, as we pointed out in the last chapter, it is easier to produce all trills with a powerful voiceless air-stream, so you might try that.

As you experiment with uvular sounds you may notice that the uvular fricatives [χ] and [ʁ] tend to develop something of a trilled quality. This is normal—it happens all the time in languages that use uvular fricatives, simply because the uvula, being small and flexible, tends to be thrown into vibration by the air-stream of the fricative. You may be able to avoid it by trying to get a strong feeling of tenseness into the rear of your soft palate and the back of the tongue as you produce [χ] and [ʁ]. An important difference between uvular fricative [ʁ] and trill [ʀ] is that whereas the tongue-back is relatively flat or convex for [ʁ], a deep longitudinal groove is formed in the back of the tongue for the trill [ʀ], and the uvula vibrates in the groove.

We have now covered all the major articulatory locations within the *oral* area. You might find it useful to run through them again. In particular, it would be useful to compare the three major tectal articulatory locations: palatal, velar, uvular. By contrasting series of sounds such as [c] [k] [q], [ç] [x] [χ], [ɲ] [ŋ] [ɴ] one becomes more clearly aware of the differences between *palatal*, *velar*, and *uvular* articulations. Finally, we must turn our attention to articulations in the pharyngeo-laryngeal area: these are articulations in the *pharynx* and *larynx*.

7. Pharyngal and glottal articulations

Articulations in the pharynx are called pharyngeal, or *pharyngal*: those performed in the larynx are *glottal* (not to be confused with 'glottalic', which is the name of a type of initiation).

The pharynx is the cavity behind the mouth, running from the back of the nose and the 'nasal port' down to the larynx. *Pharyngal* articulations can be made both in the part of the *pharynx* just behind the mouth (the *oropharynx*) and in the lower part of the pharynx, immediately above the larynx and merging with it (the *laryngopharynx*).

Here we will deal with only two types of articulation in the pharynx: one a rather generalized sphincteric compression of the oropharynx—which we shall call *pharyngal*: the other involving the epiglottis, which we shall call *epiglottal*. These are dealt with in Experiments 66 and 67 respectively.

66 The best way to induce the pharyngeal compression that we want to achieve is to activate what is called the 'gag' reflex. Unless the reader is exceptionally insensitive he can do this by sticking a finger into his mouth so that it touches, or merely approaches, the uvula. The extreme convulsive contraction of the pharynx that this induces is the starting point from which to develop a milder, less intense, contraction of the pharynx. If you send a

voiceless and then a voiced air-stream through the contracted pharynx you will produce the pharyngal sounds, voiceless [ħ] and voiced [ʕ].

These are a very common variety of the sounds of the Arabic letters ح (*ḥa*) and ع (*'ain*). They are often described in the literature as 'pharyngal fricatives', but in reality they are more often approximants. Note that the voiced sound [ʕ] has no turbulent, fricative-like, hiss although a noticeable hiss sound is heard in [ħ].

The pharyngal approximants [ħ] and [ʕ] are very characteristic of most varieties of Arabic and of a few other languages, including Somali, Berber, and some varieties of Oriental Hebrew (in modern Israeli Hebrew, the ancient Hebrew [ħ] is replaced by a velar or uvular [x] or [χ], and the [ʕ] by a glottal stop [ʔ]).

In a few varieties of Arabic and Oriental Hebrew the *'ain* (ع) appears to be pronounced, not as a simple pharyngal constriction, but as a complete closure, formed by folding the epiglottis back, as in the act of swallowing. This *epiglottal stop* is represented in the latest (1996) IPA chart by [ʡ].

67 Start by *swallowing* several times, and introspecting about what is going on. In the middle of the process of swallowing there is a feeling of complete closure when the epiglottis folds down over the larynx to prevent food from entering it. Hold that stop position for a moment. Do that several times, then try to flank that moment of closure by a vowel, for example [a], thus saying [a ʡ a] [a ʡ a]. This is an *epiglottal* stop. Once you can say [a ʡ a] fairly easily, compare it with simple glottal stop: [a ʔ a] [a ʔ a]. Notice how glottal stop [a ʔ a] is just a simple momentary 'holding of breath', a simple hiatus between the flanking vowels that hardly affects their quality.

The epiglottal stop, however, in [a ʡ a] is not only a very strong stop, but it also affects the quality of the flanking vowels, which acquire a peculiar 'squeezed' quality (pharyngalization).

Epiglottal stop [ʡ] seems to occur not only in varieties of Arabic and Hebrew as indicated above, but also in several languages of the Caucasus, for example in Chechen, where epiglottal [ʡ] contrasts with glottal [ʔ]. The existence of epiglottal stop in Arabic and Hebrew was demonstrated instrumentally by Laufer and Condax (1979).

Glottal articulation occurs, of course, in the larynx, by the juxtaposition of the vocal cords. We have already seen many examples of *glottal stop* [ʔ], articulated by making a complete closure between the vocal cords—closing the glottis. Glottal stop is sometimes used in English before a strongly stressed initial vowel, as in 'Ah!' [ʔa]. It may *accompany* final voiceless stops, producing co-articulated glottal + oral stops, in many types of English, though more frequently in the USA than in Britain, perhaps, as in *cap*, *hat*, *hack*, etc., pronounced [kæʔp͡] [hæʔt], [hæʔk], where the ligature [‿] indicates that glottal stop and oral stop are simultaneous. In some English and Scottish dialects glottal stop may totally replace an intervocalic [t], thus Cockney [baʔə], Glasgow [bʌʔər] for 'butter'.

The sound [h], as in *hot*, is often described as a *voiceless glottal fricative*, since like other consonants it occupies the marginal (initial) position in the syllable, rather than the central position in the syllable appropriate to a vowel. In terms of its articulation, however, it might also be regarded as a voiceless vowel of about the same quality as the voiced vowel that follows. The corresponding *voiced glottal fricative*, [ɦ] is essentially a brief span of *breathy voice* or *whispery voice* functioning as a consonant. Voiced [ɦ] may occur intervocalically in English in such words as *Aha!* and *perhaps*.

At the end of Chapters 2 and 3 we mentioned the prosodic features that relate to initiation and to phonation respectively, namely *stress* and *pitch* phenomena. The prosodic feature that is related to articulation is the *duration*, or length (also known as quantity) of sounds. Clearly all *maintainable* articulations can be held for a shorter or longer time. We will deal with the duration of sounds in Chapter 9, 'Prosodic Features'.

6

Co-articulation and Sequences

We completed our survey of articulatory stricture types (stop, trill, fricative, etc.) and articulatory locations (bilabial, labiodental, apico-dental, etc.) in Chapter 5. However, there are still some things that remain to be said about articulation, and we discuss them here under the headings of *co-articulation* and *sequences*.

Co-articulation. All the sounds we have dealt with so far (with one exception, [w]) have a single place of articulation: thus, [p] is *bilabial*, [c] is *dorsopalatal*, [ħ] is *pharyngal*, etc. But it is perfectly possible for articulation to occur at two different places simultaneously. As we saw in Chapter 5, the semivowel [w] involves an approximation and rounding of the lips, and consequently is *bilabial*; but, at the same time, the back of the tongue is raised towards the velum, so that there is a simultaneous *dorso-velar* articulation.

We call such simultaneous articulation at two different locations *co-articulation*. Co-articulation is an essential feature of some sounds, such as [w], but it also occurs 'accidentally' as it were in the close transition from one consonant to another. In the English word *play* for example, as usually pronounced, a little introspection will show that the tongue-tip makes contact with the alveolar ridge for the apico-alveolar lateral approximant [l] while the lips are still closed for the bilabial stop [p]. There is thus a short period of overlapping articulation—and this is a period of transitory co-articulation.

On the other hand, some consonants, like the [w] already mentioned, are co-articulated in their own right, as it were, and these are the subject of the present section.

There are two types of co-articulation: (*i*) *co-ordinate*, or *double* articulation, and (*ii*) *secondary* articulation.

1. Co-ordinate, or double, articulation

In *double* articulation there are two simultaneous articulations of the *same rank*—that is to say, of the *same degree of stricture*, hence: *stop + stop, fricative + fricative*, or *approximant + approximant*.

68 *stop + stop*. Simultaneously place the back of the tongue against the soft palate (form a velar stop, [k]), and close the lips (form a bilabial stop, [p]). Hold this double articulation [p͡k] or [k͡p] in which the ligature [‿] shows that the articulations are simultaneous, build up a little pulmonic pressure behind it, and then release it into a vowel, say [a], thus [p͡ka]. This is a *bilabial + velar* stop.

Now put a vowel before and after [p͡k] and say [ap͡ka], making sure that the two articulations are as nearly as possible coterminous, i.e. begin and end at the same time. Experiment with other co-articulated stops, [b͡g], [t͡k], [d͡g], [p͡t], [b͡d].

We label co-ordinate, or double, articulations by means of either a *plus* sign or a *hyphen*: thus [p͡k] or [k͡p] = *bilabial + velar* or *bilabial-velar*. Double articulated *bilabial + velar* sounds are sometimes referred to as 'labio-velar' or 'labiovelar'. This usage should be avoided, since the latinate prefixes *labio-*, *apico-* etc. refer strictly to *lower* articulators and should not be used to refer to the whole conjunct, lower + upper, articulation.

69 *fricative + fricative*. Simultaneously form the articulatory strictures for [f] and [s] and then say [f͡s]. Now [f] + [x], [f͡x]. You will find it is a little difficult to generate fricative turbulence simultaneously at both stricture locations. This is probably why co-ordinate fricative + fricative co-articulation is virtually non-existent in languages.

approximant + approximant. This type of co-ordinate (double) articulation is quite easy. You have already seen one example—[w]. If you experimentally lengthen [w] (which turns it into the vowel [u]), you can then decompose it into its two components. First, while keeping the [u u u . . .] going, slowly and deliberately unround the lips but *make no other change*. What is left, after you have removed the bilabial articulation, is a velar articulation—a velar approximant. Thus, the vowel [u] is a double articulation (a co-ordinate co-articulation) consisting of a rounded labial and a velar approximant. And the ultra-short [u] that is the semivowel [w] is a *bilabial-velar* semivowel.

Now, produce a palatal approximant [i] and while carefully maintaining the dorso-palatal articulation, slowly and carefully add a labial articulation—round the lips. The result will be a *bilabial-palatal* approximant, the vowel [y] as in French *lune*. Make it ultra-short, and you have the bilabial-palatal semivowel [ɥ].

Both of these double-articulated semivowels occur in French, for example in *oui* [wi] 'yes' and *huit* [ɥit] 'eight', *Louis* [lwi] 'Louis' and *lui* [lɥi] 'him'.

2. Primary and secondary articulation

The second type of co-articulation involves two simultaneous articulations of different ranks: *primary* and *secondary*. Basically, the rank order of stricture types is *stop—trill—fricative—approximant—resonant*. Secondary articulations are normally at about the rank of approximant. For example, an [f] with secondary palatal articulation is an [f] with a simultaneous articulation of the [i]- or [j]-types: since we name secondary articulations by means of adjectives in -*ized* we call this a *palatalized* [f].

The only departures from the basic ranking concern *nasalized* and *pharyngalized* sounds, and *lateral approximants*. *Any* nasal articulation is regarded as secondary to any accompanying oral articulation. For example, even though the oro-nasal orifice (the 'nasal port') may be *smaller* (and therefore apparently of higher rank) than the wide oral articulatory channel of an open vowel like [æ̃] or [ɔ̃], nevertheless the *oral* articulation is regarded as primary. We call these (and all vowels with simultaneous airflow through the nose) *nasalized vowels*—and never 'oralized nasals'.

Again all pharyngal articulations are regarded as *secondary* to any simultaneous oral vowel articulation, and, finally, any approximant-type articulation accompanying a lateral approximant is always regarded as *secondary* to the lateral. Thus, an *alveolar lateral* approximant [l] with a simultaneous *palatal approximant* ([i]-type) co-articulation would always be called a *palatalized alveolar lateral approximant* (and never an 'alveolar-lateralized palatal approximant').

The principal types of secondary articulation are *labialized* (labialization), *palatalized* (palatalization), *velarized* (velarization), and *pharyngalized* (pharyngalization).

Secondary articulations are transcribed by diacritic marks: [ʷ] for *labialized* (labialization), [ʲ] for *palatalized* (palatalization), [˷] through the letter, e.g. [ɫ], for *velarized* (velarization), and either the same [˷] or a small raised [ˤ] for *pharyngalized* (pharyngalization).

We must now carry out some experiments on secondary articulation, working systematically back from labialization to pharyngalization.

70　Say [a a a w a a a], and then [a a a k a a a]. Now say both of these *simultaneously*. The result should be [a a a kʷ a a a] with *labialized* [kʷ]. If this is done properly, the maximum approximation and rounding of the lips should be exactly simultaneous with the [k]-closure.

Now closely round the lips, simultaneously form a [k]-closure, build up a slight pressure behind the stop, and then say [kʷ a a], simultaneously releasing the labial and velar strictures. Now experiment with other labialized sounds: [tʷ] [gʷ] [dʷ] [sʷ] [zʷ], etc.—initially, medially, and finally, e.g. [sʷ a a] [a sʷ a] [a sʷ], etc. In every case note that a truly labialized consonant must have simultaneous labialization. Thus the transcription [sʷ a a] represents an initial [s] pronounced through closely rounded lips, not a sequence of [s] + [w], which would be transcribed [s w a a].

It is sometimes difficult to decide whether we are dealing with a sequence of consonants followed (or preceded) by [w], or with a single co-articulated consonant, with secondary labilization. The reason, of course, is that though in theory secondary articulation requires total simultaneity of articulation, in fact the timing-relations between two articulations are infinitely variable. We indicate this state of affairs roughly in Fig. 34.

In Fig. 34 the upper line(s) represent the primary articulatory stricture, say [k], being made, held, and then released (e.g. into a vowel). The lower line represents the degree of stricture of the secondary articulation, say, lip-approximation and rounding for labialization. The solid labial articulation lines represent unequivocal *simultaneous* (a) and *successive* (b) articulations. There is no doubt that (a) represents co-articulation secondary articulation, whereas (b) represents a labial semivowel or approximant [w] following the [k].

The broken lines represent two of the infinite number of possible states of affairs between these extremes, underlining the fact that the status of a possible secondary articulation is often ambiguous. In a real ambiguous case of this type we may finally decide whether we are dealing with a secondary articulation, say labialized [kʷ], or a sequence of distinct sounds [kw], on the basis of evidence from the general phonological structure of the language rather than on purely phonetic grounds. But the student of phonetics must be able to distinguish between the unambiguous, extreme, cases.

It would be a good idea, while looking at Fig. 34, to experiment with

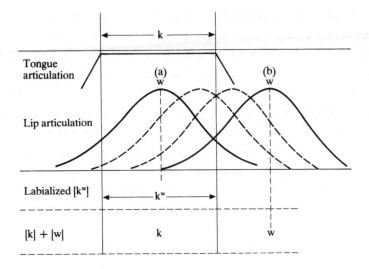

Fig. 34 Timing relations in co-articulation

producing a series of secondary articulations with different time-relations to the primary articulation, like those indicated in the figure.

We now continue working through the remaining types of secondary articulation, starting with *palatalization* in Experiment 71.

71   Palatalization is represented by a raised [ʲ] beside the symbol for the primary articulation. To produce a palatalized sound one must hold the tongue in a dorso-palatal position (approximately as for [i]) while making the primary articulation. Experiment first with pairs of voiced fricatives such as *plain* [v], *palatalized* [vʲ], i.e. [v] with simultaneous [i], *plain* [z], palatalized [zʲ], i.e. [z] with simultaneous [i].

Now place these consonants between vowels: in effect say [a a i a a] (or [a a j a a]) and [a a v a a], [a a z a a], simultaneously: thus [a a vʲ a a] [a a zʲ a a].

Next experiment with plain [l], plain [n]; palatized [lʲ], palatalized [nʲ], that is, simultaneous [l] or [n] and [i].

Voiceless fricatives can also be palatalized, but in this case, of course, the secondary articulation is not [i], but *voiceless* [i̥]: thus [f], [fʲ] (= [f] + [i̥]), [s], [sʲ] (= [s] + [i̥]).

Finally, experiment with simultaneous secondary palatalization added to stops. Say [a a a i a a a], [a a a p a a a] then combine them: [a a a pʲ a a a], and so with [a a bʲ a a] [a a tʲ a a] [a a dʲ a a] [a a kʲ a a] [a a gʲ a a].

Since palatalization consists in raising the anterodorsum of the tongue towards the hard palate, it is not surprising that sometimes, when the primary articulation also involves the tongue, the secondary palatalization slightly changes the primary articulation. Russian, which is a language with a whole series of palatalized consonants contrasting with single or non-palatalized ones, provides examples. The Russian [t] and [d], as in [tot] 'that' and [da] 'yes', are normally apico-dental. However, their palatalized counterparts [tʲ] or [dʲ] as in [tʲotʲə] 'aunt', [dʲadʲə] 'uncle' are usually lamino-alveolar or even lamino-postalveolar. The upward thrust of the anterodorsum of the tongue tends to retract and depress the apex, with the result indicated. Again, in Russian and many other languages, including English, palatalization of dorso-velar [k], as in English *key* [kʲiː], does not merely lift the anterodorsum of the tongue, but it also shifts the front edge of the area of tongue–velum contact slightly forwards.

We can now turn to *velarization*. Velarized sounds have a secondary velar-approximant-type articulation i.e. in addition to the primary articulation the back of the tongue is raised up towards the soft palate.

72   One way to achieve a velar approximant is to produce a [ɣ] (if necessary, go right back to experiment (63) and start from [x] or from [k], then [x], then [ɣ]). From fricative [ɣ] open up the articulation channel and you have the velar approximant [ɰ].

Another approach is to start from a vowel of the type [u] (more or less as in English *who* [huː]) and, while prolonging the vowel without changing it in any way, slowly and carefully *unround* the lips. The result should be a velar approximant [ɰ]. Now say a prolonged [ll..], then prolonged [ɰɰ..]. Now both simultaneously: [ɫ..].

If you compare this velarized [ɫ], and the palatalized [lʲ] you produced in Experiment 71, with the *l*s of English *feel* and *leaf*, you will probably find that these two English *l*s are somewhat similar to the velarized and palatalized *l*s you have been experimenting with, thus [fiːɫ] and [lʲiːf]. Note, however, that these two *l*s—'clear *l*' occurring before vowels and often before [j], as in *million* [mɪljən], and 'dark *l*' occurring after vowels and finally, as in *middle*—are not very strongly modified. Note, also, that there are considerable differences in the quality of *l*-sounds in different English accents. Most Scots, for example, use rather 'dark' *l*s in all positions, saying [ɫif], for example for *leaf*. Irish speakers may use a very clear *l* in all positions, saying [fiːlʲ] *feel*, etc. Americans tend to have darker *l*s than speakers of British RP ('received pronunciation'), and so on.

73   Apply velarization to some other sounds, for example [z]—say [z] and [ɰ]

simultaneously thus: [z z . . .]. Then combine velarization with voiceless fricatives, for example [s], thus: [s s . . .]. When the primary articulation is a voiceless fricative, as here, you may be able to develop the velarized form from simultaneous pronunciation of [s] and [x]. Having achieved a coarticulated [sx], try to relax the velar articulation a little, so that it is no longer fricative. This should give [s].

Now try to combine velarization with stops, e.g. [d̪]. Say [ɫ] again, several times, aloud and silently, concentrating upon what it feels like to have the back of the tongue bunched up in the velarizing position. Now, transfer that feeling to silent [d] or [da], and finally say [d̪] aloud. Do likewise with [t]. Note that the 1996 chart of the International Phonetic Alphabet shows the diacritic [ˠ] as an alternative mark of velarization.

Velarized [dˠ], [tˠ], and [sˠ] are one variety of the Arabic 'emphatic' consonants ص ط ض, which contrast with plain س ت د: [d], [t], and [s] as in [dˠiːm] 'hurt' vs. [diːm] 'perpetuate', [tˠiːn] 'mud' vs. [tiːn] 'figs' and [sˠeːf] 'summer' vs. [seːf] 'sword'. Moreover, note that velarized [ɫ] is the l-sound of Arabic *Allah* [ʔaɫɫaː], as opposed to the rather clear (slightly palatalized) [l] of [ʔallaði] 'which'.

Pharyngalized sounds. These somewhat resemble velarized sounds and used to be indicated by the same diacritic [˜]: thus [ɫ] = either velarized or pharyngalized [l]. The 1996 chart shows a more distinctive alternative, a small [ˤ] after the symbol for the primary articulation, thus: [lˤ].

74 One can achieve pharyngalization by straining the back of the tongue backwards and downwards as far as possible. Try to acquire a feeling of near-closure or near-strangulation just above the larynx. The action of swallowing may help to identify the zone in which some degree of narrowing should occur.

Say a long [l l l . . .] and while it is going on make a tentative movement towards swallowing: [l l l . . . lˤ lˤ lˤ]. Do the same with [z z z . . . zˤ zˤ zˤ] and other sounds.

Note that the Arabic 'emphatics', which we have described as velarized may also be pharyngalized. Finally we come to *nasalization*. This is usually a modification of vowels, and is symbolized by the 'tilde' [˜] placed *over* the vowel symbol, thus: [ɛ̃] [õ] not *through* it like the velarization diacritic. Nasalization was dealt with at the beginning of Chapter 5 and in Experiment 59.

We can now recapitulate the principal types of secondary articulation:

labialization, e.g. [tʷ] [dʷ] [kʷ] [sʷ] [zʷ] [lʷ] etc.
palatalization, e.g. [tʲ] [dʲ] [kʲ] [sʲ] [zʲ] [lʲ] etc.
velarization, e.g. [t] [d] [s] [z] [ɫ] etc., or [tˠ] [dˠ] etc.
pharyngalization, e.g. [t] or [tˤ], [s] or [sˤ] etc.
nasalization, e.g. [ĩ] [ɛ̃] [ã] [õ] etc.

Co-articulation, whether co-ordinate or primary and secondary, has to do
with occurrences of two different articulations *at the same time*.

We must now consider some features of successive occurrences of two
same or different articulations *one after the other*—namely sequences of
sounds.

3. Homorganic sound sequences: Geminates and affricates

It is obvious that in the stream of speech, in principle, virtually any sound
may come before or after any other sound, although there are, indeed, very
strong constraints upon the particular sound-sequences that are permitted
in particular positions in this or that language, as we shall see in Chapter 10.
However, there are certain common types of consonantal sequences which
have special names in the phonetic literature and some of which function as
single units in particular languages. All of the special sequences that we are
now about to discuss are *homorganic*, that is, they are articulated by the
same organs. The types of homorganic sequence to which we refer here are
composed of *stops, fricatives, lateral fricatives, lateral approximants, nasals*,
and the particular named sequences that we deal with are exemplified
within the numbered boxes in Fig. 35.

The first special sequence type that we shall examine is known as *gemin-*
ate (from the Latin *geminare* 'to double', *geminus* 'twin'), examples labelled
'1' in Fig. 35. As the name suggests, a geminate, or geminate sequence, is a
sequence of two identical, or nearly identical consonantal sounds.
Examples of such sequences can be observed in such English sequences as
[kk] in *book-case*, [dd] in *bad dog*, [ss] in *this set*, [nn] in *unknown*, etc. From
a purely phonetic point of view these might be called *geminates*. However,
the term 'geminate' is not usually employed with reference to such English
examples, where each of the two consonants belongs to a separate word (as
in *book case, bad dog, this set*) or to separate meaningful segments of a
word, to separate morphemes (as in *un-known*). The term *geminate* is

	e.g.	-stop	-fric.	-lat. fric.	-lat. approx.	-nasal
		-t/d	-s	-ɬ	-l	-n
stop-	t-	1 tt	2 ts	3 tɬ	4 tl	5 tn̩
fricative	s-		1 ss			
lat. fric.	ɬ-			1 ɬɬ		
lat. approx-	l-				1 ll	
nasal	n-	6 n̂d				1 nn

Named homorganic sequences: (1) geminate, (2) affricate, (3) lateral affricate, (4) lateral plosion, (5) nasal plosion, (6) prenasalized stop.

Fig. 35 Named homorganic sequences

usually applied only to those cases where there is no word-boundary or morpheme-boundary between the two sounds. There are many examples of such 'true' geminates in, for example, Italian or Arabic. Thus the sequences [tt] and [ll] are geminates in Italian *notte* 'night', *bello* 'beautiful', or Arabic *battaal* 'worthless', *Allah* 'God'. In each of these words the two consonants are clearly pronounced, in sequence, and the sequence occurs within one and the same word.

We mentioned above that a geminate is a sequence of two identical or *nearly* identical consonantal sounds. This was to cover the rather rare cases of geminates in which one of the two participating consonants is incomplete. Thus in Italian, when two *affricates* (defined below) are united in a geminate sequence, the fricative part of the first affricate is suppressed. Thus when [dʒ] + [dʒ] are united in a geminate, the first is reduced to [d], as in *oggi* 'today' pronounced [ɔddʒi].

The second type of named sequence, labelled '2' in Fig. 35, is *affricate*. An affricate is a stop released into the homorganic fricative.

75 Silently form the articulation of an apico-alveolar stop [t]. Build up a little initiatory pressure behind the stop then release it carefully *only in the centre*, i.e. release it into an [s]. That is to say, don't remove the tip and blade of the tongue as a whole, just open up that central channel. This is the affricate [ts].

Now silently form a *lamino-postalveolar* stop, build up some pressure behind it, then release the stop into an [ʃ]. This is the affricate [tʃ].

Experiment with other affricates: in each case form a stop, then, retaining all of the stop-contact except a small central channel, release the stop into the homorganic fricative: thus [pɸ] [t̪ θ] [kx] [qχ].

Now experiment with *voiced* affricates: [dz] [dʒ] [bβ] [gɣ] [ɢʁ].

Now that the mechanism of affricates is clear, we can define the term affricate more closely. An affricate is a stop released into the homorganic fricative within one and the same syllable and one and the same morpheme.

It follows from this definition that the sequence of [t] + [s] in the middle of the word *catsup* is not an affricate—the [t] and the [s] belong to two separate syllables. The [t] + [s] that occurs at the end of the English word *bits* occurs within one and the same syllable; but it still is not normally regarded as an affricate, and the reason is that the [t] and [s] in *bits* do not belong to the same morpheme: the [t] represents the end of the word *bit*, while the [s] represents the *plural* morpheme. On the other hand the [ts] at the end of the German word *Blitz* 'lightning' is normally considered to be an affricate: there is no morpheme boundary, both [t] and [s] belonging to the same word, and functioning in the structure of the German language as a single affricate unit. It is clear that the criterion for the application of both terms, *geminate* and *affricate*, is only partly phonetic: morphological considerations also play a part.

The next type of sequence is *lateral affricate*. For lateral affricates the conditions are identical with those for affricates except that the stop is released into a homorganic lateral fricative. Such sounds are rather common in American Indian languages: thus in Navaho we have not only [tsah] 'needle' with an *alveolar affricate*, but also [tɬah] 'ointment' with an *alveolar lateral affricate*, and incidentally also a glottalic pressure lateral affricate [tɬ'] in e.g. [tɬ'ízí] 'goat' (no. 3 in Fig. 35).

4. Lateral plosion, nasal plosion, and prenasalized stops

When a stop is released into a homorganic *lateral approximant*, the sequence is usually said to involve *lateral plosion* (no. 4 in Fig. 35). 'Lateral plosion' means simply that the stop is released, or 'plodded' (i.e. exploded or imploded) laterally rather than centrally. The distinction between (normal) central plosion and lateral plosion was, in fact, demonstrated in Experiment 48.

When lateral plosion occurs at the end of English words like *little* and *middle* the final lateral approximant is usually syllabic, i.e. forms a syllable by itself, and this is shown by the diacritic mark [ˌ] placed under it: thus [lɪtl̩], [mɪdl̩]. It should be noted that young children and some Scots speakers do not use lateral plosion here, but insert a very short vowel-like sound between the stop and the lateral, thus: [lɪtəl], [mɪdəl].

Nasal plosion (no. 5) is analogous to lateral plosion. In nasal plosion the articulatory closure for the stop is continued on into the following homorganic nasal. The stop is thus 'exploded' through the nose—the transition from the stop to the nasal being marked only by the sudden dropping of the velum to open the nasal orifice.

English examples are [dn̩] and [tn̩] as in *sudden* [sʌdn̩], *button* [bʌtn̩] (same proviso as for [dl] [tl] about children and some Scots). Other examples in English are [pm̩] as in *Clapham bus* [klæpm̩ bʌs], [kŋ] as in *bacon grease* [beɪkŋ gɹiːs].

The last of the named homorganic sequences is *prenasalized stop* (no. 6). These are homorganic sequences like [mb-] [nd-] [ŋg −] occurring at the beginning of a syllable and functioning as a unit in a language. They are particularly common in Austronesian languages.

These, then, are the principal named types of homorganic sequences: geminate, affricate, lateral affricate, lateral plosion (laterally released stop), nasal plosion, and prenasalized stop.

5. Heterorganic sequences and contiguous sequences

In the preceding section we have dealt only with *homorganic* sequences, that is, sequences of articulations formed by the same articulators. Now we turn our attention to all types of sequence: *homorganic, heterorganic*, and *contiguous*. Homorganic sequences are illustrated by such English sequences as [ʃʃ] in *fishshop*, [dt] in *bad time*, [θð] in *both these*, [zd] in *these days*, [ŋg] in *anger*, [ds] in *dead centre*, etc.

A *heterorganic sequence* is one in which the articulators used in the successive sounds are quite different. 'Quite different' means that the articulators can be freely manipulated independently of each other. Thus [kp] in *back part* is a heterorganic sequence, since the *tongue*, which is the lower articulator in [k], can be moved into the *dorso-velar* position for [k] quite independently of what the lips are doing in [p]. Articulations made by the apex or blade of the tongue can be made quite freely no matter what the back of the tongue is doing. So, in spite of the fact that the *blade* and the *back* (posterodorsum) of the tongue are, in fact, parts of the same organ, we regard such sequences as [sk] (lamino-alveolar + dorso-velar) in *asking*, as *heterorganic*.

The third type of sequence is *contiguous*. In a contiguous sequence we use adjacent parts of the same organ, with the result that the articulators cannot be manœuvred freely in total independence of each other. For example, velar and palatal articulations are contiguous since they involve the posterodorsal and anterodorsal parts of the tongue. Consequently, one cannot simultaneously articulate a velar and a palatal without the one articulation affecting the other. We saw, above, that a palatalized [k] has its primary articulation shifted forward by the palatalization. Other contiguous articulations are bilabial and labio-dental, alveolar and dental, alveolar and postalveolar.

In our discussion of *sequence* so far we have referred only to consonantal sequence. However, there is one type of *vocalic* sequence, or sequence of vowels, that we must take note of in passing, although we do not take up the analysis and description of vowels till Chapter 7.

In the chain of speech, in principle, any vowel may be followed by any other. When two identical vowels succeed one another we might well refer to this as a 'geminate' vowel sequence, although, in fact, this term is not normally used of vowels. Sequences of identical vowels occur in English in such examples as *bee-eater* [i] + [i], *spa-artist* [a] + [a], *new ooze* [u] + [u]. The vowels in such sequences tend to coalesce into a single very long vowel, which we can compare with the vowels in *beater* [i], *spartan* [a], *news* [u].

6. Diphthongs

A sequence of two *different* vowels can occur in two successive syllables, as in *see Ann* [i] + [æ], *too eager* [u] + [i] . . . etc. Such a sequence has no particular name. But a sequence of different vowels, within one and the same syllable, is called a *diphthong*. English examples are [aɪ] in *high*, [aʊ] in *how*, [ɔɪ] in *boy*, and in very many types of English [eɪ] in *day*, [oʊ] or [əʊ] in *go*, etc. In a diphthong, the two vowels, the starting point (or 'first element') and the finishing point ('second element'), such as [a] and [ɪ] in *high*, are not perceived as two separate vowels, but the diphthong is perceived as a transitional, gliding, sound starting at the first element and gliding towards the second element. A diphthong, as we have said, occurs within a single syllable—is performed with a single stress-pulse (or pulse of initiator power). In English diphthongs, the stress-pulse is a *decrescendo* one, starting rather strong and then fading away: thus the stress-pulse of *high* [haĭ] may be represented as >. The mark [˘] over the [ɪ] indicates the weak or unstressed element of the diphthong. A decrescendo diphthong like this is often called a 'falling' diphthong because of the fact that the stress falls away from a peak near the beginning of the diphthong. *Crescendo*, or 'rising', diphthongs, which start weakly stressed and build up to a peak near the end, represented by <, are also possible. Some people might describe such English words as *yes* [jes], *yawn* [jɔn], *you* [ju], *war* [wɔɹ], etc., as containing rising diphthongs [ĭe] [ĭɔ] [ĭu] [ŭɔ], but it is more usual to describe them (and transcribe them) as we have done, that is as sequences of the semivowels [j] and [w] + a vowel.

7. Close and open transition

Before leaving the subject of sequence phenomena we must consider one more topic, namely two different ways of making the transition from one consonantal articulation to another: what we call *close transition* and *open transition*.

In *close transition* the successive consonants are articulated as closely together as possible. What this means differs according to whether we are talking of a homorganic, heterorganic, or contiguous sequence. In a homorganic sequence, close transition simply means that the articulation is maintained, unbroken, through both of the successive sounds: thus the [pp] in *top part*, is articulated with the lips closed for the duration of the two [p]s, the [ff] of *half fare* holds the labio-dental fricative articulation throughout both [f]s, and so on.

In *open transition* between homorganic consonants there is a momentary and minimal relaxation of the articulation which is reformed immediately. Thus in 'take the top apart' in English there is normally no vowel between the [p]s, just an open transition which we can represent as [·]: thus *top · part* (as opposed to *toppart*). Similarly in *half a fare* there is a mere open transition between the [f]s, thus, *half · fare*.

76 Experiment with making close and open transitions between homorganic consonants. Thus, say [a f f a] [a s s a] [a v v a] [a f v a] in each case articulating the two consonants as a *prolonged* articulation with a syllable division in the middle of it. Do the same with pairs of homorganic stops: [a p p a] [a b b a] [a t t a] [a d d a] [a t d a] [a d t a], etc. Notice that in each case (even when there is change of phonation, as in [a t d a] [a d t a]) what you have is long articulation, maintained unchanged for the duration of *two* successive sounds. These are all close transitions.

Now say the same sequences with an absolutely minimal release and remake of the articulation. Say [a f · f a], for example with a slight relaxation of the lower lip between the [f]s. The relaxation need be no more than sufficient to insert a momentary voiceless approximant between the [f]s, thus; [a f ʋ̥ f a]. Notice that this is what happens, in rapid speech at least, in saying *half a fare*, *tough affair*, etc. in English.

Carry out similar experiments with the other examples just given, [a s · s a] [a v · v a], etc. and then with the stops [a p · p a] [a d · d a], etc. Note that the minimal open transition between [p] and [p] may take the form of a momentary bilabial approximant or wide fricative [ɸ], thus [a p ɸ p a].

These were examples of close and open transitions between homorganic consonants. In the case of *heterorganic* sequences, the difference between close and open transition is somewhat more marked. In *close transition* between heterorganic consonants there is a moment of *articulatory overlap*: in other words, the articulatory stricture for the second consonant is formed *before* the stricture for the first is released.

77 Say [a k] and hold the final [k]. Now, while still holding that final [k] form a bilabial stop articulation. Silently release the [k] and only after that release the [p]. The whole sequence might be transcribed [a a k k p p a], where [k p] represents the moment of co-articulation—of articulatory overlap—in the middle of the sequence. Now say the English words *back part*, slowly and silently, giving particular attention to the articulation of the sequence [k p]. In virtually all varieties of English, this will be an example of close transition.

Carry out similar experiments with [t k] in *that car*, [p t] in *top ten*, [f k] in *staff car*, [s f] in *asphalt*, etc.

Notice how, in every case (in normal English), there is close transition—in every case the second stricture is formed before the first is released.

If you are not a native speaker of English you may have to carry out this series of experiments with particular care, to ensure that you are, in fact, using close transitions.

Next, experiment with *open transition* between heterorganic articulations. Use the same examples, but this time, make sure that the first stricture is *released* a moment before the second stricture is formed. The actual transition between the consonants must be absolutely minimal: there must be no vowel inserted between the consonants. The *approach* of the articulators to the second articulation must have started by the moment when the first stricture is released.

Observe that, in rapid speech at least, English utilizes open transition between consonants in such phrases as: *back apart* [k · p], is *that a car* [t · k], *top a ten* [p · t], *half a can* [f · k], *this affair* [s · f], etc.

Finally we must consider the transitions that occur between consonants with *contiguous articulation*. In *close transition* between contiguous articulations there is accommodation: the place of articulation (and sometimes the phonation) of one consonant *accommodates* to the articulation (or phonation) of the other. In many languages, including English, the place of articulation of a velar is shifted forward slightly before a palatal semivowel [j] or a palatal vowel [i]. In other words, the velar articulation is accommodated to the contiguous palatal articulation: the velar, that is, is somewhat palatalized.

In *open transition* between contiguous articulations there is little or no accommodation. The stricture for the first consonant is made at the normal location, and the movement of accommodation to the location of the second consonant is actually made during the momentary period of transition.

78 Say the English word *backyard*, containing [k j] several times, aloud and silently. Note the accommodation of [k] to [j]. Now say *eighth*, containing [t̪ θ] several times, aloud and silently. Note the accommodation of [t] to [θ]. The articulation [t̪] is apico-dental. Compare its alveolar articulation in *eight*. Say *train*, containing [t r] aloud and silently, and note how the apico-alveolar [t] accommodates to the post-alveolar [r]. The [t] is either articulated completely post-alveolarly [t̠], or the tongue-tip slides rapidly backwards from the apico-alveolar to the apico-postalveolar position.

Now compare all these examples of *close* transition between contiguous articulations, with *open* transitions between the same consonants. In English, at least in rapid speech, there is open transition (rather than the actual presence of a vowel) in the sequences [k · j] in *back a yard*, [t · θ] in *ate a thing*, [t · r] in *terrain*. Say these aloud and silently, and note how in this second, open-transition series there is no articulatory accommodation.

CONSONANTS (PULMONIC)   © 1996 IPA

	Bilabial	Labiodental	Dental	Alveolar	Postalveolar	Retroflex	Palatal	Velar	Uvular	Pharyngeal	Glottal
Plosive	p b			t d		ʈ ɖ	c ɟ	k g	q ɢ		ʔ
Nasal	m	ɱ		n		ɳ	ɲ	ŋ	N		
Trill	ʙ			r					ʀ		
Tap or Flap				ɾ		ɽ					
Fricative	ɸ β	f v	θ ð	s z	ʃ ʒ	ʂ ʐ	ç ʝ	x ɣ	χ ʁ	ħ ʕ	h ɦ
Lateral fricative				ɬ ɮ							
Approximant		ʋ		ɹ		ɻ	j	ɰ			
Lateral approximant				l		ɭ	ʎ	L			

Where symbols appear in pairs, the one to the right represents a voiced consonant. Shaded areas denote articulations judged impossible.

CONSONANTS (NON-PULMONIC)

Clicks		Voiced implosives		Ejectives	
ʘ	Bilabial	ɓ	Bilabial	ʼ	Examples:
ǀ	Dental	ɗ	Dental/alveolar	pʼ	Bilabial
ǃ	(Post)alveolar	ʄ	Palatal	tʼ	Dental/alveolar
ǂ	Palatoalveolar	ɠ	Velar	kʼ	Velar
ǁ	Alveolar lateral	ʛ	Uvular	sʼ	Alveolar fricative

OTHER SYMBOLS

ʍ   Voiceless labial-velar fricative   ɕ ʑ Alveolo-palatal fricatives

w   Voiced labial-velar approximant   ɺ   Voiced alveolar lateral flap

ɥ   Voiced labial-palatal approximant   ɧ   Simultaneous ʃ and x

H   Voiceless epiglottal fricative

ʢ   Voiced epiglottal fricative

ʡ   Epiglottal plosive

Affricates and double articulations can be represented by two symbols joined by a tie bar if necessary.

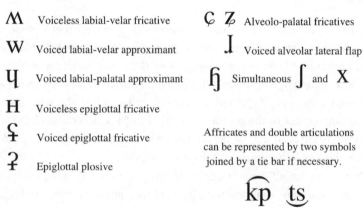

k͡p t͡s

Fig. 36 The International Phonetic Alphabet (revised to 1993, corrected 1996)

VOWELS

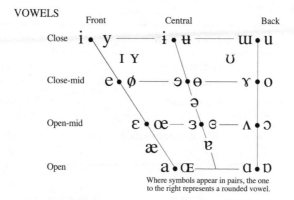

Where symbols appear in pairs, the one
to the right represents a rounded vowel.

SUPRASEGMENTALS

ˈ	Primary stress
ˌ	Secondary stress
	ˌfoʊnəˈtɪʃən
ː	Long eː
ˈ	Half-long eˈ
˘	Extra-short ĕ
|	Minor (foot) group
||	Major (intonation) group
.	Syllable break ɹi.ækt
‿	Linking (absence of a break)

TONES AND WORD ACCENTS

LEVEL		CONTOUR	
e̋ or ˥	Extra high	ě or ˇ	Rising
é ˦	High	ê ˆ	Falling
ē ˧	Mid	e᷄ ˈ	High rising
è ˨	Low	e᷅ ˈ	Low rising
ȅ ˩	Extra low	e᷈ ˈ	Rising-falling
↓	Downstep	↗	Global rise
↑	Upstep	↘	Global fall

DIACRITICS   Diacritics may be placed above a symbol with a descender, e.g. ŋ̊

◌̥	Voiceless	n̥ d̥	◌̤	Breathy voiced	b̤ a̤	◌̪ Dental	t̪ d̪
◌̬	Voiced	s̬ t̬	◌̰	Creaky voiced	b̰ a̰	◌̺ Apical	t̺ d̺
ʰ	Aspirated	tʰ dʰ	◌̼	Linguolabial	t̼ d̼	◌̻ Laminal	t̻ d̻
◌̹	More rounded	ɔ̹	ʷ	Labialized	tʷ dʷ	◌̃ Nasalized	ẽ
◌̜	Less rounded	ɔ̜	ʲ	Palatalized	t dʲ	ⁿ Nasal release	dⁿ
◌̟	Advanced	u̟	ˠ	Velarized	t dˠ	ˡ Lateral release	dˡ
◌̠	Retracted	e̠	ˤ	Pharyngealized	t dˤ	◌̚ No audible release	d̚
◌̈	Centralized	ë	◌̴	Velarized or pharyngealized	ɫ		
◌̽	Mid-centralized	e̽	◌̝	Raised	e̝	(ɹ̝ = voiced alveolar fricative)	
◌̩	Syllabic	n̩	◌̞	Lowered	e̞	(β̞ = voiced bilabial approximant)	
◌̯	Non-syllabic	e̯	◌̘	Advanced Tongue Root	e̘		
◌˞	Rhoticity	ɚ a˞	◌̙	Retracted Tongue Root	e̙		

Table 3

Sequence type	Open transition	Close transition
Homorganic	Articulatory non-continuity	Articulatory *continuity*
Heterorganic	No overlap	Articulatory *overlap*
Contiguous	No accommodation	Articulatory *accommodation*

We can sum up the differences between close and open transition as shown in Table 3.

We have devoted some time to the two different ways of making the transition between successive consonants because this is a feature that differs somewhat from one language to another—thus in [k t] in English *actor* there is close transition, but in French *acteur* there is, usually, open transition.

With this survey of co-articulation and sequence phenomena we come to the end of our study of what are usually called consonants. It will be noted that we have given no formal definition of consonants though it will be clear that by consonants we mean chiefly sounds functioning as *syllable margins*. In the word *cat* [kæt], [k] and [t] form the margins of the syllable, while the vowel [æ] is its centre or nucleus. Again, the *dorso-palatal approximant* [i] is clearly a vowel when it is the centre of a syllable as in *seat* [siːt], but when essentially the same sound is reduced to a mere glide away from the dorso-palatal approximant position, in the palatal semivowel [j] as in *you* [juː], it is a syllable margin, and consequently a consonant. We shall have a little more to say about this at the beginning of Chapter 7.

In order to recapitulate most of what has been discussed up to now, look at Fig. 36. This is a chart of the phonetic symbols of the International Phonetic Association, and it will be advisable to read through it several times, both silently and aloud, both horizontally along the rows of stops, fricatives, and so forth, and vertically down the columns. To assist in this we provide some notes here.

Terminology. Reading across the top (location labels) of the main chart we find the headings *Dental, Alveolar* and *Postalveolar*. The symbols [t] [d] [n] [r] [ɾ] [ɬ] [ɮ] [ɹ] [l] are listed under *Alveolar*, but with no vertical lines separating them from *Dental* and *Postalveolar*. This means that these symbols can be used to represented sounds articulated at any of the three locations. If it is necessary to specify that such sounds are in fact dental the appropriate dental diacritic can be used (see under the list of DIACRITICS); if they are retracted alveolars, or postalveolars, the underline meaning 'retracted' can be used (illustrated on the diacritics list only for a vowel). Note that special symbols are provided for fricatives at all three locations. But note also that dental [s] and [z] can also occur, and can be symbolized by means of the dental diacritic. Dental [s] and [z] differ from [θ] and [ð] in terms of the size and shape of their articulatory channels: for [s] and [z] this is a narrow, grooved central channel; for [θ] and [ð] a wide, flat channel.

Note that under OTHER SYMBOLS [ɕ] and [ʑ] are labelled *alveolo-palatal*. This older term violates the strict rule of systematic phonetic terminology in which the prefixed term refers to the *lower* articulator. We should prefer to call them *lamino-prepalatal* or *palatalized lamino-postalveolar*.

For the present the display of VOWELS, SUPRASEGMENTALS and TONES AND WORD ACCENTS can be passed over, since we are going to deal with these matters in subsequent chapters.

7

Vowels: Introduction

1. Vowels and consonants: Importance of silent study of vowels

In Chapter 6 (p. 116) we partially distinguished between consonants and vowels on the basis of their different functions, marginal and central, in the structure of syllables. For general phonetic purposes, however, that distinction is inadequate. There are, for instance, certainly syllabic central units that we would prefer not to describe as vowels: for example the syllabic trilled [r] that forms the syllable centre in Czech words like [krk] 'neck' or [prst] 'finger', not to mention syllabic [l] and [n] in English *middle* and *button*.

In order to mark off a class of articulations that corresponds closely to what are traditionally called *vowels*, we have to be somewhat arbitrary. So by *vowels*, we understand a class of pulmonic pressure sounds normally voiced, with a maintainable central oral approximant or resonant dorso-domal, or pharyngal, articulatory channel.

We have already seen, more than once, that the articulation of one vowel at least, namely [i], can be perfectly well described in accordance with the same principles that we use in describing consonants: that is as a *dorso-palatal approximant*. In fact, all vowels can, in principle, be described as approximants or resonants articulated at various oral and pharyngal locations.

However, it has long been the custom to define vowels in terms quite different from those used in defining consonants. This traditional description of vowels, instead of specifying stricture type and location, as for consonants, seeks, in effect, to define the shape and size of the resonance chambers of the mouth and pharynx by specifying the position of the tongue and lips. The traditional way of classifying vowels works well in practice, and, indeed, is the only basis for the successful acquisition of practical skill in producing, identifying, and classifying vowels.

Vowels, or, more precisely, the mouth-shapes for vowels, are specified in terms of three variables—three *parameters: vertical tongue-position* (high–low), *horizontal tongue-position* (front–back), and *lip-position* (unrounded–rounded).

It is essential for the student of phonetics to become intimately acquainted with the tactile and proprioceptive sensations associated with these parameters in his own vocal tract. It is absolutely useless merely to be aware of them intellectually. Consequently, one must carry out a great deal of *silent* introspection concerning these sensations, and *silent* practice of vowels. This was the recommendation of the great English phonetician Henry Sweet, over a century ago: 'The first and indispensable qualification of the phonetician is a thorough practical knowledge of the formation of the vowels. Those who try to learn new sounds by ear alone, without any systematic training in the use of their vocal organs, generally succeed only partially.' (Sweet (1877), p. 21.) Considerable experience (and at least one small experiment—see Catford and Pisoni (1970)) confirms Sweet's view. In all experimentation on vowels it is helpful to use a hand mirror (and a small flashlight where necessary) so that one can correlate the visible movements and positions of the tongue and lips, with the proprioceptive sensations, and also with the auditory sensations when they are whispered or voiced.

2. Lip- and tongue-positions for vowels

The most obvious and most easily controlled of the vowel parameters is *lip-position*, so we start with that.

79 Silently alternate a vowel of the [i]-type (as in English *see*) with a vowel of the [u]-type (as in English *too*). Concentrate attention on the position of the lips in articulating these vowels. Speakers of many varieties of English may notice that in saying a word like *too* there is no fixed degree of lip-rounding. At the start of the word the lips may be more or less spread, but as the utterance of the word proceeds, they become more and more closely rounded. We are, for the moment, interested only in the most extreme rounding of the lips, as at the *end* of *too*. Say a long [uː] vowel with the lips fixed in this closely rounded position.

Having silently produced this rounded [u], switch to [i] (as in *see*). Silently alternate [u i u i]. At this point one must *detach* the lip movements from the vowel sounds. In other words, it is necessary to experiment with slowly and deliberately rounding and spreading the lips as an activity by itself, with no particular vowel sounds in mind.

Having discovered experimentally that lip-rounding is an independently controllable parameter, one can make further experiments to discover the effect of rounding or its absence on various types of vowel.

80 Say a prolonged [i i i . . .] aloud and silently, and introspect about the lip-position, which you will probably find to be moderately spread. Exaggerate the lip-spreading a little, so that the [i]-vowel is being said through a broad smile. Now while silently saying a prolonged [i i i i i . . .] slowly and deliberately round the lips, taking care to 'think [i]' all the time, rigidly maintaining the tongue-position of [i]. Having reached maximum lip-rounding, with the tongue still in the [i] position, produce whisper, and then voice. The audible result is an [i]-type vowel with rounded lips, which we symbolize by [y]. This is approximately the French *u* of *lune* and the German *ü* of *Bühne*.

Say a prolonged [u u u . . .]—roughly the vowel of *too*, only take care to say it through *fully rounded lips*. While holding a prolonged silent [u u u u u . . .], slowly and deliberately unround the lips, taking care to 'think [u]' all the time, rigidly maintaining the tongue-position of [u], with tongue bunched up at the back of the mouth. The unrounding process begins chiefly with a relaxation of the closely rounded lips, but this is followed by an increasing tension at the corners of the mouth, as they are drawn back into a wide smile. Having reached a state of completely unrounded, widely spread lips, with the tongue still firmly in the [u]-position, produce whisper, and then voice. The audible result is a totally unrounded [u] (a vowel that doesn't sound at all like [u]), for which the phonetic symbol is [ɯ]. This is somewhat similar to the Russian vowel *ы* of *мышь* [mɯʃ] 'mouse' or the Scots Gaelic *ao* of *laogh*, [ɬɯɣ] 'calf'. Experiment further, silently and aloud, with adding and subtracting lip-rounding, saying [u ɯ u ɯ u ɯ . . .] etc.

Now experiment silently in a whisper and with voice, adding lip-rounding to [ɛ], as in *head*, and taking lip-rounding away from [ɔ] as in *saw*, and so on.

By now you should have good control of the parameter of lip-position, and the ability to pronounce any vowel at will with the lips unrounded or rounded. If this is not so, repeat Experiment 80 as often as necessary, until you feel that your lip-control is perfect.

The second parameter of vowel description that we shall examine is that of 'tongue-height', as it is often called.

81 Say a series of vowels, [i] [e] [ɛ] [a], roughly as in English *beat bait bet bat*—at this stage the precise quality of the vowels is not important. Say this series of vowels several times, silently, [i] [e] [ɛ] [a], [i] [e] [ɛ] [a]. It will be obvious that in progressing through this set the mouth becomes more and more open.

Experiment with a comparable series of vowels articulated at the back of the mouth [u] [o] [ɔ] [a], very roughly as in *too toe paw pah*. Say this series silently and make the same observations as you did on [i] [e] [ɛ] [a]. Once again, it should be clear that the mouth gets progressively more open as you go from [u] to [a]. Repeat the series again several times.

In carrying out these experiments in varying vowels in the vertical dimension—the parameter of 'tongue-height'—you will probably become aware that the opening of the mouth in going from, say, [i] to [a] can be done in three different ways: (*i*) by keeping the lower jaw still and progressively lowering and flattening the tongue, (*ii*) by fixating the tongue with respect to the lower jaw, and simply lowering the jaw, (*iii*) by a bit of both.

From the phonetic point of view the important thing is the varying distance between the surface of the tongue and the roof of the mouth, however achieved, since that determines in large part the size of the oral resonance chamber. For the student of phonetics, however, the most important thing is to develop awareness of the position and shape of the tongue, and this can be done most readily by fixating the jaw and concentrating attention on the proprioceptive and tactile sensations associated with lowering and raising the tongue.

82 Bite the end of a pen or pencil, or any other convenient object that will hold the teeth about $\frac{1}{3}$ in., or 1 cm., apart. Of course it is important to make sure that the tooth-separator does not project into the mouth to interfere with movements of the tongue.

Now, holding the jaw rigid in this manner, experiment repeatedly with silent vowels of the types [i] [e] [ɛ] [a] and [u] [o] [ɔ] moving through the series upwards and downwards slowly and quickly, many times. Try to become clearly aware of the different degrees of tongue-raising through the proprioceptive sensations from the tongue-muscles, and (for the front series of vowels) the tactile sensations of contact between tongue sides and molar teeth, at least for [i] and [e]. Finally, as far as you can by looking, with flashlight and mirror, through the narrow space between the teeth, try to see the different positions of the tongue. In order to see the tongue-positions well you will have to experiment with going through as nearly as possible the same series of tongue postures with the mouth rather wide open.

In Experiment 82 the vowels were all articulated silently. Experiment 83 adds whisper and voice to them.

83   While carrying out the same experiments as in Exp. 82, first *whisper* and then *voice* the vowels. You may find at first that the auditory sensations of the vowels completely mask the proprioceptive sensations. Whisper is a good compromise, however. In whisper you can hear, more or less, the auditory qualities of the vowels, but you can still feel the tongue-position pretty clearly. If necessary, repeat the last few experiments again until you are confident that you can clearly *feel* the differences of 'tongue-height'.

The third parameter used in the description of vowels is what we have called 'horizontal tongue-position'—the relative advancement or retraction of the body of the tongue.

84   Say a silent [i], then carefully round it to a silent [y]. Be careful to preserve exactly the tongue-position of [i] even after you have closely rounded the lips.
    Now rigidly maintain the lip-position, but silently shift from rounded [i], that is [y], back to [u]. Silently alternate [y u y u] several times slowly and deliberately. As you introspect while doing this you will observe that in going from silent [y] to silent [u] the tongue moves backwards, deeper into the mouth. As you silently alternate [y u y u], etc. you can feel the tongue sliding backwards and forwards. If you are a speaker of many types of English, and if you are using a (closely rounded) version of the *oo* in *too* as your [u], you will probably notice that the tongue doesn't move back very far in going from [y] to [u]. This is because in most varieties of English the *oo* vowel is not a very back vowel. To indicate this 'non-back' quality of *oo* we can write two dots over the letter *u*: [ü]. So, in carrying out the present experiment, see what happens if you silently go from [y] to [u] as before, and then strive your hardest to pull the tongue even further back. Keep the tongue fully bunched up, close to the roof of the mouth, as it was for [i] [y] and [ü], but strive to prolong the backward slide of the tongue beyond [ü] to a fully back [u]: [y]–[ü]–[u].

The reason we started Experiment 84 by closely rounding [i] to [y], and then sliding back from [y] to [ü] (and subsequently [u]) was this: the proprioceptive sensations of lip-movement tend to mask those of tongue-movement. So if you had started from *unrounded* [i] and then slid silently back to *rounded* [ü] and [u] the strongly perceived feeling of change of lip-position would have tended to blot out your perception of the tongue movement. Consequently, it was necessary to keep the lip-position constant in order to concentrate attention on the tongue movement.

We can, of course, eliminate change of lip-position in another way: by starting with unrounded [ɯ] and sliding forward to [i], and in Experiment 85 we do that.

85   Say a silent [u] and try to make it a really back one, i.e. a back [u] rather than an English non-back [ü]. Now slowly and deliberately unround and spread the lips, while 'thinking [u]' all the time, and carefully maintaining quite rigidly the tongue-position of [u]. The result is silent [ɯ]. Now from this [ɯ] position silently slide forward to [i]. All this time the lips must be kept spread in a broad smile, so that there is no distracting change of lip-position. Silently slide back and forth, slowly then more quickly, between [ɯ] and [i]: [ɯ i ɯ i], etc.

As you do this repeatedly you should begin to identify the proprioceptive sensations of having the body of the tongue pushed as far forward in the mouth as possible, as for [i] or [y], and pulled far back in the mouth as for [ɯ] or [u].

Carry out similar experiments with lower or more open vowels, for example, silently produce an [ɛ], roughly as in *head*: while carefully retaining the tongue-position of [ɛ] add lip-rounding, changing [ɛ] to [œ], which is roughly the vowel of French *neuf*. Now, without changing the lip-position, silently slide back to [ɔ], as in *saw*, and alternate slowly, quickly, at first silently, then later whispered and voiced [œ ɔ œ ɔ] . . .

This should give you once again the feeling of moving the tongue back and forth in the mouth: varying, that is, along the parameter of *horizontal tongue-position*.

If you still have some uncertainty about the feeling of moving the tongue to the front and back of the mouth, do Experiments 84 and 85 again and again, until you are absolutely confident about the feelings of horizontal tongue-movement.

Now you have a clear idea, intimately experienced in your own vocal tract, not merely intellectually known, of how vowels can be described and classified: in terms of vertical and horizontal tongue-position, and position of the lips.

We have seen, and verified experimentally, that vowels differ in terms of three parameters, and can thus be classified as (*i*) *rounded* or *unrounded*, (*ii*) *high* or *low*, or to use the terms we shall use henceforth *close* or *open*, (*iii*) *front* or *back*.

Table 4

Front		Back	
Unrounded	Rounded	Unrounded	Rounded
Close: (*beat*) i	y (*lune*)	ɯ (*laogh*)	u (*too*)
(*bait*) e			
Open: (*bet*) ɛ	œ (*neuf*)		ɔ (*saw*)

We can lay out this scheme of classification as shown in Table 4, with a few examples.

The general outline of vowel-description that we have presented is not sufficiently detailed or specific to enable us to unambiguously specify fine distinctions between the vowels of different languages and dialects. For that purpose we have to learn a rather precisely defined set of universal reference-vowels, known as 'the Cardinal Vowels'. This system was invented by the great English phonetician Daniel Jones.

3. Introduction to Cardinal Vowels

The Jones system of Cardinal Vowels is based upon the idea of a 'vowel limit', and of a 'vowel space' delimited by it. It is easy to discover experimentally what is meant by the vowel limit.

86 Produce a silent close front vowel, a vowel like that heard in English *see*, French *si*, etc.: [i]. Note, as you have frequently done before, how the tongue is bunched up very high in the front of the mouth, leaving only a narrow channel between the dorsal surface of the tongue and the hard palate and prepalatal arch. Voice this vowel [i]. As we have observed before, [i] is a dorso-palatal approximant. Now, while pronouncing a prolonged [i i i i i ...] vowel, make the tongue very tense and push its dorsal surface up closer and closer to the hard palate, until audible turbulence can be heard. At this point the approximant [i] has obviously turned into the fricative [j]. By making very fine adjustments in the tenseness and convexity of the tongue-surface, pass back and forth several times between the approximant [i] and the fricative [j]: [i j i j i j i j i].

Experiment 86 has shown that there is a limit to the 'closeness' of a vowel: if you raise the tongue any further, the vowel will turn into a fricative.

87 Produce a prolonged voiced [i] once again, noting particularly its extreme *frontness*, the fact that the anterodorsum of the tongue is pressed very far forwards in the mouth. Now strive to push the anterodorsum even further forwards, coming closer and closer to the prepalatal arch (immediately above and behind the alveolar ridge). Once again you will find that as the channel between the tongue-surface and the palate-surface narrows, the hiss of turbulence becomes audible and the approximant [i] has turned into a fricative: not exactly the [j] we reached by pushing upwards from [i], but rather an anterodorso-prepalatal fricative, which we can represent by [ʑ], and which sounds like [j] modified in the direction of lamino-postalveolar [ʒ]. Carefully alternate [i ʑ i ʑ i ʑ].

A similar experiment with [u] (or better, its unrounded counter-part [ɯ]) gives results of the same kind.

88 Produce an [u]-type vowel—somewhat like a tense, monophthongal (i.e. completely unchanging throughout its duration) version of the English vowel in *too*, or better, the German vowel in *du*—which is generally more *back*. From this very back [u] silently, and while rigidly retaining the close back tongue-position of [u], slowly and deliberately unround the lips: be careful to retain *exactly* the close back tongue-position while doing this. Silently maintain the [ɯ] position, noting how you can feel the tongue bunched up towards the back of the mouth with part of its dorsal surface very near the soft palate. Carefully maintaining the close back position, initiate and voice a prolonged [ɯ]: this, like [i], is an approximant. Now, while continuing to produce prolonged [ɯ], tense the tongue-back and strive to push it upwards, coming still closer to the soft palate. As you do this, the hiss of turbulent airflow will begin to be heard: the approximant [ɯ] is being converted into the fricative [ɣ]. Carefully alternate [ɯ ɣ ɯ ɣ ɯ ɣ].

A similar experiment with a very open very back vowel will help to define the vowel limit further. The kind of vowel to aim at is roughly of the type of [ɑ] in *far* or the [ɒ] of *cot* in British RP or the [ɔ] of *caught* in some varieties of American English. But it must be much deeper—more retracted—than any vowel you are familiar with.

89 Draw the tongue down and back, particularly back. Get the sensation of pulling the tongue as far down and as far back into the pharynx as possible. Retain this very low back position, and voice it, producing a very low back [ɑ]-type vowel. Prolong this vowel and while doing so force your tongue even further back. As the space between the tongue-root and the back wall of the

pharynx narrows, the quality of the [ɑ]-vowel will become somewhat strangu-
lated, and you may hear it turning into a pharyngal fricative or possibly a
kind of pharyngalized uvular fricative. It is clear, at least, that you ultimately
reach a point where the clear vowel-like quality of [ɑ] is lost.

Experiments 86, 87, 88, and 89 have served to demonstrate that, at least
in the upward and backward direction, there is a kind of boundary in the
mouth and pharynx beyond which approximant-type vowel sounds become
fricatives: this boundary delimits the 'vowel space' in these two dimensions,
as indicated by the broken line in Fig. 37.

It is more difficult to specify, in a precise manner, the forward and downward limits of tongue position. Fig. 37, which is based on X-ray photo-
graphs of the author's articulations, shows the 'vowel limit', represented by
a broken line, continuing down the prepalatal arch to just behind the postalveolar zone. This is quite in accordance with the findings of Experiment
70, in which the convex anterodorsal surface of the tongue was brought as
close as possible to the concave prepalatal arch. But it is not so easy to
indicate the vowel limit for completely open vowels in an analogous manner. The problem is that the tongue is a mobile and polymorphous mass:
that is to say, a mass that can take up different positions and somewhat
different shapes. Since it is difficult to describe and compare the positions
of the tongue-mass as a whole it is convenient to select some easily identified *reference-point* for purposes of comparison. For over a century it has
been traditional to define relative tongue-positions in terms of the location

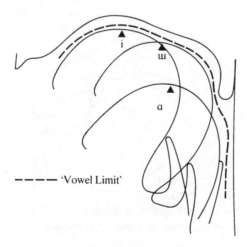

Fig. 37 The vowel limit

of the summit of the convex tongue-mass—the *highest point of the tongue*. In Fig. 37 the highest point of the tongue for each of the vowels [i] [ɯ] and [a] is indicated by the tip of a small black triangle. It must always be remembered that the highest point of the tongue is no more than a convenient *reference-point*; it has no significance other than that. Indeed, as we have already seen, another location on the tongue-surface is more important in defining the vowel limit, and indeed, in other ways: this is the location of the narrowest linguo-tectal or linguo-pharyngal articulatory channel. Anticipating a little, look at Fig. 38. This shows the tongue-configurations for the Cardinal Vowels that we are about to study. The black dots here show the highest point of the tongue for each vowel, while broken lines round the periphery show the location of the narrowest articulatory channel for some of the approximant-type vowels. This shows that the highest point (a mere reference-point) does not always coincide with the location of the articulatory stricture.

As we have already pointed out, the underlying idea of the Cardinal Vowels is that of a 'vowel limit' within the mouth, and, consequently, a 'vowel space' inside that limit. In theory, any vowel of any language must have its tongue-position either *on* the vowel limit itself, or within the vowel space. The problem, then, is to define that space, and to specify a set of reference-points on the vowel limit, in a way that is independent of any particular language.

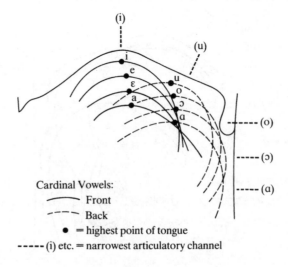

Fig. 38 Tongue-configurations for Cardinal Vowels

The key reference-points for the Cardinal Vowels are two that we have already experimented with, namely the closest and most front vowel possible [i], and the openest and most back vowel possible [ɑ]. The vowels [i] and [ɑ] represent relatively fixed points, that anyone can locate for himself by following the directions given in Experiments 86, 87, and 88, without ever having heard the sounds.

Between [i], which we will call Cardinal Vowel 1, and [ɑ] which is Cardinal Vowel 5, are three intermediate Cardinal Vowels: 2 [e], 3 [ɛ], and 4 [a], which are sometimes said to represent equidistant points between 1 [i] and 5 [ɑ]. The system is completed by continuing the series of 'equidistant' vowels on past [ɑ] up to [u], with Cardinal Vowels [6] [ɔ], 7 [o], 8 [u].

Daniel Jones, the inventor of the system, described the Cardinal Vowels of the sets 1–4 and 5–8 as being *organically* (articulatorily) equidistant, i.e. separated by equal steps of tongue-lowering/raising, and also acoustically (by which he meant *auditorily*) equidistant. On the whole, he emphasized the articulatory equidistance more, though the question whether it is better to regard the Cardinal Vowels as an *articulatory* or an *auditory* scale is still disputed. The present writer's view (like that of Henry Sweet) is that for the purpose of learning the Cardinal Vowels it is essential to concentrate on their *articulatory* characteristics: make correct tongue-configurations and the correct sounds will automatically follow.

Daniel Jones emphasized the articulatory (and auditory) equidistance of the separate series [i–e–ɛ–a] and [ɑ–ɔ–o–u], not the equidistance of the entire set. This is important because, as many users of the system have observed, the distance between [a] as the openest possible extremely front vowel, and [ɑ], as the most retracted possible open vowel, clearly seems to be greater than the distance between the successive 'equidistant' vowels within the separate front and back sets.

Partly because of this, it is desirable to learn the front series and the back series as two distinct, though related, sets. This helps to avoid a problem that arises if one tries to produce [i-e-ɛ-a-ɑ] as a single set of equidistant vowels. This problem is the tendency to let the more open front vowels slip back from the fully fronted position as one begins, as it were, to aim for [ɑ]. Fig. 39 shows schematically what I mean. The solid line through [i] [e] [ɛ] [a] indicates the progression by equal steps through a purely front series of vowels: the broken line suggests the kind of deviation from frontness that often occurs when a student tries to say [i–e–ɛ–a–ɑ] as a single series of equidistant vowels.

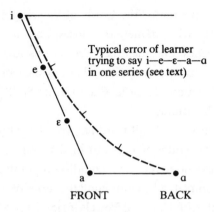

Fig. 39 Error to avoid in pronouncing front CVs. Typical error of learner trying to say i–e–ɛ–a–ɑ in one series (see text)

Before finally beginning to study the Cardinal Vowels we must introduce a type of diagram that is commonly used to represent the Cardinal Vowels and the universal vowel space that they surround and define. This diagram (Fig. 40) is a simplified version of earlier diagrams that purported to correspond more closely to the actual tongue-positions of the Cardinal Vowels. It is easy to draw the Cardinal Vowel diagram if you observe the length proportions 2:3:4 for the bottom, right, and top sides of the diagram. The slope of the left side, representing front vowels, is supposed to correspond more or less to the fact that the location of the highest point of the tongue retreats backwards into the mouth the more the tongue is lowered, but, as is shown by comparison with Fig. 38, this retreat is exaggerated. The fact that the top line, connecting [i] and [u], is twice as long as the bottom line, connecting [a] and [ɑ], reflects the fact that the *acoustic* (and auditory) difference between [i] and [u] is more than twice the difference between [a] and [ɑ]. The very great acoustic difference between [i] and [u] results largely from the fact that [u] is rounded while [i] is unrounded. As can be seen from the symbols used to label the eight (primary) Cardinal Vowels, three out of four back vowels, namely [u] [o] and [ɔ], are rounded: only the most open back vowel, [ɑ], is unrounded. The reason for selecting rounded vowels for the back series is that, more often than not, in natural languages all but the most open of back vowels are rounded. There is a second series of 'secondary' Cardinal Vowels which have the opposite lip-positions, that is, the front vowels and the most open back vowels are rounded, while the closer back vowels are unrounded.

So, then, the commonly used Cardinal Vowel diagram is a hybrid, to a

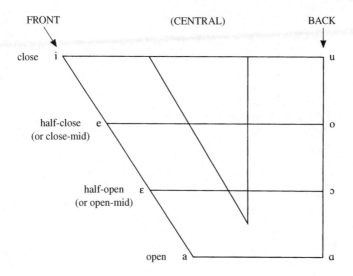

Fig. 40 The Cardinal Vowels

large extent reflecting the relative tongue-positions of the vowels, with front vowels down the left side, back vowels on the right side, and with its vertical spacing reflecting equal articulatory steps of tongue-lowering in going from [i] to [a] or from [u] to [ɑ], but at the same time reflecting the different *acoustic* distances between [i] and [u], and between [a] and [ɑ] in the different lengths of the upper and lower horizontal lines.

In spite of its curious hybrid nature, the diagram works very well in practice. Since the tongue-position of any vowel must lie on the periphery of the figure or somewhere within it, dots placed on its periphery or within it can indicate the position of any vowel in relation to the Cardinal Vowels, which serve as universal reference-points. This is why the Cardinal Vowel system is an essential tool of all practical phoneticians, who must learn these universal reference-vowels as well as they possibly can.

It has often been stated that the Cardinal Vowels can only be learned orally, from a teacher who already knows them. This is only partly true. Perhaps a final polish can best be applied to one's Cardinal Vowels by appealing to the judgement and the corrective hints of a competent teacher. But all students can go a very long way towards accuracy in the Cardinal Vowels—and some can achieve virtual mastery of them—without a teacher, providing they carry out experiments and exercises on them with meticulous care. In Chapter 8 we introduce the system of Cardinal Vowels in detail through a series of experiments.

8

The Cardinal Vowels (CVs)

1. General characteristics of cardinal vowels: Errors to avoid

There is some divergence of opinion among phoneticians as to whether the system of Cardinal Vowels (which, from now on, we shall refer to as CVs) should be regarded primarily as an articulatory or as an auditory scale of reference-vowels. From the practical point of view, however, it is best to proceed as if the system is basically an articulatory one, and to familiarize oneself thoroughly with the 'feel'—the proprioceptive and tactile sensations—of the CVs.

As indicated in Chapter 7, the CVs are a set of eight tongue-configurations, five of them with unrounded lips, the remaining three with rounded lips. There is also a set of eight secondary CVs with exactly the same tongue-configurations, but opposite lip-positions. Finally, there are a few additional vowel articulations, which, though not usually considered part of the CV system, are essential for the student of phonetics to get to know.

The CVs are not the vowels of any particular language, but are, as we have seen, a set of systematically established, language-independent, universal reference vowels. Naturally, some of the vowels of some languages happen to coincide with, or to approximate closely to, some of the CVs. Thus, typical French vowels, of *si* [si], *ces* [se], *sait* [sɛ], are rather close to the CVs [i], [e], [ɛ]. Practically no English vowels are at all close to CVs. This means that the English-speaking reader must start from the assumption that not a single one of the vowels used in the English language is exactly a Cardinal Vowel. Moreover, the vowel-sounds of English, and of other languages, vary very considerably from one dialect to another.

All of this means that in learning or teaching the CVs we must use the vowels of the reader's language with the greatest care. From time to time they provide useful starting-points for arriving at CVs, but readers must always assume that the CVs are not by any means the same as any vowel of their own language.

Two characteristics of the CVs must be emphasized at the outset. First, they should all be pronounced in a rather energetic, tense, manner. They are, after all, *peripheral* vowels—that is, vowels produced with the tongue thrust as far forward as possible or pulled back as far as possible, and the close ones have the tongue pushed up as far as possible. It is therefore reasonable to assume that if you do not at times feel some degree of strain, or tiredness, in some of the muscles within, or attached to, the tongue, you are not exerting yourself sufficiently to produce good CVs. Secondly they are all *monophthongs*—that is, they are simple or 'pure' vowels, that can be prolonged for as long as possible with absolutely no change of tongue- (or lip-) position, and consequently no change of quality. This is very important for English speakers to remember (and we shall remind them repeatedly), since many of the vowels of English, in most dialects of English, are *diphthongs*. That is, they are gliding vowels that start with one tongue- and/ or lip-position, and end up with another. Obvious diphthongs are the sound of *I* [a ɪ] and the *ow* of *how* [aʊ]. If you say these words aloud, in a whisper, and silently, several times, the gliding movement of the tongue will be obvious in both of them, and in [aʊ] a radical change of the lip-position will also be obvious.

But some other English vowels are less obviously diphthongal. Thus, many speakers—it is probably safe to say most speakers—of English pronounce the vowels of such words as *day* and *go* in a decidedly diphthongal manner. Experiment 90 deals with the vowel of *day* (normally a diphthong) and with the production of a rigidly fixed *monophthong* somewhat resembling it.

90 Say the word *day* aloud, in a whisper and silently. Pronounce it silently, quickly, slowly, and at an intermediate rate. As you introspect about it, it is very probable that you will discover that your pronunciation of the *ay* in *day* is diphthongal. If you come from Scotland, Ireland, Wales, India, or some parts of the North of England, it is possible that you will find your *ay* to be an unchanging monophthong. Most probably, however, you will find that *ay* starts with mouth slightly open, and then, as the sound progresses, the mouth closes somewhat. The tongue rises slightly (when you are doing it silently, you may feel an increasing contact between the sides of the tongue and the

molar teeth). The auditory effect is likely to be that of a vowel that changes its quality throughout its duration: its exact starting and finishing points vary very widely according to dialect, and the diphthong might be represented as [ei], [ɛɪ], [æɪ], and so on: you will learn the precise values of these letters later.

If you find that your *ay*-vowel is, indeed, diphthongal, even to a very slight degree (as you probably will), it will be necessary to start training your tongue to adopt and hold a rigid, fixed, position which will produce a vowel having, roughly, the quality of your *ay* diphthong (a kind of average or mid-point between its beginning and end) but with an absolutely fixed, unmoving, tongue-, jaw-, and lip-position.

91 Make the tongue very tense, and press its sides against the back molar teeth. Hold the tongue, silently, in this position, anchored, as it were, to the molar teeth, for several seconds.

After you are confident that you are able to hold the tongue rigidly in this position, initiate an air-stream and produce a prolonged vowel, first whispered, then voiced.

It should be something roughly of the type represented phonetically as [e]. Make sure that your tongue is pushed well *forwards* to ensure that you are producing a truly front vowel, as well as *upwards* to maintain contact with the molar teeth. Listen and feel very critically. If the sound changes in the slightest, or if there is the slightest movement of the tongue during the utterance of the vowel, stop and go back to the stage of silently holding the fixed position of the tongue, anchored to the molar teeth.

Then concentrate hard on holding that fixed tongue-position and just incidentally, by stealth, as it were, begin to voice it, keeping almost all of your attention on the fixed tongue position. The trick is to break the association with that old diphthongal vowel sound, and the way to do it is to concentrate entirely on the articulation. You have to say to yourself NOT, 'I'm producing an *ay*-type vowel sound', BUT, 'I'm holding a certain articulatory posture— and I'm going to hold it, whatever sound comes out when I voice it.'

We next carry out a similar procedure with the diphthong of *go*, or better, the isolated diphthong of *Oh!* This, again, is almost certain to be a diphthong (unless you speak certain varieties of Scottish, northern English, Irish, Welsh, or Indian English), involving progressive raising of the tongue and a progressive increase in lip-rounding as the vowel proceeds. The exact starting and finishing point of the diphthong varies very widely according to dialect: you may be saying an only slightly diphthongal [oʊ] or a very diphthongal [ɜʊ], which starts with the tongue low in the mouth and the lips in a neutral position and ends up with the tongue bunched up quite high and the lips quite closely rounded: or anything in between. In any case, the task now is to produce some kind of [o]-like vowel articulation, prolonged for several seconds, with absolutely no change of tongue- or lip-position from beginning to end. Taking your diphthongal English *oh* as a starting point, try, as you did with the *ay*-vowel, to produce a kind of average or mid-way [o]-sound.

92 Draw the tongue well back into the pharynx and keep it raised rather high (there should be some feeling of strain at the base of the tongue and just above the larynx as you do this), with the lips rather closely rounded. The lips should be as close as they were at the end of your diphthongal *o* (or closer, if you feel that your *o* really involves very little lip-rounding, as some do). Now, silently hold this position rigidly: tongue bunched up and drawn back, lips well rounded. Continue to concentrate hard on holding that tongue and lip configuration while stealthily initiating an air-stream, and starting up whisper, then voice. Once again, the aim must be to hold a tongue- and lip-position: the voicing, and consequent audible sound, are incidental. Concentrate almost entirely on the articulation, and merely casually and incidentally notice the vowel-sound that is produced: nevertheless, be quick to stop the performance at once if you feel (or hear) that the sound is not a rigidly maintained unchanging monophthongic vowel.

Some students quickly get to the point where they are producing a good maintained monophthong but then they spoil it by finishing it off with a brief diphthong-like glide away from that fixed position. Watch out for that. When you produce a long, monophthongal [e e e e e] or [o o o o o], as in Experiments 91 and 92, concentrate on holding that fixed tongue- (and lip-) position right up to the end. Let the initiation and phonation stop BEFORE you relax the tongue or lips. Now go back over 91 and 92 once again, checking that you are not spoiling your monophthongs in this way.

It is, of course, not only the vowels of *day* and *go* that are commonly diphthongal in English. There are varieties of English in which virtually *every* vowel is diphthongal, and speakers of these varieties must be particularly careful to discipline their tongues (and lips) into absolute rigidity in producing the Cardinal Vowels. In the experiments that follow, which are designed to lead the reader to discover all the CVs, we will repeatedly warn against diphthongization. But it may be useful for English-speaking readers to run through a series of English vowels aloud, and then silently trying to discover which, if any, of them are truly monophthongal in their pronunciation.

The following words provide examples of all the front and back vowels of English:

(1) *he, heed*; (2) *hid*; (3) *hay, hayed*; (4) *head*; (5) *had*; (6) *ha!, calm*; (7) *hod*; (8) *haw, hawed*; (9) *hoe, hoed*; (10) *hood*; (11) *who, who'd*.

Nos. 2, 4, 5, 7, and 10 occur only with a consonant after them in English, which is why only one example of each is given. In experimenting with these English vowels, try to cut off the final consonant of nos. 2, 4, 5, 7, and 10, saying first *hid*, then (carefully preserving the same vowel quality) *hi* . . ., and likewise *head* and then *he* . . ., etc. In other words, try to isolate these (and all the other) vowels, the better to be able to introspect about them, and feel exactly what is going on when you produce them. Note that nos. 4, 6, 7, 10 are virtually never diphthongal. All the others may be, in various varieties of English.

Having determined which of your English vowels are diphthongal, be particularly careful to avoid diphthongizing CVs that resemble them to some extent.

2. The front CVs

We are now ready to start acquiring the articulations of the CVs.

93 Produce CV 1 [i]. Make your tongue very tense and bunch it up in the front of the mouth as *high* and as far *forward* as you can without actually producing a fricative. Maintain the articulation silently and feel the following: the tip of the tongue is in contact with the backs or roots of the lower teeth, the anterodorsum of the tongue is pushed up very high and very far forward—you can feel quite strong contact between the sides of the tongue and the upper teeth on both sides, from the *molars* to the *canines*—the canine tooth is the third upper tooth from the centre on either side. Now voice the vowel and note that it is a very 'sharp' [i]-sound, noticeably higher and tenser and 'sharper' than the vowel of English *me*, or *heed*. This is CV 1 [i].

We now proceed to CV 2 [e].

94 Produce a tense, silent CV 1 [i], and then deliberately lower the tongue a very little, keeping it quite tense, and keeping the tip of the tongue in contact with

the backs or roots of the lower teeth. Lower the tongue only to the point where contact with the canine and front molar teeth is lost, but you can still feel contact between the sides of the tongue and the back molars. This should be approximately CV 2 [e]. Slowly and deliberately move back and forth between this new, very slightly lowered position, and the [i] position, then try to fixate the tongue in the [e] position. The tongue should be tense, tip touching the backs of the lower teeth, thrust well forward, sides pressing against upper molars. Produce voice with the tongue fixated in this position, and maintain the resultant [e e e e . . .] vowel for several seconds. The tongue must be rigidly fixed, the lips spread, and there must be absolutely no movement of tongue or lips during this prolonged [e e e e . . .]. Be specially careful at the end of the utterance: don't let it finish with the tongue slipping up to the [i] position (producing [e e e . . . i]), nor with the tongue slipping back and down to the [ə] position (producing [e e e . . . ə]). Let the voicing stop before you relax or move the tongue in any way. Concentrate on the *fixed tongue position*, not on the sound that is produced: let that be merely incidental. If you think about the sound too much you may find yourself equating it with your [eɪ] or [ɛɪ] in *hay*, which is almost certainly a diphthong.

Having consolidated the tongue-postures for the CVs [i] and [e] by repeated silent positioning of the tongue for these vowels, with occasional voicing to see what they sound like, we move on to the *half-open front* CV 3 [ɛ].

95   One way to approach [ɛ] is this: silently articulate [i] then [e], several times, concentrating on the perceived *distance* between the close [i] and the *half-close* [e]. Now start at silent [i], silently drop down to [e], then try to drop down the same distance, keeping the tongue in a very front position. Repeat this manœuvre silently many times: tongue *close, half-close, half-open*. When you are confident that you can reliably do this, carry out the same moves in a whisper, and then aloud, trying all the time to produce *equal steps* of tongue-lowering, resulting in *equal steps* of sound, in going from [i] to [e] and from [e] to [ɛ].

The third CV, [ɛ], is closely similar to the French [ɛ] vowel of *bête*. For a few speakers of English, particularly in the North of England, the vowel of *head* is about the same as CV 3. For most others it is not. Speakers of RP usually have a vowel between CV 2 and CV 3 in *head*, that is, one that is too high for CV [ɛ]. Many Americans, specially in the Middle West, have a vowel in *head* that is about the same height as CV 3 [ɛ], but not nearly *front* enough. On the other hand, such people often have a vowel in *had* which starts off rather close to CV 3, but then slides backwards: type [ɛ·ə], [hɛ · əd]. So although these vowels of French and English may be some kind of guide to CV 3, do not rely on them. CV 3 is simply a tense, rigid, monophthongal vowel, two steps down from [i], as it were. This is what we tried to achieve in Experiment 95.

96   A further equal step downwards, with tongue still pressed well forwards, gives us the tongue-configuration of CV 4 [a]. The commonest error here is to let the tongue slip back, so that the vowel produced no longer belongs to the front series. Remember that in going from CV 3 [ɛ] to CV 4 [a] the movement must be only *downward*—a slight lowering of the tongue and/or of the jaw—not inward at all.

It will be well now to experiment with the four front CVs [i–e–ɛ–a] as a series. The points to bear in mind are: (*i*) all are very *front* vowels: from this point of view they form a single, unified, group, all produced with the tongue thrust as far forward in the mouth as possible. (*ii*) CV 1 [i] is the highest frontest possible vowel. (*iii*) CV 4 [a] is a very low vowel—it may be thought of as the 'lowest possible' front vowel, though that is not so clearly defined as 'highest possible'. A feeling of 'lowest possible' can be achieved by lowering the jaw somewhat (not excessively, front teeth not more than about 1 cm. or $\frac{1}{2}$ in. apart) and drawing the body of the tongue down to the bottom of the mouth, always being careful to keep it thrust as far forward as possible. At the same time, note that having the tongue 'as low as possible' does not mean that the tongue is hollowed: it must retain essentially the same convexity as it has for all the other front vowels. Americans may find it helpful to note that CV 4 [a] is something like the [aː] vowel that many speakers of South Midland and Southern dialects use for [aɪ] in such words as *time* [taːm].

97   Having repeatedly switched (in silence) from CV 1 [i] to CV 4 [a] to get a clear feeling of the two extremes of front vowel positions, now go from CV 1 to CV 4 silently, in *equal steps*: CV 1, 2, 3, 4. Do this repeatedly, watching in your mirror, and concentrating on *frontness*, and the feeling of *equal steps*.

Finally, do the same thing aloud: [i] [e] [ɛ] [a], many times. Combine the feeling of equal steps with extreme frontness and rigidly monophthongal pronunciation of all the vowels. Repeat the series many times, quickly and slowly, maintaining each position for a moment, and then for a longer period of time. Listen and feel in an extremely critical way. The tongue must not slip back from the extreme front position as it goes down, and each vowel must, as already pointed out many times, be *absolutely monophthongal*. If you find yourself diphthongizing any of the vowels (saying, for example, [eɪ] instead of [e], [ɛə] instead of [ɛ]), immediately stop, and *silently* practise the articulation of that vowel, then tentatively whisper and voice it, taking care to concentrate *primarily* on the *feeling*—not the sound—because it is the proprioceptively and tactilely perceived tongue-position that you must control: the sound will take care of itself. Watching in your mirror, compare your lip-positions with those shown in Fig. 41.

3. The back CVs

Assuming that the front CVs [i] [e] [ɛ] [a] have been acquired, approximately at least, we turn to the back vowels 5 [ɑ], 6 [ɔ], 7 [o], 8 [u].

The first problem is to make sure that all four vowels of the series 5–8 are as much *retracted* as possible. In articulating all of them there must be a distinct feeling of muscular strain as you pull the tongue-mass as far back

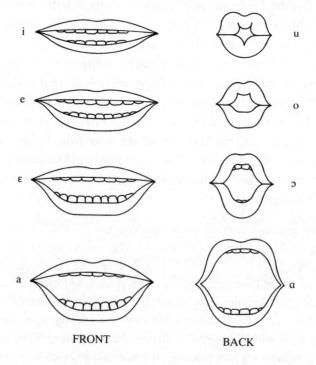

FRONT   BACK

Fig. 41 Schematic representation of lip-positions of Cardinal Vowels

in the mouth as possible. Even before carrying out detailed experiments on the back CVs, silently articulate many times a set of vowels of the type [ɑ] [ɔ] [o] [u] with tongue pulled as far back as possible.

98 Start with [ɑ], with the tongue absolutely as low and as far back as possible, with the lips in a more or less neutral position. Then, move the tongue (silently) upwards, by equal steps—about equal, as nearly as you can judge, to the steps you made for the front vowels—to three more positions, roughly those of [ɔ] [o] and [u].

Note that [ɔ], [o], and [u] have rounded lips—progressively more rounded as you move up. Fig. 41 shows the lip-positions of the four back vowels. Compare these repeatedly with your own lip-positions as you articulate the series, and as you practise individual vowels.

We must now take a more careful look at the individual vowels.

99 CV 5 [ɑ] is, as we have seen, as low and as back as possible, with neutral lips. Moving the tongue and/or jaw up one step, and bringing forward the corners of the mouth to form the typical kind of open rounding, articulate CV 6 [ɔ]. Make an attempt at this position, then whisper it, and finally voice it. The resulting sound must be absolutely monophthongal, and it must *sound* as well as *feel* about one-third of the way between the most open [ɑ] and the closest [u].

As usual, we cannot use the vowels of any particular language as an absolute guide, but they can provide some hints. A typical RP [ɔː] as in *saw* is not far off CV 6: Americans, however, have more difficulty. In some American dialects the typical vowel of *saw* is much too open. It is [ɒː], with a vowel almost as open as [ɑ], rather than [ɔː]. On the other hand, some New Yorkers have a vowel more like [ɔ]: but here again, there are problems. First they tend to *diphthongize* their [ɔ], to something like [ɔə]: and the starting point in what one might call 'broad NY' is much too high, so that the diphthong is something like [oə], specially in words ending in a consonant, such as *caught* [kɔət] or [koət]. French typically has a vowel of about the right height, but not nearly far enough back, in words like *note* [nöt], where the two dots indicate a strongly centralized vowel.

These negative indications may help the reader to avoid some of the worst errors.

Leaving [ɔ] in a possibly uncertain state, to be improved later if necessary, we progress to [o]. As this suggests, the learning of the CVs is a matter of making closer and closer approximations.

100   CV 7 [o] has the tongue raised by two equal steps from [ɑ], or about two-thirds of the way to [u]. The lips are rather closely rounded. Assuming that you can articulate a very close, very back, very rounded [u], you should experiment by silently moving from [ɑ] to [u] by equal steps: silent [ɑ] [ɔ] [o] [u]. Having arrived, by this kind of experimentation, at a rather closely rounded, very back vowel, about two-thirds of the way from [ɑ] to [u], whisper it, and then voice it, maintaining a prolonged, unchanging [o o o . . .] for some seconds.

Most English speakers will realize that CV 7 [o] is somewhat reminiscent of the vowel of *go*. As we have already pointed out, a monophthongal [o]-type vowel very close to CV 7 is used by many Scots, northern English speakers, and by Irish, Welsh, and Indian speakers. Speakers of RP and of most types of American English have a diphthongal sound, usually starting considerably forward from the back position, and involving a progressive raising of the tongue, and a progressive rounding of the lips, e.g. [əu]. Clearly, this is very remote from the rigidly monophthongal, fully back, half-close, rounded CV 7. That is why such people must try to acquire the articulation of this vowel, as suggested, in a manner totally unrelated to thoughts about the vowel of *go*. However, if one can accurately imitate one of the monophthongal [o]-type vowels mentioned above, that may be a useful guideline. The French [o] in *beau* is of about the right height, but usually not back enough.

101   CV 8 [u] is the closest possible very back vowel. It may be arrived at, as we have already mentioned, from an English [u] vowel, but only with great care and conscious effort: it must be *as back as possible* (which English [ü] is far from being), *rigidly monophthongal*, and *strongly rounded*. Another starting point for arriving at the articulation of CV 8 [u] is [w], as in English *wall*. Whisper that word, several times, and do the same with a prolongation of the initial [w]: silently make and hold that [w]-articulation. It will probably be close to CV 8 [u]. It may require some tensing and some retraction, to make it as back as possible.

Figure 40, which we introduced in the last chapter, shows the eight primary Cardinal Vowels on the commonly used diagram. You should now go through the whole series many times, while looking at the diagram, which you will find at the end of Chapter 6.

Go through the CVs from 1 to 8 several times, silently. Remember, all are rigidly monophthongal. Be careful to make 1–4 very front—don't start slipping away from the front position as you get down towards 4 [a]—thrust the tongue energetically forward all the time, and take equal steps between 1 and 2, 2 and 3, 3 and 4. Take care to make 5–8 very back—the tongue must be strained, tiringly, back towards the pharynx—and there should be equal steps between 5 and 6, 6 and 7, and 7 and 8.

Next, whisper the whole series, taking exactly the same precautions, but now that the articulations are made audible by whispering, try to see that the *auditory impressions* are as equally spaced as possible, as you say 1, 2, 3, 4 and then 5, 6, 7, 8.

Finally, say the CVs aloud, taking the same precautions.

Having acquired a close approximation to the eight primary Cardinal Vowels, the next step is to acquire the eight secondary CVs. This is not difficult, since it merely entails changing the lip-positions of the CVs.

Figure 42 shows the CV diagram with both primary and secondary CVs indicated. A short arrow points out from the symbol for each primary CV to that for the corresponding secondary CV.

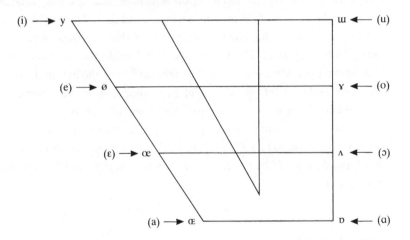

Fig. 42 (Primary) and secondary Cardinal Vowels

4. Types of lip-rounding

Before we go through all the secondary CVs it is necessary to make two remarks about lip-rounding. The first point to note is that (as we have already seen to some extent) there is normally a close correlation between tongue-height and degree of rounding: the closer the vowel the smaller the labial aperture and vice versa. Close vowels like [y] and [u] have very close rounding—a very small aperture barely the diameter of a pencil; opener vowels, like [œ] and [ɔ] have a much bigger aperture. In other words, corresponding to the different levels of 'tongue-height' we have *close rounding, half-close rounding, half-open rounding,* and *open rounding.* The second point is that the form of the lip-rounding often differs according to whether it is applied to back vowels or to front vowels.

102   We can easily discover these two types of rounding experimentally. Silently round the lips as if for a very round [u] vowel. Note that the corners of the lips are pushed in towards the centre so that both lips are pushed forwards, or 'pouted'. They form a kind of small tunnel in front of the mouth. In this type of rounding you can feel that the cheeks are pulled inwards, and also that the channel between the lips is formed by the inner surface of the lips rather than their outer surface: it is distinctly 'endolabial' (cf. pp. 80–1). Rounding of this type is called 'inner rounding', and it is characteristic of rounded back vowels like [u] and [o].

For the second type of rounding do not 'pout' the lips, but vertically compress the corners of the mouth, leaving a small central channel between the lips, of a slit-like flat elliptical shape rather than actually round. This type of rounding is called 'outer rounding', and unlike the 'inner rounding' that we have just seen, it involves the outer surface of the lips, and so may be called 'exolabial' (cf. pp. 80–1). Outer rounding is more characteristic of front rounded vowels, like [y] and [ø], though not all vowels of this type in all languages have outer rounding. The specific type of rounding to be applied to the secondary CVs [y] [ø] [œ] [ɶ] is not usually specified, but front rounding would be rather natural. In any case, you should experiment with both types.

5. Secondary CVs

We can now proceed to go through all the CVs, primary and secondary, silently, whispered, and voiced. We abbreviate secondary CV as 'SCV'.

103   CV 1 [i] → SCV 1 [y]. Silently articulate [i], add close rounding (preferably close outer rounding) to form [y]. Silently switch back and forth between [i] and [y] many times, taking care to keep the tongue absolutely fixed in the close front position of [i] all the time. Do the same with whisper and then with voice. Prolong the SCV [y].

As we have already pointed out, vowels rather close to SCV [y], though not so close and so front, include French *u* in *lune*, German *ü* in *Bühne*, and we might add Chinese *ü* in *yu* meaning 'mud', 'fish', 'rain', 'to meet' according to tone.

104   CV 2 [e] → SCV 2 [ø]. Silently articulate half-close front [e] (one step down from [i] in the series of equal steps that go from [i] to [a]), remembering to keep it very tense and very front: add lip-rounding, a very little less close than that of [y] (half-close outer rounding) to form [ø]. Silently switch back and forth between [e] and [ø], taking care to keep the tongue all the time rigidly fixed in the half-close front position of [e]. Do the same with whisper and then with voice.

SCV 2 [ø] is closer and more front than the French *eu* in *feu*, the German *ö* in *schön*.

105   CV 3 [ɛ] → SCV 3 [œ]. Silently articulate half-open front [ɛ] (one step down from [e]) taking great care to make it very front and rigidly monoph-thongal; add lip-rounding somewhat more open than that for [ø], to form [œ]. Silently switch back and forth between [ɛ] and [œ], taking care to keep the tongue all the time rigidly fixed in the half-open fully front position of [ɛ].

CV 4 [a] → SCV 4 [œ]. Silently produce the most open front vowel [a]. Remember it must be very open, the tongue lying right down on the floor of the mouth, but still convex (i.e. the centre of the tongue must not be pulled down), and as front as possible. Run silently or in a whisper through the whole front series [i] [e] [ɛ] [a] and take care that you keep the same feeling throughout—particularly the feeling that [a] belongs to exactly the same front series, with the tongue-mass thrust forward in the mouth, not in any way pulled back, as for [ɑ].

When you are sure you have got a good [a] position, hold the tongue in that position, and gradually bring the corners of your mouth inwards somewhat to the open rounded position, in reality a kind of vertically placed oval shape. Whisper and then voice this [œ] vowel, and compare it with the one next above it, [œ].

Go through the whole front series again, silently, with whisper and with voice, as often as you need in order to feel that you really have control of all the front CVs, both primary and secondary.

Now we can turn to the back CVs, and derive the secondaries from the primaries as we did with the front ones.

106   Throughout all of these experiments on the back CVs make sure that they really *are* back. You must, in other words, maintain throughout that feeling of straining the whole mass of the tongue backwards into the pharynx.

CV 5 [ɑ] → SCV 5 [ɒ]. Having silently achieved a good maximally open maximally back vowel [ɑ], slowly 'round' the lips as you did for [œ]: that is, move the corners of the mouth inwards to form a kind of oval 'open rounding'. Do this with whisper, then with voice. You will probably observe that there is really not much difference between the neutral position of the lips for [ɑ] and the open rounding of [ɒ]. Concomitantly with this there is also not a great difference in sound. Nevertheless, there is a slight difference and you must become aware of this.

Speakers of British RP and various South English dialects may note that SCV 5 [ɒ] is not unlike the vowel of *hot*, *cot*, etc. This may also be true for some New England Americans, but for most Americans the vowel of *hot*, *cot*, etc. is *unrounded*, and may not even be very back: for instance, one may hear such words pronounced with a vowel nearer to CV 4 than CV 5, as [hat] [kat], or nearly so.

For some Americans the nearest vowel to SCV 5 [ɒ] may well be the vowel of *caught*, which is often pronounced as something approaching [kɒːt] with a rather open back rounded vowel (though not actually as open as SCV 5).

For the remaining three back vowels, the change from primary to secondary is effected by *un*rounding, not rounding the lips. Some people find it a little more difficult to *remove* rounding from a given vowel than to add it. Consequently, you may find it useful to re-practise the deliberate, slow, silent rounding and unrounding of the lips before going on to experiment with converting primary CVs [ɔ], [o], [u] to their secondary counterparts [ʌ], [ɤ], and [ɯ].

107   CV 6 [ɔ] → SCV 6 [ʌ]. Make sure that your [ɔ] is really back, and one whole step above [ɑ] (silently running through the series [ɑ]–[ɔ]–[o]–[u] may help to ensure that it is about the right distance from [ɑ]). Silently articulate [ɔ] and slowly and deliberately unround it: relax the lips, then pull the corners of the mouth back in the direction of a smile, but not too far; the opener unrounded vowels (both back and front) do not have the extreme retraction of the corners of the mouth that is characteristic of the close vowels [i] and [ɯ]. Now unround [ɔ] to [ʌ], with whisper and with voice, taking care all the time to retain the *tongue-position* of [ɔ].

The SCV 6 [ʌ] has a sound that is noticeably different from that of [ɔ], but while saying it, with the lips consciously spread, not rounded, it may help to think of the sound of [ɔ] as well as its articulation. Say to yourself, in effect, 'I am now going to say [ɔ]', but keep the lips widely spread: i.e. deliberately say [ɔ] through wide-spread lips.

The symbol [ʌ] has often been used to represent the English vowel in words like *cut* and *bud*. This is a convention that goes back to the nineteenth century, but it must be noted that, apart from a few Scottish dialects, no variety of English has a fully back vowel in such words.

Some varieties of American English have a *cut* vowel that is half-open and almost completely central, more appropriately represented by the symbol [ɜ] (see below). In RP the *cut* vowel is usually more open than [ʌ], perhaps about half-way between open and half-open, and very much further forward.

Bearing this in mind, one must learn SCV 6 [ʌ] purely by deriving it from [ɔ], without guidance from vowels of English or any other language.

108   CV 7 [o] → SCV 7 [ɤ]. Make a silent [o]. Make sure it is really *back*, and strongly rounded. Silently remove the rounding, taking care to retain exactly the tongue-position of [o]. Do this with whisper and voice. Note that the place of articulation (the narrowest stricture) of [o] → [ɤ] is pretty much in the uvular zone. You can test your articulation of [o] → [ɤ] by producing voiced [o], unrounding it to [ɤ], then slightly closing up the articulatory channel. This should produce a fricative [ʁ], or thereabouts. If you believe you have a good [o], you can also aim at [ɤ] by saying [o] through wide-spread lips.

Once you have achieved a good thoroughly back [ɤ] you might experiment by allowing it to slip forward a little, becoming a somewhat centralized [ɤ̈]. Now place a [g] before that [ɤ̈] and a [d] after it: [gɤ̈d]. This is a rather widespread American pronunciation of the word *good*.

109   CV 8 [u] → SCV 8 [ɯ]. Silently articulate a good close, back, strongly rounded [u]: remember, this cardinal vowel is very *back* (unlike most varieties of English [u]), and very *close*, and tense. Taking care to maintain that close back tongue position, slowly and silently remove the lip-rounding. Do the same thing with whispered, and then voiced, [u] → [ɯ]. Having reached [ɯ], maintain it, then experimentally close up the articulatory channel a little. The result should be the voiced velar fricative [ɣ].

We have now completed our survey of all the CVs. It is important to consolidate these by repeatedly going through the primary CVs, silently, whispered and voiced, always taking care to make *all* of them rigidly monophthongal, to make nos. 1–4 very, very front, and nos. 5–8 very, very back, and to aim at approximately equal steps in going from close [i] to open [a], and from open [ɑ] to close [u].

It takes a great deal of practice to reach the stage where secondary CVs can be independently controlled. Consequently, it is best to practise them always as derivates of the primary CVs, i.e. by saying [i] → [y], [o] → [ɤ], etc. This has the advantage, too, of firmly linking them to the primary CVs, with which, of course, they are identical in tongue-position.

6. Central vowels and other additions to the CVs

We now have to experiment with a number of other important, or basic, vowel-sounds which are not usually regarded as part of the CV system, though they might well be. These are the central vowels, [ɨ] [ʉ], [ɘ] [ɵ], [ɜ] [ɞ] and [ä]. (See Fig. 43.)

After one has acquired virtual mastery over the extreme front and extreme back vowels of the Cardinal system, it is useful to experiment with vowels exactly half-way between front and back. These central vowels can be arrived at by sliding back and forth between front and back vowels and trying to stop half-way.

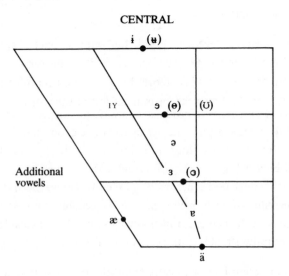

Fig. 43 Additional vowels

110 Close central [ɨ] and [ʉ]. Make a silent, very back [u]: remember, the tongue must be strained back towards the pharynx. Now, while retaining exactly the same lip-position slide the tongue forward to the very front vowel [y]. (An attempt to switch from inner rounding with [u] to outer rounding with [y] would merely be distracting in this experiment.) Slide back and forth between silent and whispered [u] and [y] many times, taking care to maintain the strongly bunched up, close, tongue-height throughout. Now, while silently sliding back and forth, try to stop about mid-way between [u] and [y]. This should be the position of the close central rounded vowel [ʉ]. Having stopped the tongue at this mid-point, produce voice and the sound should be [ʉ], auditorily (as well as articulatorily) about half-way between [u] and [y]. Repeat this procedure many times, and see if you can consistently arrive at approximately the same sound of [ʉ]. When you have achieved this, unround [ʉ] to the corresponding unrounded close central vowel [ɨ]. Now cross-check your [ɨ] by arriving at it by silently sliding back and forth between close unrounded front [i] and back [ɯ]. Stop half-way between these two vowel-positions, voice the sound and see if it is the same as the [ɨ] arrived at by unrounding [ʉ]. It ought to be.

111 Half-close central [ɵ] and [ɵ]. Carry out the same type of experiment at the half-close level. Repeatedly slide between half-close back rounded [o] and half-close front rounded [ø]. Take care to retain, as precisely as possible, the same half-close height of the tongue throughout, and the same degree of lip-rounding (with no distracting change in the type of rounding).

Now, while carefully maintaining the rounding and the tongue-height, stop the slide at about the mid-point between [o] and [ø] and produce voice. The sound should be half-close central-rounded [ɵ]. Repeat the procedure with the unrounded half-close vowels [e] and [ɤ]. Slide back and forth between them silently, and then with whisper, stop at the mid-point and voice the resultant half-close central unrounded [ɘ]. Cross-check by rounding this [ɘ], which should produce [ɵ], which should produce [ɘ].

When you can produce a good half-close central rounded [ɵ], try putting a [b] before it and a [k] after it, saying [bɵk]. This should be fairly close to a common pronunciation of the English word *book* in both RP and many types of American English. The only differences are that the English *book* vowel (for which the symbol [ʊ] is often used) is usually a little back from [ɵ] and may have less lip-rounding.

112 Half-open central [ɜ] and [ɞ]. It is probably easiest to start, as usual, with the rounded vowels: half-open back rounded [ɔ], and half-open front rounded [œ]. Silently slide back and forth between these vowels, taking care to maintain the half-open position of the tongue. Now, try to stop at the half-way point, produce voice, and the sound ought to be half-open central rounded [ɵ]. This is something like the French vowel, commonly transcribed [ɔ], in *bock*, 'beer-glass', *fort*, 'strong', etc. (Actually, the French vowel may be somewhat less advanced, lying between [ɔ] and [ɵ].)

Now silently slide between half-open front [ɛ] and half-open back [ʌ], and try to stop half-way between the two. Voice this sound, which ought to be half-open central [ɜ]. Cross-check by rounding this to [ɵ], and by unrounding [ɵ] to [ɜ]. This half-open unrounded [ɜ] is one variety of the RP vowel of *bird*, [bɜːd].

Open central [ä]. By sliding back and forth between CV 4 [a] and CV 5 [ɑ], and then stopping in the middle, one can reach an open central vowel which may be represented by [ä]. The *a*-type vowels of many languages are of an open more or less central type. In RP and many types of American English the vowel of words like *cart, father* is often about [ä], or between central [ä] and back [ɑ].

We have now completed our survey of central vowels, and hence of all those vowels that may be regarded as reference points for the Cardinal Vowel system, namely, CV 1–8, secondary CVs 1s–8s, and the central vowels.

There are six other vowel-types for which the IPA supplies special symbols, in the case of the first three (it seems) because they are English vowels, that are not very close to CVs. These special symbols are [ɪ] (also represented by [i]), [ʊ] (also represented by [u]), [æ], [ə], [ɐ]. The sixth is [ʏ], which represents a rounded [ɪ], which is commonly the sound of German short ü as in *hübsch* 'pretty'.

[ɪ] half-close (raised), front-retracted, unrounded. This is the vowel of *hit, hid*, etc., and in RP it is usually as indicated in the short description just given. It is quite close to CV 2 [e], but noticeably retracted, i.e. produced with the tongue-mass drawn back towards, but not to, the central position. A good deal of variation occurs with this vowel in varieties of English, which, though always distinctly centralized, ranges in height from about half-way between close and half-close, to half-way between half-close and half-open. In some varieties of 'advanced' (sp. younger generations) RP, and American, the vowel [ɪ] is diphthongized, so that *hid* is pronounced [hɪəd].

[ʊ] represents an advanced slightly raised half-close back rounded vowel. It is typically heard in words like *book, pull*. In *good* it is often completely unrounded, particularly in American English. The rounded and unrounded varieties, as we pointed out above, are very similar to rounded [ɵ] and its unrounded counterpart.

[æ] represents a fully front vowel about half-way between half-open [ɛ] and open [a]: it is traditionally found in the RP pronunciation of words like *bat*, *bad* [bæt] [bæd]. A good deal of variation occurs, however, even within RP, and closer, opener and centralized varieties occur. In some varieties of American English the relation between the vowels of *bed* and *bad* is almost the reverse of what it is in traditional RP. In RP those words are *bed* [bɛ̣d] and *bad* [bæd], where [ɛ̣] represents a vowel somewhat raised from half-open [ɛ]. In this pronunciation we have *bed* [bæ̈d] with a vowel about half-way between CVs [ɛ] and [a] but strongly centralized, and *bad* [bɛəd] with a vowel starting about CV 3 [ɛ] somewhat lengthened, and gliding towards a central vowel.

The symbol [ə], traditionally known as *schwa*, which is the German spelling of the name of a Hebrew letter representing a vowel of this type, is used for any mid-central vowel, i.e. a vowel of the central type between half-close and half-open. It is often used for any obscure-sounding, unstressed vowel of this general type. For example, it is commonly used for the most weakly stressed vowel in such English words and phrases as *potato*, *back again*, *sofa*, [pəˈteɪtɵʊ], [ˈbækəgɛn], [ˈsɵʊfə], even though the [ə] of *back again* is very close and rather back (resembling [ɯ]), and the [ə] of *sofa* is a very open central vowel perhaps accurately represented by [ɐ]. The symbol [ə] is also used very often to represent the 'e-muet' or unstressed and fugitive [ə] of French, although this vowel is usually slightly advanced from the central zone and slightly rounded.

The symbol [ɐ] is occasionally used for a central vowel, between half-open and open, as at the end of *sofa* in RP. It should be noted that this symbol is not very commonly used, since [ə] can usually be substituted for it, particularly in representing unstressed vowels.

The symbol [ʏ] represents a rounded [ɪ]—a common form of the German.

We have now gone through all the Cardinal Vowels, a set of Central Vowels, and a few additional ones. The Cardinal Vowels are normally presented as we have shown above, as consisting of a *primary* series, all unrounded except for the last three (6, 7, and 8), and a *secondary* series, all rounded, except for the last three (6s, 7s, and 8s).

We mentioned this feature of the CV system in Chapter 7, pointing out that the reason for switching from unrounded to rounded for the last three primary CVs is because vowels with these tongue-configurations are most commonly rounded in the world's languages. Consequently, for most students, unrounded front vowels, like [i] [e] [ɛ], and rounded back vowels, like [ɔ] [o] [u], are more familiar and hence easier to learn than vowels with the opposite lip-position ([y], [ø], [œ], [ʌ], [ɤ], [ɯ]). Not only in the learning situation, but also when one is trying to identify and specify the vowels of some language by reference to the CVs, it is more likely that one will be dealing with vowels like [i] [e] . . . [o] [u] than with vowels like [y] [ø] . . . [ɤ] [ɯ]. This particular assignment of rounding among the primary and secondary CVs is therefore determined by practical considerations.

For certain purposes it is more useful, and it is certainly more 'logical', to present the CVs (and the additional vowels that we have dealt with) on two separate but correlated diagrams, one representing unrounded vowels, the other rounded vowels. We shall see a use for CV diagrams of this type in a moment. Meanwhile we turn our attention briefly to the *acoustics* of vowel sounds.

7. The acoustics of vowels: Vowel formants

For a basic practical command of phonetics no deep knowledge of the *acoustics* of speech is necessary. However, it is of interest to see how the mouth shapes we have been studying convert the sound of voice into specific vowel sounds.

The vibration of the vocal folds—the regular repeated rapid opening and shutting of the glottis—releases regular and repeated little bursts of air, generating a sound-wave. The rate at which the little air-bursts escape from the larynx (that is, the number of bursts per second) determines the *frequency* of the sound-wave, expressed in *cycles per second* (the 'cycle' being one complete vibration), or *Hertz* (Hz). Thus, a rate of glottal vibration of 100 openings-and-shuttings per second is described as a frequency of 100 cycles per second, or *100 Hz*, and the sound-wave thus generated is described as having a *frequency* of 100 Hz. A rate of glottal vibration of 200 openings-and-shuttings per second generates a sound-wave with a frequency of 200 Hz, and so on.

It is the number of vibratory cycles per second—the frequency—of the sound-wave that we perceive as the *pitch* of the voice: a sound with a frequency of 200 Hz is perceived as having a higher pitch than one with a frequency of 100 Hz, one with a frequency of 300 Hz has a still higher pitch, and so on.

The majority of the sounds that we hear are, in fact, produced by complex sound-waves. This means that, in addition to the basic, or *fundamental*, frequency (the determiner of perceived pitch) there are regular, lesser, or *partial* vibrations which give rise to numerous higher frequency (higher pitched) components, known as *harmonics*. Each of the harmonics is a whole-number multiple of the fundamental frequency. Thus for a fundamental frequency of 100 Hz there will be harmonics at frequencies 100×2, 100×3, 100×4, i.e. 200, 300, 400 Hz, etc. The sound-wave generated by the vibrating vocal folds is of this complex type, rich in harmonics.

The quality of any particular vowel-sound is determined by its acoustic *spectrum*. The acoustic spectrum is the way in which the amplitude peaks are distributed over the frequency scale—that is, the locations of the loudest or most prominent frequencies or frequency-bands in the complex sound. As the complex wave-form of voice passes through the cavities above the larynx—the pharynx and mouth—these cavities act as a series of resonators, which pick out and reinforce some frequencies in the sound-wave and subdue others. Since it is precisely these resonances that determine the spectrum, or form, of the complex sound-wave, they are called *formants*, and their frequencies are called *formant frequencies*. The natural frequencies of the resonators do not necessarily correspond with the frequencies of any of the harmonics. This is not surprising, since the harmonic frequencies are determined by the frequency of the vibrations of the vocal folds, whereas the resonance frequencies are determined by the shape and size of the cavities above the larynx.

Each tongue- and lip-configuration for a particular vowel-sound shapes the mouth and pharynx into a resonator system that picks out certain formant frequencies that are characteristic of that particular vowel. There may be a number of formants, all at frequencies above the fundamental, and we number them Formant 1, Formant 2, Formant 3, Formant 4, etc., in order of rising frequency, usually abbreviating them to F1, F2, F3, F4, etc. Thus, Cardinal Vowel 1 [i] has F1 at about 240 Hz, F2 at about 2400 Hz, F3 often at about 3000 Hz, and so on. It turns out that we can characterize most vowel-sounds rather well in terms of the first two formants—the two lowest resonance frequencies above the fundamental. So we often describe vowels in terms of F1 and F2.

Reasonable average frequencies of F1 and F2 of the Cardinal Vowels for a male voice would be about as follows:

[i] F1 240   F2 2400   [y] F1 235   F2 2100
[e] F1 390   F2 2300   [ø] F1 370   F2 1900
[ɛ] F1 610   F2 1900   [œ] F1 585   F2 1710
[a] F1 850   F2 1610   [Œ] F1 820   F2 1530
[ɑ] F1 750   F2 940   [ɒ] F1 700   F2 760
[ʌ] F1 600   F2 1170   [ɔ] F1 500   F2 700
[ɣ] F1 460   F2 1310   [o] F1 360   F2 640
[ɯ] F1 300   F2 1390   [u] F1 250   F2 595

Figure 44 shows the frequencies of the first and second formants (F1 and F2) of the primary CVs plotted against a frequency scale.

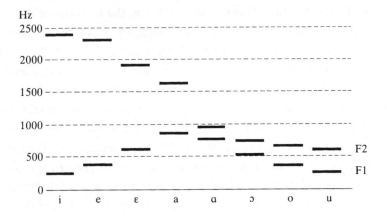

Fig. 44 First and second formants of Cardinal Vowels

Figure 45, on the other hand, shows the CVs on two Cardinal Vowel formants charts (CVF charts): that is, regular CV diagrams (one for unrounded vowels, the other for rounded vowels) with the addition of lines indicating the frequencies of F1 and F2. For this purpose the unrounded and rounded vowels must be charted separately, because of the differences between the frequencies of their formants, particularly F2.

These CVF charts show how the formants relate to the articulatory con-figurations for the vowels. F1 has the lowest value for the closer vowels, increasing as the vowels get more and more open. F2 has the lowest value for back vowels, increasing as the vowels become more and more front. Comparing the CVF charts for unrounded and rounded vowels one can

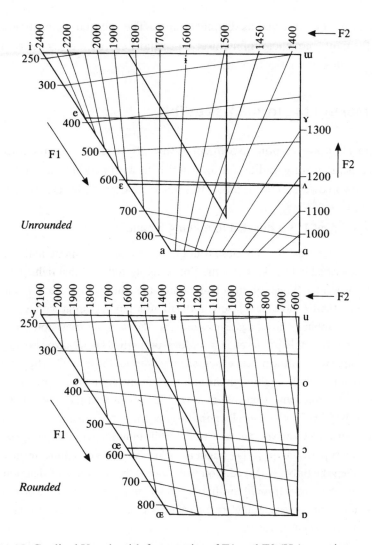

Fig. 45 Cardinal Vowels with frequencies of F1 and F2 (Hz) superimposed

also see the very noticeable effect of lip-rounding upon the formants, particularly F2, and more especially for the back vowels.

When you pronounce a voiced vowel, normally you cannot hear the separate formants: the fundamental and the audible harmonics are all sounding together, so that what you hear is simply a vowel spoken on a particular pitch (determined by the frequency of the fundamental) and of a particular quality (determined by the frequencies of the formants, especially F1 and F2). As a rule, the individual formants that characterize the vowel are not perceived as distinct sounds. The accurate determination of the formant frequencies of a vowel is normally carried out by instrumental analysis in a phonetics laboratory.

8. Making the formants audible

There are, however, non-instrumental ways of getting to hear the formants, and it is interesting and useful to experiment with making the formants of one's own vowel sounds audible, and this is what we do in Experiments 113 and 114.

Experiment 113 is directed to making F1 audible.

113   You can hear F1 if you close your glottis and tap your throat, in the manner described in Exp. 11. Close the glottis tightly and hold that tight closure for some time. While carefully maintaining the glottal closure, and taking care that there is no other closure in the mouth, tap the throat with a pencil, or by snapping a finger against it, and note the relatively clear note, of definite pitch that this produces, if you do it properly. Having acquired the technique with a little practice, now silently produce the front CVs [i] [e] [ɛ] [a]— that is, silently go through the motions of articulating these vowels, tapping your throat, with your mouth in position for each of the vowels in turn. If your CV 1 [i] is a really close one (as it ought to be) you may not hear a very clear note when you tap your throat while mouthing [i]. But the subsequent vowel positions, [e] [ɛ] [a], ought to yield clear notes of a quite distinct pitch when the throat is tapped. You will observe that the pitch of that note goes *up* as you pass from [i] through [e] and [ɛ] to [a]. What you are hearing is a tap-pitch corresponding to the frequency of F1, rising as you pass from closer to opener vowels.

Now carry out the same experiment with the back vowels [ɑ] [ɔ] [o] [u], and note how the tap-pitch goes down, indicating the lowering of the frequency of F1 as you go up from open (and unrounded) [ɑ] to close (and rounded) [u]. Experiment further with rounding and unrounding vowels, such as [e]–[ø], [ɛ]–[œ], [u]–[ɯ], etc., noting how lip-rounding affects the formant frequency (and hence the tap-pitch).

Experiment 113 shows that F1 corresponds to the parameter of tongue-height. The frequency of F1 is lowest with close vowels, highest with open vowels. In addition, it is somewhat affected by lip-rounding. Rounding lowers the frequency of all formants, the formants of back vowels somewhat more than those of front vowels, and F2 more than F1.

Having made F1 audible by throat-tapping we now carry out an experiment that will enable us to perceive F2. This can be done by *whispering*
vowels. Whisper is a somewhat complex noise, but within the rather rich
hushing sound of whisper we can generally pick out the sound of F2.

114 Go through the CVs in a strong whisper, listening carefully to the pitch of
the dominant note of the whisper. As you go through the primary CVs—[i]
[e] [ɛ] [a] [ɑ] [ɔ] [o] [u]—you can hear the whisper-pitch (representing the
frequency of F2) steadily going down as you proceed from CV 1 to CV 8.
The most striking changes in the frequency of F2 can be heard (*i*) when you
alternate between unrounded and rounded versions of whispered vowels
which are otherwise the same, e.g. [e]–[ø], [ɛ]–[œ], [u]–[ɯ], [o]–[ɤ] etc., and
(*ii*) when you go in a whisper through a *horizontal* series of vowels.

You should carefully carry out the following experiment. Form a very
back, strongly rounded, whispered [u]. Now, taking care to maintain the
lip-rounding throughout, slowly slide the bunched-up tongue forwards
(carefully retaining the *close* tongue-position) from fully back [u] through a
somewhat centralized [ü], fully central [ʉ], and retracted [ÿ] to a fully front
[y], doing all of this in a whisper. Repeat this manœuvre several times,
noting how the whisper-pitch starts quite low for [u] then gets higher and
higher as the tongue slides further and further forward. Slide back and
forth several times between the extreme back and front vowels [u] and [y].
Now try the same experiment with the close *unrounded* vowels [ɯ]–[ɨ]–[i] (it
may be easiest to start by forming [u] then unrounding it to [ɯ] before
starting the whispered forward slide to [i]).

Note once again how the frequency of F2 (heard as the whisper-pitch of
the successive vowels) goes up and up as you go forward from [ɯ] to [i].
Now carry out similar experiments at different tongue-heights—with the
half-close series [o]–[ɵ]–[ø], [ɤ]–[ə]–[e], the half-open series [ɔ]–[ɜ]–[œ], [ʌ]–
[ɜ]–[ɛ], and the open series [ɑ]–[a].

Experiment-series 114 demonstrates the relationship between F2 and the
parameter of horizontal tongue-position. As you move from back to front
the frequency of F2 gets higher.

Take another look at Fig. 45. There you see the actual frequencies (in Hz)
of F1 and F2. The charts in this figure will be more meaningful now that
you have actually discovered the relationships between formant frequencies
and tongue- and lip-positions by experimentation in your own vocal tract.
You will also understand why it is necessary for unrounded and rounded
vowels to be plotted on separate CV formant charts. Lip-rounding, as

Experiments 113 and 114 demonstrated, has considerable effect on formant frequencies, particularly on F2. Note how the frequency of F2 for the close back unrounded vowel [ɯ] is almost 1400 Hz, whereas the frequency of F2 for the rounded vowel [u], with exactly the same tongue-position, is only about 600 Hz. Because of such great differences in values of F2, clearly the lines representing frequency have to be differently oriented in the two charts.

It should be noted, by the way, that formant frequencies are not absolute: the specific values for the frequencies of the formants depend upon the size of the vocal tract that is producing the sound. The values given here (approximately my own) are correct for a moderately large man. A small woman's formants would all have somewhat higher frequencies (increased by a factor of about 1.2), a child's would be higher still, and those of a man with a very large vocal tract would be lower. However, the values given here are a reasonably useful average.

Readers with some musical knowledge will observe that it is quite easy to equate the series of larynx-tapping pitches (F1), and the series of whisper-pitches (F2), with musical notes, either on the diatonic scale, centred on middle C, or, perhaps more usefully, on the sol-fa (doh-ray-me) scale. Using the latter scale, it is interesting to go once again through the series of whispered vowels, from [u] to [y] (as in Experiment 114).

Call the whisper-pitch [u] doh and then move up the scale by shifting the bunched-up tongue forwards, exactly as in Experiment 114. Assuming that the reader has not yet quite got the knack of producing a truly, fully back [u] (as is highly probable) we may take it that his starting-point—his doh—will have a frequency of about 700 Hz. With the starting doh at 700 Hz, the 'high doh' (d', an octave higher) will have exactly twice the frequency, that is 1400 Hz, which, as Fig. 45 shows, is about the frequency of F2 for the close central vowel [ʉ]. By the time [y] is reached, the frequency of F2 is about that of la or ti of the second octave.

Figure 46 shows the CVF charts for unrounded and rounded cardinal vowels with approximate sol-fa scales added. The bold italic letters (*d*, *r*, etc.) indicate the doh-ray-me values of throat-taps representing F1. The plain letters (d, r, etc.) indicate the doh-ray-me values of dominant whisper-pitch, representing F2.

You should experiment with these scales, trying in each case to make your scales start at about the point indicated as doh on the charts, remembering, of course, that if you shift the starting point (the doh) all the other

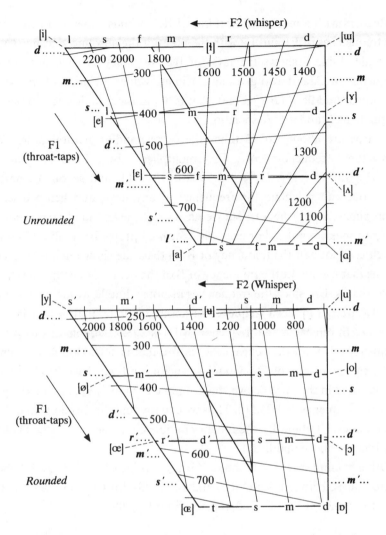

Fig. 46 Cardinal Vowel charts with doh-ray-me superimposed

notes will be shifted accordingly. You will probably find it easier to work
with F2 (whisper) than with F1 (throat-taps), and in particular you may
discover that whisper-pitch is a useful guide to locations along the 'horizontal' dimension: front, central, back. Starting with doh as about the
furthest back whispered vowel you can produce on each level (close, half-
close, half-open, open) slide slowly forward on that level and observe that
you can estimate roughly when you have reached the central vowel and then
the front one from the pitch of the whisper. This, in fact, is a good way of
learning the central vowels.

Readers with a more technical knowledge of music may want to equate the frequencies of F1 and F2 with the notes of the absolute, diatonic (A, B, C) scale. Table 5 shows the ratio of the frequency of each note to the frequency of C, and also gives approximate values for notes of the octave starting at middle C (261.63 Hz), that is, C_4 in the notation recommended by the USA Standards Association.

Sharps are about 1.0595 times the corresponding natural note. Thus $C^4\# =$ the frequency of C_4 multiplied by 1.0595, that is $261.63 \times 1.0595 = 277$, $D_4^\# = 293.5 \times 1.0595 = 311$, and so on. Using this table, one can calculate the frequency of any note, and hence discover approximately how the formant frequencies of the Cardinal Vowels correspond to musical notes. For example, Cardinal [i] has F1 at about 240 Hz, which is about half the frequency of B_4 in the scale shown in Table 5. That means that it is about the frequency of B of the octave *below* the one shown here (that is, B_3), since the frequencies of notes double within each octave. F2 of Cardinal [i] has a frequency of about 2400 Hz, that is, a little more than D_7. In our table, the frequency of D_4 is 293.5. Double this to get the frequency of D_5 (of the octave next above), that is, 587. Double it again to 1174, the frequency of D_6. Double it again, and you have 2348, the frequency of D in the third octave above middle C, namely D_7, and this is quite near the frequency of F2 of [i]. Thus we can say that the formants of [i] have these values: F1 about B_3 (the B below middle C), F2 about D_7 (the D of the third octave above middle C).

Other examples are [ɛ], F1 about 610, that is, nearly $D_5^\#$ (622), F2 about 1900, that is, between $A_6^\#$ (1865) and B_6 (1975), [ø] F1 about 500, that is, about B_4 (493.95), and F2 700, that is, about F_5 (698).

Table 5

	USA Standards Association Notation							
	C_4	D_4	E_4	F_4	G_4	A_4	B_4	C_5
Ratio of note frequency to C	1.000	1.122	1.260	1.335	1.498	1.682	1.888	2.000
Approx. values for notes starting at middle C in Hz	261.63	293.5	329.65	349	391.92	440	493.95	523.26

9. Additional vowel modifications

We have now almost finished with vowels, but a few points still have to be made. Although the system of Cardinal Vowels is an indispensable tool for the practical phonetician, it does not take account of all possible features that may characterize the vowels of particular languages.

Three modifications of vowels not covered by the Cardinal Vowel system by itself are *nasalization, retroflexion*, and *rhotacization*.

Nasalization has already been mentioned, so here we need only remind the reader that any vowel, whether Cardinal or other, can be pronounced with the soft palate raised or lowered. The raised soft palate closes the entrance to the nose and characterizes *oral* vowels, [i] [e] [ɛ] [a], etc. Most vowels of most languages are basically of this type, though they often become nasalized in the neighbourhood of nasal consonants. Thus English [æ] in *bad* is normally purely oral. In the word *man*, however, where it is flanked by nasal consonants, it will commonly be nasalized, hence [mæ̃n]. In some languages, of which French is the best-known example, there is a series of obligatorily nasalized vowels that contrast with purely oral vowels. Thus, in French we have such word-pairs as *paix* 'peace'/*pain* 'bread' = [pɛ]/ [pɛ̃], *beau* 'beautiful'/*bon* 'good' = [bo]/[bõ].

Retroflexion as a modification of vowels most commonly affects opener vowels. Thus, in dialects of South-west England and some parts of Midwest America, the vowel [ä] in a word like *far* may be pronounced with retroflexion throughout, as [fäɻ] (or in some rural dialects of South-west England [väɻ]) where the raised symbol for a retroflex approximant indicates retroflexion throughout the vowel.

To produce a retroflexed [ä] simply say a long [ɑ]-type vowel, and while trying to maintain it, deliberately curl the tip of the tongue up and backwards a little, and note how this modification affects the quality of the vowel. Carry out the same modification with other vowels, e.g. [ɛɻ] [ɔɻ] [eɻ] [oɻ].

Rhotacization: The term 'rhotacized', which means, in fact, 'r-coloured', has been applied to the very peculiar sound represented by *ir* in the word *bird* in a common American pronunciation of this vowel. This vowel was formerly described as 'retroflexed' but this is not a correct description. It does not usually have the upward curling of the tongue that is characteristic of retroflexion. Instead, the main body of the tongue is bunched up into a kind of half-close-central position, but with two peculiar modifications: one modification is a moderate degree of deep pharyngalization: the root of the tongue is drawn back into the pharynx just above the larynx. The second modification is a fairly deep depression in the surface of the tongue opposite the uvular zone. This sub-uvular concavity can be acquired as follows. Produce a uvular trill. Note that in order to do this you have to form a longitudinal furrow in the tongue within which the uvula vibrates. Now move the whole body of the tongue slightly forward, while retaining precisely that deeply furrowed configuration. The result should be a close approximation to the typical American '*bird* vowel', for which the phonetic symbols [ɝ] and [ɚ] have been used—both representing a central vowel with an *r*-like modification.

As we saw, this very strange American vowel involves not only a concavity—or 'sulcalization' (from the Latin *sulcus* 'a furrow, or trench')—of the tongue in the neighbourhood of the uvula, but also some slight degree of pharyngalization. It is because of this that a series of vowel-sounds with modifications of this rhotacized type in some languages spoken in the Caucasus area of Russia, notably Tsakhur and Udi, are known as 'pharyngalized' vowels.

These additions to the basic parameters of vowel classification complete our survey of vowels.

9

Prosodic Features

1. Initiatory prosodies: Initiator power (= stress)

Up to now we have been looking at speech-sounds as isolated phenomena. In reality, of course, spoken sounds occur strung together, one after the other. More precisely, speech is a *continuum*; a continuous flux of initiatory, phonatory, and articulatory states and movements, constantly changing, often overlapping and interpenetrating and influencing each other. When we look at isolated sounds we are artificially cutting up that flowing chain of events into a series of *segments* or *segmental sounds*, as we sometimes call the speech-sounds that we isolate out of the continuum.

Although the segmentation of speech is an artificial procedure, we are obliged to do it—to arrest the flow, as it were—in order to pin down individual sounds for detailed study. We must, however, also give attention to those phonetic phenomena that are characteristic not so much of the individual segments as of their relations to each other, or of stretches of the speech-continuum that are greater than one segment in length. Because such phenomena take account of more than just segments they are sometimes called *suprasegmental* features. Another name for them is *prosodic features*, or *prosodies*, and these are the terms we shall use.

We have already noted in passing that the prosodic features of speech can be related to the three basic components of speech—initiation, phonation, and articulation. We therefore study them under these three headings. The prosodic features *stress* and the division into *syllables* are features of initiation; prosodic phenomena of *pitch* are features of phonation; and the *duration* of sounds is a feature of articulation.

The *initiatory prosodies*, that is, stress and syllabification, relate to the way in which the bursts of muscular energy that drive the initiator (the organ that initiates airflow for speech) are organized and distributed.

We saw in Chapter 2 that stress can be defined as *initiator power*, and, moreover, that this definition is applicable to all types of initiation. It is possible to initiate not only pulmonic sounds but also glottalic and velaric sounds with greater or lesser initiator power, that is, greater or lesser stress. Nevertheless, stress as a prosodic feature of languages is virtually always manifested in terms of *pulmonic pressure* initiation.

As we saw in Chapter 2, it is desirable to begin learning about stress by experimenting with voiceless fricatives. This is the best way of 'getting the feel' of the difference between stressed and unstressed syllables, so we start from there.

115　Say a prolonged [s s s s . . .]. Now deliberately superimpose some variations of stress upon that prolonged [s s s s . . .]. That is, while continuously producing this voiceless fricative sound, vary the amount of energy you use in initiating the air-stream. Deliberately drive the air out in an alternating series of stronger and weaker bursts of initiator power. Representing moments of increased power by bold capital **[S]** we can indicate the alternation of initiator power as [s s **S S** s s **S S** s s **S S**] etc. Experiment with varied patterns of stress: [**S S** s s **S S** s s **S S** s s], [s **S** s s **S** s s **S S**], [s s s **S** s s **S S**], etc., and with different voiceless fricatives: [**F F** f f **F** f f], [f f **F F** f **F** f f **F F**], etc. Now try the same experiment with sequences of voiceless stops, e.g. [pʰ pʰ **Pʰ** pʰ **Pʰ Pʰ**], etc. Note that, whereas the sequences of voiceless fricatives could be produced while retaining the articulation unchanged throughout the utterance of each set, in the case of the stops it is necessary to release each one into a momentary puff of breath (symbolized here by superscript [ʰ]).

The IPA diacritic for stress is a short vertical line ['] placed *before* the symbol for the stressed sound or syllable. Thus the examples in Experiment 115 are properly transcribed as [ss 'ss ss 'ss ss 'ss], ['ss ss 'ss ss], etc. Note that this convention is different from that used in many dictionaries and other publications where the stress-mark, often an accent [´], is placed on, or after, the stressed syllable. The IPA practice of placing the stress-mark before the sound or syllable to be stressed is of some practical advantage. It means that as you read along a phonetic transcription (which students at first cannot do very fluently) you are being warned in advance: 'the next syllable is to be stressed'. The IPA supplies diacritics for various degrees of stress, but for the present we shall use only ['], meaning 'stressed' as opposed to 'unstressed' (which is unmarked).

As you experimented with ['s s s 's s '. . .] etc. you probably noticed that stressed ['s] sounds distinctly louder than unstressed [s]. This is because the velocity of airflow through the articulatory channel is higher for the stressed sound, and consequently the turbulence is greater and the resultant hiss is stronger, that is, has greater acoustic intensity. Any particular sound-type appears louder when stressed than when unstressed: thus a strongly stressed ['s] sounds louder than a weakly stressed (unstressed) [s], and a strongly stressed ['f] sounds louder than a weakly stressed [f].

However, the *range* of loudness varies from one sound-type to another: thus a strongly stressed ['f] may sound no louder than a weakly stressed [s]. Try this, saying ['f] and then ['s] with, as nearly as you can judge, the same initiator power: the ['s] will probably sound a little louder than the ['f]. Then experiment further with strongly and weakly stressed ['f], [f], ['s], [s], ['ʃ] [ʃ], and compare the apparent loudness of these sounds. You will probably discover that, for the same degree of initiator power (i.e. stress), [ʃ] sounds louder than [s], and [s] sounds louder than [f]. This shows that, while all speech-sounds exhibit variations of loudness under different conditions of stress, nevertheless some sounds are always louder than others for a given degree of stress. Speech-sounds differ from each other in terms of their inherent loudness, or inherent *sonority*. This is equally true of vowel-sounds. The vowel [a] for instance, has greater inherent sonority than [i]: for the same initiator velocity (same stress) [a] sounds louder than [i], and again, a strongly stressed [i] may sound no louder than a rather weakly stressed [a].

This is why it is unwise to talk of stress (as some people have done) in terms of degrees of *loudness*, since loudness is in part a product of the inherent sonority of sounds. It is much more reliable to think of stress entirely in terms of *degrees of initiator power*—the amount of energy expended in pumping air out of the lungs.

Incidentally, we often talk as if there were two clearly distinct degrees of stress—called 'stressed' and 'unstressed'. This, of course, is not the case. Initiator power is infinitely variable, from zero (when the initiator is inactive and, consequently, there is no airflow and no sound) to an indefinite maximum (depending on the size and muscular strength of the speaker) when the initiator is operating at full power, forcing the air out at the highest possible velocity against the resistance imposed upon the airflow by phonatory and articulatory strictures. However, many languages make meaningful, linguistic, use of only two distinct degrees of stress, namely a relatively strong stress, characterizing what are called 'stressed' syllables, and a relatively weaker stress, characterizing what are called 'unstressed' syllables.

This is one reason why it is often useful to talk *as if* there were a clear-cut distinction between stressed and unstressed sounds.

So far we have experimented chiefly with voiceless sounds. There is a good reason for this, namely, that with voiceless sounds it is particularly easy to get the feeling of stress—that is, to become aware of the kinaesthetic sensations associated with the production of different degrees of stress. There is also another reason that we will refer to again in a moment.

Having acquired a basic feeling for stress as initiator power, we must now experiment with producing *voiced* sounds with varying degrees of stress.

116   Say a prolonged [z z z z z z z] and then impose different stress-patterns upon it, just as you did with [s s s s s] in Exp. 115, thus: ['z z 'z z 'z z] etc. You may find it easier to separate the successive [z]-segments by a glottal stop, thus: ['zˀ zˀ 'zˀ zˀ] etc. but you need not do this. Continue with varying patterns, such as: [z 'z z 'z z 'z], [z 'z z z 'z z z], ['v v 'v 'v v], etc.

Next, experiment with vowels, preferably separated by consonants, in such sequences as ['la la 'la la 'la la], [la la 'la la la 'la], [ba 'ba ba ba 'ba], [li 'li li 'li], ['bi bi 'bi bi bi 'bi] etc.

It is a little more difficult to be aware of the feeling of stress-variations with voiced sounds, and you may find it helpful to try whispering the examples of Experiment 116 as well as voicing them.

As I hinted above, there is another reason why it is simplest to begin the study of stress with voiceless fricatives. This is the fact that with voiced sounds, particularly vowels, attention may be distracted from stress by the presence of concomitant differences of *pitch*, and in real-language examples—for example, in English—there are often differences in *duration* as well. These concomitants of stress sometimes confuse people, since they tend to conceal the true nature of stress, as simply initiator power.

If you experiment briefly with stressed and unstressed voiced syllables, such as ['la la 'la la], [la 'la la 'la], ['da da da], [da 'da da], etc., you will probably find that you pronounce the stressed syllables—particularly if you stress them strongly—on a higher pitch than the unstressed syllables, and you may also make them longer.

There is a natural, physical, connection between stress and pitch, as we shall see below. Consequently stressed syllables are often pronounced on a different pitch from neighbouring unstressed syllables. If you say the English words 'abstract (noun), ab'stract (verb), or 'pervert (noun), per'vert (verb), you will notice that in the *nouns* the first syllable is stressed, whereas in the *verbs* the second syllable is stressed. But at the same time, as you say these words in isolation, you will probably notice a difference in the pitch-scheme of each word-pair. In the nouns, the first syllable starts on a fairly high pitch: the pitch falls and the second syllable is quite low-pitched. In the verbs, however, the first syllable is probably said on a mid-pitch, while the second syllable has a falling pitch, possibly starting a little higher than the first syllable. Using a rather obvious kind of pitch notation, we can represent these pitch-schemes as shown in Fig. 47.

If you whisper the words, the difference of pitch is abolished and you can then become more clearly aware of the stress difference. You will also notice, incidentally, that the unstressed syllables tend to be of shorter duration than the stressed syllables. You can, incidentally, get an even clearer impression of the stress difference, in a relatively pure state, by mimicking the stress patterns of the word pairs with a voiceless fricative such as [s] saying: *noun* ['ss], *verb* [s's].

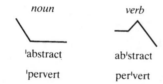

Fig. 47 Pitch-schemes of nouns and verbs

It is, indeed, quite easy to manœuvre the English words into a position where, in normal English speech, the pitch differences are eliminated. This happens, for instance, in such sentences as "*I* said abstract or "*I* said pervert, where the *I* is spoken very emphatically (the double stress-mark ["] indicating extra strong stress) meaning *I said it . . . not you.* Here there is strong stress and a *high-falling tone* on 'I'. In such a sentence the quoted word at the end is pronounced on a uniform low pitch, but its stress pattern is preserved. We can indicate the pitch pattern and the stresses of such sentences as shown in Fig. 48.

Try saying these sentences, and note how the stress differences are preserved, in '*abstract* vs. *ab'stract* etc., even though these words are spoken on a monotone. Thus, though pitch phenomena and stress are often related to each other in the pronunciation of a language, they are, in fact, distinct and isolatable features which are independently controllable. The fact that in many languages, of which English is one, stress is associated with pitch and duration has led to some confusion. 'Is stress really pitch,

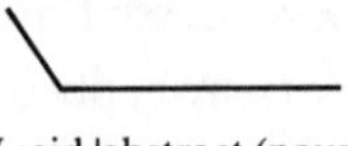

ᵘ**I** said ˈabstract (noun)
ᵘ**I** said abˈstract (verb)
ᵘ**I** said ˈpervert (noun)
ᵘ**I** said perˈvert (verb)

Fig. 48 Stress differences on uniform pitch

or duration, or energy, or what?' is the kind of muddled question that has often been asked. The answer is that all of these features, pitch, duration and energy of utterance, as well as the inherent sonority of a sound, may contribute to the perceptual *prominence* of a sound or syllable—that is, the degree to which it appears to stand out from its neighbours. However, from a general phonetic point of view, to prevent confusion, it is best to confine the application of the term *stress* to initiator power as we have defined it here.

2. The syllable

We have frequently used the term syllable without defining it, and we have stated, or implied, that stress is a feature of syllables rather than of segmental sounds. This, indeed, is why stress is treated as a prosodic rather than a segmental phenomenon.

In a general way, speakers of most languages can tell how many syllables there are in a word, even if they cannot define the syllable. Thus the words *see* and *man* have one syllable, *paper*, *today* have two, *phonetic* has three, *impetuosity* has six, and so on. A definition of the syllable for general phonetic purposes, like the definition of stress, has to take account of initiatory activity, and it is instructive, once again, to begin with pulmonic pressure voiceless sounds.

If you say a prolonged [s s s . . .] there are several different ways of doing it. First, one may utter a smooth continuously flowing stream with more or less unvarying initiator power. This gives the impression of a prolonged unbroken hiss, forming, as it were, a single very long syllable. Secondly, one may utter this prolonged [s] not with smooth unvarying initiator power, but in a series of separate pulses with the power rising to a peak for a moment, then diminishing somewhat, then peaking again and so on. In this utterance we still have a continuous, unbroken [s]-sound, but there is also some effect of discontinuity, because the loudness of the hiss rises and falls with the rising and falling of the initiator power. In other words we get the feeling of a series of syllables—a series of *power peaks*, or peaks of initiator velocity separated from each other by moments of diminished velocity.

117 Say a prolonged, unbroken [s s s . . .], getting the feeling of a single, very long syllable. Now say the same sound on a series of pulses, or surges, of initiator power, so that you get the feeling of a series of syllables (but without ever interrupting the continuous hiss of [s]—only varying its loudness) [s. s. s. s. . . .].

Now do the same with [z], that is pronounce [z. z. z. . . .] with a pulsating series of syllabic [z]s. Finally, do the same thing with a vowel, say [a. a. a. a.]. There should be no break here between the vowels (do not insert a glottal stop between them) just a continuous stretch of voicing with a periodic rise and fall of initiator velocity that seems to cut up the continuum into a series of syllables.

In these experiments the division between syllables was made by a self-imposed momentary retardation of the movement of the initiator. But it is also possible, and, in fact, much more usual, to impose that retardation from above, as it were, by articulatory activity, as in Experiment 118.

118 First, say a series of syllabic [s]-sounds, as in Exp. 110, separated only by momentary retardations of the initiator: i.e. a continuous, unbroken [s]-hiss, divided by pulmonic pulses into a series of syllables [s. s. s. s. s. s. . . .]. Now produce a prolonged [s], this time broken up by a series of [t]s: [s t s t s t s t . . .]. Once again, you will get the impression of a series of separate syllabic [s]-sounds, but this time the division into syllables is imposed by the successive stop articulations. Now, do the same kind of thing with a prolonged vowel-sound. On a long continuous pulmonic pressure air-stream say [a d a d a d a d a . . .]. You will hear and feel that as a series of syllables separated from each other by [d]-sounds. You can do the same kind of thing with other consonants: [a p a p a p a . . .] [a s a s a s a . . .] [a s p a s p a s p a . . .], etc.

We arrive, then, at a definition of the *syllable* as a *minimal pulse of initiatory activity* bounded by a momentary retardation of the initiator, either self-imposed, or, more usually, imposed by a consonantal type of articulatory stricture.

Every syllable has a central part, or *nucleus*: this is most commonly a vowel, as in English *cat, stop, slept,* and so on, but occasionally it is a sound that we would usually regard as a consonant, such as the [r] that forms the nucleus of Czech [krk] 'neck', or the syllabic [n] that forms the nucleus of the final syllable of English *sudden* [sʌdn]. Since the syllable-nucleus is normally a vowel we shall represent it here as V. A syllable may consist of nothing but the nucleus, as, for instance, the English words *awe, ah,* the name of the letter *E,* and so on, which we can represent as simply V. On the other hand, there may be a *consonantal beginning* or *end* to the syllable, which we can represent as C. We can thus indicate various kinds of syllable structures that occur in English as: V, e.g. *awe ah*; CV *saw go*; VC *eat up*; CVC *cat mad,* etc. If there is more than one consonant at the beginning or end of a syllable, we can show this by simply adding as many Cs as may be necessary, thus: CCV *play stay,* VCC *apt end,* CCVC *stop brought,* CCVCC *stopped* [stɒpt] *plant,* CCCV *stray screw,* CCCVCC *strand,* and so on. Languages differ greatly as to the types of syllable structure that they permit, and we will refer to this again when we discuss the sound-systems of languages.

We have now seen that, in the course of speaking, the activity of the initiator—most commonly, indeed nearly always, the pulmonic initiator—is parcelled out, as it were, into short chunks, or small peaks of initiator power separated from each other by slight retardations of the initiator. These chunks are *syllables,* and the momentary retardations that mark the boundaries between syllables are most commonly imposed by consonants, but they can also be self-imposed. Moreover, each syllable may be produced with greater or lesser initiator power, or *stress* as it is called, than its neighbours. The word *phonetics,* for instance, clearly has three syllables—is delivered in three chunks of initiatory activity, each bounded by consonants, thus: CVCVCVCC. Moreover, it is clear that the second syllable is delivered with greater initiator power than the others, and consequently we describe it as stressed, and so we can represent the syllabic structure of that word as CV'CVCVCC where 'CV marks the stressed syllable, and finally, we can transcribe it as [fə'nɛtɪks].

There is one further matter to discuss concerning prosodic features associated with initiation. This is the question of what is often called the *rhythm* of speech. This is partly a matter of the alternation or distribution of short and long syllables, but it is also a matter of the timing of the initiator pulses.

3. The foot

In many languages, of which English is a good example, in addition to syllables, such as we have discussed, initiatory activity seems to be parcelled out into relatively equal chunks that are often longer than the length of a syllable.

Here are three English sentences with a stress-mark ['] inserted before each stressed syllable:

1. 'That's what 'John bought 'yesterday 'morning.
2. 'That's the 'book John bought 'yesterday 'morning.
3. 'That's the 'model John bought 'yesterday 'morning.

We tend to deliver each of these sentences in four bursts of initiator activity. Each burst, or 'chunk', has the initiator power rising to a peak in the syllable that is marked as stressed, then the power falls off to a low value, then rises again to a peak at the next stressed syllable, and so on.

Representing the rise and falls of initiator power by a rising-falling line, and the division into chunks by vertical lines, we can represent the initiatory pattern of these sentences as in Fig. 49.

If you read these sentences aloud in a properly English way, with what we describe as an English rhythm, you will probably get the feeling that all the 'chunks' are, in some respect, equal, or nearly so. Consider the second one in particular. In sentence (1) it contains two syllables, in (2) it has three syllables, and in (3) it has four. As you say each sentence you will notice that there is some attempt to pack all these syllables, two, three, four into about the same space of time. Not exactly the same of course, but there is obviously a tendency in that direction—a tendency, that is, to give about the same amount of time to each chunk. At the same time, you may feel, as you

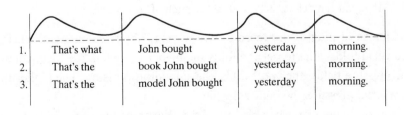

Fig. 49 Stress-groups, or feet

repeat the three sentences, voiced and whispered, that you expend about the same energy on each chunk.

Each of these chunks is what we call a 'stress-group' or 'foot' and you will notice that each contains one major stressed syllable, because the distribution of initiator power within each foot follows approximately the curve shown. English speech tends to be delivered in a series of *feet*, each containing from one to several syllables, each with a power curve of the type shown. Within short stretches of speech, feet in English tend to be *isochronous* (i.e. of equal duration) and *isodynamic* (each involving about the same output of initiator power).

Not all languages are like English. In French and Japanese for example, the parcelling out of initiator power is done differently. In these languages, if there is any isochrony (equal timing) or isodynamism (equal powering) it applies rather to syllables, than to those longer stretches called 'feet' that may be several syllables in length.

4. Phonatory prosodies: Pitch variation (= intonation and tone)

We turn now to those prosodic features that relate to *phonation*. These include features of *voice-quality*, that may, in some languages, affect stretches of speech longer than the segment, and features of *pitch*. We concentrate here on the second type of phonatory prosody, *pitch*.

It is obvious that the vocal folds can vibrate at different frequencies, and that voice can thus be produced at different pitches.

119 Experiment with deliberately varying the pitch of your voice. Keeping pretty much within the normal compass of your speaking voice (unlike Exp. 12, where you had to go as high and as low as possible), say the syllable [la] on a low level pitch, on a rising pitch, and so on. This is just to verify that you can deliberately control the pitch of your voice.

Change of pitch is produced in two ways: (*a*) by stretching and tensing the vocal folds—the tenser the folds the higher the pitch. (*b*) By changing the pressure below the vocal folds, the subglottal pressure. The higher the subglottal pressure, the higher the pitch.

You probably won't be able to *feel* the tension of the vocal folds, but if you say, or sing, a series of notes, starting low and going higher and higher with, as far as possible, the *same initiator power* throughout, then you can be pretty sure you are raising the pitch by tensing the vocal folds.

The second method of changing pitch—changing subglottal pressure—can be demonstrated this way. Say, or sing, a very prolonged vowel on one unchanging pitch (any pitch that is comfortable for you). Arrange with a friend that, while you are producing that long unchanging note, he should suddenly give your chest (at about the level of the diaphragm) a short sharp squeeze. The result will probably be a short sharp rise in pitch. This demonstrates the second method of pitch change. The short sharp squeeze momentarily increased the pressure of the air below the vocal folds, and this sudden increase in subglottal air pressure caused the vocal folds momentarily to vibrate faster and produce a higher pitched note. This demonstrates in a simple way that relationship between pitch and pressure that we referred to above.

This is why strongly stressed syllables have a tendency to be pronounced on a higher pitch than unstressed syllables. But this tendency may be overruled by specific rules of a particular language. There are languages, including dialects of English, in which most stressed syllables are actually pronounced on a *lower* pitch than the neighbouring unstressed syllables. This is true, for example, of the English of Aberdeenshire in Scotland, and some varieties of Welsh English, Jamaican English, and Indian English.

Pitch and pitch changes are utilized in languages in two distinct ways. On the one hand, variations of pitch may be related to relatively long stretches of speech, which may be many syllables in length, and which correspond to relatively large grammatical units such as the sentence. Pitch variation used in this way is called *intonation*. On the other hand, the pitch variations of a language may be related to short stretches of speech, typically of syllable length, and to small grammatical units such as words and morphemes. Pitch variation used in this way is called *tone*.

Examples of *intonations* are the pitch patterns of an English sentence like the following, for which the intonations are indicated by means of a rather obvious notation, in which lines represent the pitch levels of the stressed syllables that occur at the start of each foot, and the dots represent the unstressed syllables that follow them.

1. 'Jane was here 'yesterday [⁻ ˙ ˙ ＼ ˌ ˌ]
2. 'Jane was here 'yesterday? [＿ ˌ ˌ ⌣ ˙ ˙]
3. 'Jane was here '*yesterday*? [⁻ ˙ ˙ ＿ ˌ ˙]

In the three versions of this sentence the changes in the pitch pattern or *intonation contour* in no way change the meaning of the individual words in the sentence—not even of the word *yesterday*, which is the carrier of the major pitch differences. What it does do, is change the function of the sentence as a whole, from a statement (1) to a question (2), to a question with incredulous emphasis on 'yesterday' (3). Using terms that are currently rather popular in linguistics we might say that *intonation*, as here, has a *pragmatic* rather than a *semantic* function.

Examples of *tones* might be the following words in Mandarin Chinese. Here the pitch movement of the tones is indicated impressionistically as the intonational pitch movements were in the last example.

1. *ba* [➖] 'eight'
2. *ba* [➚] 'to uproot'
3. *ba* [➘➚] 'to hold'
4. *ba* [➘] 'a harrow'

It is clear that this is quite different from the last example, because here, first, the pitch differences occur on a single syllable, and secondly, they completely change the meaning of the word. In other words, *tone*, as in these examples, has a *semantic* rather than a pragmatic function, and is a permanent or inherent feature of the word.

5. Articulatory prosody: Duration of articulation (= length)

The third basic component of speech is articulation, and this is particularly relevant to the prosodic feature of *length* or *duration*.

Of course, it is clear that in speech both initiatory and phonatory events can be shorter or longer. You can obviously produce a series of pulmonic pressure pulses of longer or shorter duration. Going back for a moment to Experiment 117, you can pump out that series of syllabic [s]-sounds very rapidly [s. s. s. s. s. . . .], or in a more leisurely fashion [s̄ . s̄ . s̄ . s̄ . . .], etc. And it is clear that, during speech, there can be longer or shorter stretches of voicing or voicelessness. Thus, in such a sentence as *They stopped splashing* [ðeɪ 'stɒpt 'splæʃɪŋ] we have a long stretch of voicelessness in [-ptsp-]: in *They stopped talking* the stretch of voicelessness is shorter [-ptt], in *They all talk* [ðeɪ ɔːl tɔˑk] it is quite short; only during [t]. But differences in duration of a phonation type are not what we normally have in mind in talking about length, or duration.

When we talk about duration in phonetics we are referring to the *duration of particular articulatory postures*. In Chapter 4 we saw that there were two types of stricture that are *essentially* momentary, namely: *flap* and *semivowel*. A flap (or tap) is an approach to, immediately followed by a departure from, a momentary contact. If you prolong the contact the sound will no longer be a flap, but a stop. A semivowel is likewise an approach to and/ or departure from an approximant position: if you prolong that position you have an approximant, or approximant-type vowel [i] [u], etc.

All other stricture types are, as we saw in Chapter 4, *maintainable*. It is these strictures that can be maintained for a shorter or longer time, i.e. can have different durations. Thus we can have shorter or longer *stops*, *fricatives*, *approximants*, *vowels*, etc.

We already noted earlier in this chapter that there is some tendency, at least in English, to make stressed syllables (or, rather the vowels that form their nuclei) longer than unstressed syllables. It is, however, perfectly possible to control duration quite independently of stress.

120   Say a series of syllables such as ['la la 'la 'la la . . .] alternating stressed and unstressed. Now, experiment with varying the duration of the syllables. The IPA symbol for *long* duration is two dots placed after the symbol for the lengthened sound: thus: [i] [ɛ] [u], etc. represent short vowels. [iː] [ɛː] [uː] represent long vowels, and [s] [l], etc. represent short consonants, [sː] [lː] etc. represent long consonants.

    Now say ['laː la 'laː 'la laː la] and then ['la laː 'la laː 'la laː] and [laː 'la 'la laː 'la . . .] etc. In languages like Czech and Hungarian, both of which contrast long and short vowels, and both of which have stress on the first syllable of a word, such stress and duration patterns as 'CVVCV 'CVCVV 'CVCV 'CVVCVV freely occur.

Though duration is an independently controllable variable in speech, there is some degree of 'natural' or universal relationship between duration and vowel quality. It has been observed in many different languages that, other factors being equal, open vowels tend to be longer than close vowels. It is assumed that the reason for this is that open vowels require a bigger articulatory movement, and it naturally takes longer to execute this than the shorter movement of close vowels.

10

Sound-systems of Languages

1. Phonology: The utilization of speech-sounds

In the preceding chapters we have talked about speech-sounds for the most part as things-in-themselves—that is, as so many isolated physiologico-acoustic events without much reference to the way in which they are used in different languages. But now we must look at how sounds are utilized—how they are organized into the sound-systems of languages.

The study of the physiological, aerodynamic, and acoustic characteristics of speech-sounds is the central concern of *phonetics*. The study of how sounds are organized into systems and utilized in languages is the central concern of *phonology*. Neither of these two linguistic disciplines is independent of the other. A knowledge of what features of sound are most utilized in languages determines what aspects of sound production are most worth studying in depth. Thus phonetics depends to some extent upon phonology to indicate areas of linguistic relevance and importance. Phonology, on the other hand, is heavily dependent on phonetics, since it is phonetics that provides the insights that enable one to discover what sound features are linguistically utilized, and it is phonetics again, that supplies the terminology for the description and classification of the linguistically relevant features of sounds.

Apart from very minor anatomical differences, all human beings have the same vocal apparatus. Consequently, all human beings are capable of producing the same sounds. In other words, the human sound-producing potential is universal, it is also capable of infinite variation. Consonants can be articulated in a great variety of ways at any of the locations within the vocal tract described in Chapter 4, or at any intermediate point. Vowels can be articulated anywhere in the entire vowel-space defined in Chapter 6.

However, out of the infinite range of possible sounds, every language utilizes only a fraction of this rich phonetic potential, and, moreover, languages differ greatly as to which parts of this potential they make use of. English, for example, has the glottal fricative [h] but otherwise makes no use at all of the whole pharyngo-laryngeal tract in the articulation of consonants. By contrast, Arabic exploits that part of the vocal tract much more extensively, with the pharyngals [ʕ] and [ħ] and the glottals [ʔ] and [h], and there are a few languages which make even more use of that area, for example, the Burkihan dialect of the North Caucasian language Agul, with no fewer than *seven* consonants articulated in the pharyngo-laryngeal area.

On the other hand, Arabic has only two labial obstruents, [b] and [f], where English has four, [p], [b], [f], [v]. French has three rounded front vowels [y], [ø], [œ], and Mandarin Chinese has one such vowel, [y], but English never combines lip-rounding with the articulation of front vowels, i.e. has no rounded front vowels.

English makes absolutely no use of pitch to distinguish one word from another, but Chinese, for example, makes considerable use of pitch for this purpose, with 4 word-tones in Mandarin, and 6 tones in Cantonese.

2. A continuum of vowel-sounds

Not only do languages contrast with each other in terms of the different parts or aspects of the phonetic potential that they utilize, they also differ in the ways in which they divide up any particular range, or *continuum*, of possible sounds. What is meant by 'continuum' in this context will be made clearer by Experiments 121 and 122.

121   Produce a *continuum of vowel sounds* by starting at CV 1 [i] and then carefully sliding along the periphery of the CV diagram in an unbroken slow glide. Keeping the body of the tongue bunched well forward in the mouth, so as to retain a truly *front* position throughout, slowly and continuously lower the tongue from [i] to [a]. You may find yourself at first wanting to proceed by a series of steps or jumps, from [i] to [e], [e] to [ɛ], [ɛ] to [a]. You must resist this. If you do find yourself jumping from one CV to another, go back to [i] and start over again. The tongue must move downwards, always maintaining its very front position, at a uniform slow pace. When you reach [a] try to continue the slow uniform-paced glide back to [ɑ]. This whole procedure is represented by the broken line in Fig. 50.

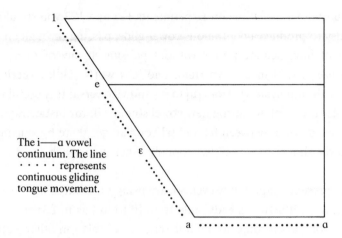

The i——ɑ vowel continuum. The line · · · · · represents continuous gliding tongue movement.

Fig. 50 The i–ɑ vowel continuum. The line . . . . . . represents continuous gliding tongue movement. For the same, represented as a straight line, see Fig. 51

We saw in Chapter 7 that tongue-height can be varied in one or both of two ways: (1) by fixating the lower jaw and passing from a closer to an opener vowel by lowering and flattening the tongue, and (2) by fixating the tongue in relation to the lower jaw and changing tongue-height solely by lowering the jaw. You will probably find it easiest to carry out the present procedure by controlling only one set of muscles at a time, as suggested in Experiment 122.

122   Fixate the lower jaw, if necessary by gripping the end of a pencil or of a small cork between your teeth. Now, using first whisper then voice, start at [i] and slowly and uniformly lower your tongue through all possible positions—not stopping at any—to [a]. Having completed this slow continuous tongue-lowering from [i] to [a], continue slowly and continuously retracting it to [ɑ]. Try to carry out the whole operation again, from [i] through [a] to [ɑ], in one slow, controlled, continuous movement.

Now try to do the same thing in the second manner. Start with a very tense, close front [i]. Keep the tongue rigidly in that close front position, and slowly and continuously lower the jaw. If you produce voice while doing this you will hear how the vowel quality continuously changes, passing slowly through all possible vowel sounds between [i] and [a] as you lower your jaw more and more. When you get down to [a] with the tongue still fixated, you will, of course, have to retract the tongue in order to continue the unbroken slide back to [ɑ].

If you spend a little time on Experiments 121 and 122 you should find it quite easy to produce a continuous vowel-glide, passing through an infinite number of intermediate points without pausing at any of them. This is quite a useful skill in its own right, and it is worth while experimenting further with sliding slowly from [u] to [y] and vice versa. It is useful because it provides a way of acquiring new vowel sounds: if, for instance, you want to produce a vowel between [e] and [ɛ] you can get there by starting at [e] and slowly sliding downwards, stopping when you reach the vowel you want.

In the present chapter, however, we are using this skill in a different way. If you carry out a slow steady slide from [i] to [ɑ], as in Experiments 121 and 122, you pass through an infinite series of vowels—in other words, you experience a *vowel continuum*. Having got the idea of a vowel continuum, not as a mere intellectual concept, but as something you can produce and feel and hear in your own mouth, you can more readily understand when we say that different languages dissect the vowel continuum in different ways, that is, select different bits within it for linguistic use.

3. The vowel continuum differently dissected by English and Spanish

English divides up the peripheral vowel continuum from [i] to [ɑ] into six divisions—or, to put it differently, selects six bits on or near that continuum for use in words of the language. These six selected bits of the continuum are the following: [i] as in *beet*, [ɪ] as in *bit*, [eɪ] as in *bait*, [ɛ] as in *bet*, [æ] as in *bat*, and [ɑ] as in *part*. (In British RP the sixth vowel, [ɒ] in *pot*, lies beyond the short vowel continuum given here.) Spanish, on the other hand, selects only three bits out of that continuum, namely [i] as in *ibis*, [e] as in *eres*, and [a] as in *acá*.

It would be reasonable to suppose that vowel-sounds would be more or less evenly spaced along the continuum, and to some extent this is the case. The more widely spaced out they are, the more room there is for variation. For example, the Spanish vowel represented by [e] has variants ranging from about CV [e] to about CV [ɛ]. But these variants do not occur at random; they are systematically related to different environments—to different locations within the syllable. Generally speaking, the closer variants of the Spanish [e] vowel occur in open syllables—that is, in syllables

not closed by a consonant—while the opener variants occur in closed
syllables, i.e. those that end in a consonant. Examples, with a hyphen
indicating the division between syllables, are *pe*-ro 'but', with [e], but
per-ro 'dog' with [ɛ].

We can represent the vowel continuum that we have been talking about,
and the different divisions imposed upon it by English and Spanish, as in
Fig. 51.

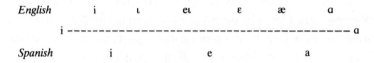

Fig. 51 The i–ɑ vowel continuum: English and Spanish divisions

4. Voice-onset-times differently exploited by different languages

A different kind of phonetic continuum is represented by the 'voice-onset-
time' (VOT) of stop consonants. As we saw earlier, a characteristic feature
of initial *aspirated* stops is that, after the moment of release of the oral
closure, the vocal folds take some time to come together and start vibrating
for the following vowel. This time-lapse before the onset of voicing is what
we call the VOT. Taking the moment of release of the oral closure as
reference time, aspirated stops, with a delayed voice-onset, have a *positive*
VOT. For example, if the voicing does not begin until 100 thousandths of a
second—a hundred milliseconds—after the release of the stop, we have a
VOT of + 100 ms. If the voicing begins simultaneously with the release of
the oral closure, the stop is *unaspirated*, and the VOT, of course, is *zero*. If
the vocal folds start vibrating *before* the release of the stop (as they do in
voiced stops) we have a *negative* VOT. For example, if the voice-onset precedes (rather than follows) the stop-release by 100 ms., then the VOT
is – 100 ms.

So it is clear that there is a *continuum* of possible durations of the time-
difference between the release of a stop and the onset of voicing, running
from, say, + 100 ms. to, say, – 100 ms. with any conceivable value in
between. This kind of continuum is, of course, a purely conceptual one—a

continuum of possibilities, composed of all conceivable VOTs that might occur. You cannot actually run unbrokenly through it in your own vocal tract as you did with the vowel continuum. You can, however, pronounce, one after the other, a series of discrete examples illustrating different points along that conceptual continuum, which is what we will do in Experiment 123.

Meanwhile, look at Fig. 52. In this figure the vertical lines represent the start and finish of lip-closure for a labial stop. The horizontal lines represent, conventionally, the state of the glottis, the dotted line indicating voicelessness—the glottis being either wide open (as for aspirated stops), or narrowed to the whisper, or prephonation, position (as for unaspirated stops, see p. 56)—and the wavy line indicating voicing. The broken diagonal line running from top to bottom represents the whole conceptual continuum that we have been talking about—it suggests that there is, in principle, a continuum, an infinite number, of possible VOTs.

Now, while looking at Fig. 52, carry out Experiment 123.

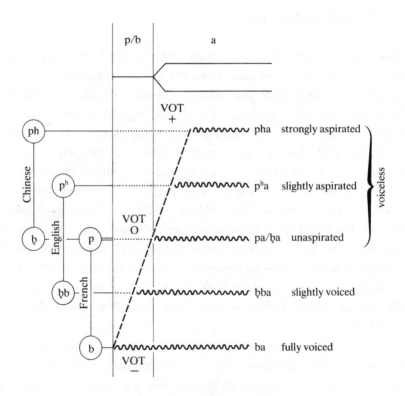

Fig. 52 The VOT continuum

123   Close your lips as for a [p] and build up pulmonic-pressure behind them. When the pressure is really high, suddenly open the lips and release a considerable blast of air before the vocal folds finally come together and start vibrating. This high pressure [p] has a long VOT, i.e. it is strongly aspirated, and we represent the utterance as [pha].

Now do the same again, but this time build up less pressure so that the air-blast following the release lasts a shorter time before the voicing begins, i.e. the VOT is shorter. This is a moderately aspirated [p], perhaps such as you would normally use in English, and the utterance is represented as [pʰa].

Next, produce a quite unaspirated [p]. Remember that for an unaspirated stop the glottis is already 'throttled down' to about the size of the whisper orifice during the closed phase of the stop: consequently, the vocal folds can start vibrating immediately upon release of the oral closure, i.e. the VOT is (virtually) zero. You can achieve this by *imagining whisper* during the closed phase of the stop. Remember what it feels like to whisper a [v] and get this same glottal feeling into the closed phase of the stop—i.e. *whisper* the stop, but there will, of course, be no audible whisper, so that voicing starts immediately the lips burst open. This is [pa], with unaspirated [p], i.e. with zero VOT.

The three [p] sounds produced in Experiment 123 are all voiceless. Two of them, strongly aspirated [ph] and moderately aspiratedly [pʰ], have positive VOTs. Plausible values might be something like 120 ms. for [pha] and 60 ms. for [pʰa], but of course, the actual VOTs that you achieved might differ quite widely from these values, and could only be established by instrumental measurement. The unaspirated stop [p] in [pa] is still voiceless, since the vocal folds are not vibrating at all during the closed phase of the stop.

In our next experiment we continue our progress along the conceptual continuum of VOTs into increasing *negative* values of VOT. Whereas in the aspirated stops there was a *delay* in voicing, which did not begin until a noticeable time after the release of the stop, in the next two examples there is an advance, or *anticipation* of voicing, which starts while the labial closure is still firmly in position. It is because we assigned positive values to delayed voice-onset that we now have to assign negative values to the anticipated onset.

124   Now produce a 'slightly voiced' [b]. Close the lips, hold them closed, and contrive to get the vocal folds vibrating *just before* the release of the labial closure. This kind of [b] starts out as a totally voiceless stop, and then, just at the last moment before the lips part, it turns into a voiced stop. We can represent it in transcriptions as [b̥ b a], that is, voiceless [b̥] passing (momentarily) into voiced [b] just before the lips open up into the vowel.

Finally, produce a fully voiced [b], i.e. get the voicing going well before the release of the stop, as in Exps. 31 and 32.

Experiments 123 and 124 exemplified five different points along the continuum of possible voice-onset-times. Figure 52 represents the VOT continuum by a slanting broken line, and labels these five different VOT values. It also suggests how three different languages exploit different parts of the VOT continuum in their contrasting pairs of initial stop consonants.

Some further comments on Fig. 52 are necessary. First, it will be noted that both French and Mandarin Chinese have a voiceless unaspirated stop, but they are represented differently in the transcriptions—the French one by [p] and the Chinese one by [b̥]. This indicates that the voiceless unaspirated stops of the two languages are not identical. French [p] (and likewise [t] and [k]) is relatively 'strong'—the pulmonic pressure behind the stop is relatively high, and it is tensely articulated. The Chinese [b] (and likewise [d̥ and g̥]) is articulated in a more lax way. The Chinese sounds, though totally voiceless just as the French ones are, have a lower air pressure behind the stop and probably require less muscular tension in the articulators than the French sounds. This relatively low pressure and rather lax articulation is reminiscent of voiced [b], [d], [g], where some of the energy in the air-stream has been absorbed in setting the vocal folds in vibration. Consequently we represent the Chinese voiceless unaspirated stop as [b̥], as a reminder that, though completely voiceless, it has something like the laxness of a [b].

The English unaspirated stop is represented as [b̥b] to underline the fact that it starts out as a laxly articulated voiceless stop, like the Chinese [b̥] but then it momentarily (i.e. for not more than 20 or 30 ms.) turns into a voiced stop [b] just before the release of the oral closure.

It should be noted that Fig. 52 represents *initial* stops. This is particularly relevant to the English examples, for in English moderately to strongly aspirated voiceless stops occur initially (before stressed vowels) but usually not elsewhere. Thus the medial [p] and [k] of *paper* and *baker* are much less aspirated than the initial stops of *pay* or *Kay*. In most types of American (and some types of British) English the medial consonant of *better*, *butter*, etc. is not a stop at all, but a (voiced) apico-alveolar tap [ɾ], though in British RP it is usually a voiceless slightly aspirated [t].

In many types of English syllable-final voiceless stops, as in *hop*, *hot*, *hock*, *stopgap*, etc., are unreleased (i.e. have no audible release) [p̚], [t̚], [k̚], and may be preceded, and accompanied, by glottal closure, [ʔpˀ], [ʔtˀ], [ʔkˀ]. Moreover, as we pointed out in Chapter 3, after [s] as in *spar*, *star*, *scar*, the English stops are unaspirated, like the French [p] or Chinese [b̥].

We have now seen how three different languages select different parts of the VOT continuum for use in building up the phonological forms of their words. The VOT continuum is universal. That is to say, all human vocal tracts are capable of producing stops with voice-onset-times at any point along that continuum. But different languages utilize different parts of the continuum. Thus, Chinese utilizes points towards the 'positive' end of the continuum; French utilizes points nearer the negative end of the continuum, while English utilizes an area between those two.

When we looked at the vowel continuum, above, we saw how two different languages, English and Spanish, used different parts of that continuum—just as the three languages we have now been looking at use different parts of the VOT continuum. But we also noted that the two languages, English and Spanish, divide up the vowel continuum into different *numbers* of bits, different numbers of vowel-units—English 6, Spanish 3.

It so happens that Chinese, English, and French each divide up the VOT continuum into the same number of bits, the same number of different VOT-types, namely two. But there are languages that utilize not just two bits of the VOT continuum, but three. Such a language is Thai. Thai utilizes three different types of initial stop consonant, which can be exemplified by voiceless aspirated [ph], voiceless unaspirated [p], and voiced [b]. Thus, with respect to the *number* of types of stop consonant that they utilize, the three languages, Chinese, English, and French, are the same. They each have just two types of stop, though they differ with respect to the precise quality of these stops: that is to say, the stop-types of these languages are differentiated from each other in different ways, as utilizing different parts of the VOT continuum. Thai, on the other hand, differs from all three of these languages in that it utilizes *three*, not just two, different types of stops— three different bits of the VOT continuum.

We can capture this similarity and difference by transcribing the two types of labial stop of all of the first three languages as /p/ and /b/, but the three types utilized by Thai as /ph/ /p/ and /b/. Here we are representing facts about the *phonology* of these languages rather than about *phonetics*, we are representing phonological units, or phonemes, as they are called, rather than speech-sounds. This is indicated (following the normal practice of linguistics) by placing the symbols within slant lines / / rather than within square brackets [ ]. The distinction between phonemes and speech-sounds will be made clearer below. Meanwhile, we can display this very small fragment of the sound-systems of Chinese, English, and Thai showing how the contrastive phonological units, the phonemes, correlate with their different phonetic realizations, as shown in Table 6.

Table 6

Language	Phonetic realization				
	[ph]	[pʰ]	[p]/[b̥]	[b̥]	[b]
Chinese	/pa/ 'to crouch'		/ba/ 'eight'		
English		/paɪ/ 'pie'		/baɪ/ 'buy'	
French			/pɑ/ 'step'		/bɑ/ 'low'
Thai	/phaa/ 'cloth'		/paa/ 'aunt'		/baa/ 'crazy'

Other languages have *more* than the three types of stop of Thai, but the additional ones do not represent simply further subdivisions of the VOT continuum since they involve other features. Thus Hindi and many other Indian languages have four types of stop, by adding a voiced aspirated stop (type [bɦ]) to the series. The sound [bɦ] does not fit on the VOT continuum we have been looking at, since it involves whispery voiced or 'murmured' aspiration, not the purely voiceless aspiration of these other languages.

Still other languages have *five* different types of stop, but the fifth one is distinguished by something other than VOT, namely a difference of initiation type. Thus Sindhi of Pakistan and NW India has voiced implosives as well as all the types of stop that Hindi has. The systems of labial stops of these additional languages thus are shown in Fig. 53.

Hindi: /ph/   /p/   /b/   /bɦ/
Sindhi: /ph/   /p/   /b/   /bɦ/   /ɓ/

Fig. 53 Labial stops in Hindi and Sindhi

5. Phonemes

We have seen how different languages exploit the universal human sound potential in different ways. Every language uses a particular set of phonemes for the purpose of building up the phonological forms—the audible realizations—of its words, and we have seen some examples of these. Now we must look more closely at the nature of phonemes and at the sound-systems of English.

Phonemes are the minimal sequential contrastive units of the phonology of languages. Each of the three terms *minimal, sequential,* and *contrastive* requires explanation.

We will take *contrastive* first. Phonemes are *contrastive* in the sense that they are the bits of sound that distinguish one word from another. Consider the English word *bit*, transcribed phonemically as /bɪt/. It is distinguished from the word *pit* /pɪt/ solely by the contrast between the initial consonants /b/ and /p/. Again, *pit*, is distinguished from *fit* by the contrast between /p/ and /f/; and *bit* is distinguished from *bet* /bɛt/ by the contrast between the vowels /ɪ/ and /ɛ/ and so on. The bits of sound that carry, or manifest, these contrasts are phonemes.

Phonemes are *minimal* sequential units, because if you take a stretch of speech and chop it up into a sequence of phonological units, the *shortest* stretch of speech that functions as a contrastive unit in the buildup of the phonological forms of words is the phoneme. The phonological structure of English, like that of other languages, can be described as a hierarchy of units. The largest, or most inclusive, unit in English is the intonation contour or *tone-group*. For example, each of the three versions of the sentence *Jane was here yesterday*, given on p. 173, exemplifies a single tone group.

1. ‖ ▬ ‧ ‧ ➘ ‥ ‖   2. ‖ ▬ ‥ ‧ ▬‧‧ 3. ‖ ▬‧‥ ▬ ‧‧ ‖

Each of these utterances represents a single phonological unit of pitch—a single *tone group*, here marked off by double vertical lines.

We can, however, chop up each tone group into smaller units—namely into two successive rhythmic units, or *feet*, shown here as separated by single lines, thus:

‖ ▬‧▬ | ➘‧▬ ‖   ‖ 'Jane was here ‖ 'yesterday |

That these feet are contrastive, meaning-differentiating, units is demonstrated by the fact that we could divide the utterance into feet differently, and this would convey a slightly different meaning:

|| ━ · | ＼ ﹍,﹍|| 　 || 'Jane was 　 | 'here yesterday ||

Next, we can divide each foot into still smaller chunks, namely into a sequence of *syllables*, shown here as separated by hyphens within each foot, thus:

|| 'Jane-was-here | 'yes-ter-day ||

Finally, we can divide up each syllable into a sequence of still smaller units—and here it is necessary for us to go into phonetic transcription, separating each unit from the next by a dot, thus:

|| 'dʒ.eɪ.n-w.ə.z-h.ɪə | 'j.ɛ.s-t.ə.-d.ɪ ||

That represents a possible British, RP, pronunciation. The corresponding American form might be:

|| 'dʒ.eɪ.n-w.ə.z.-h.ɪ.ɹ | 'j.ɛ.s-t.ə.ɹ-d.eɪ ||

At this point we can do no further chopping. We have reached the lowest rank in the phonological hierarchy, the smallest sequential or linear units—*phonemes*. There are no smaller meaning-differentiating units: we don't built up the phonological shapes of words out of only half an [s] or a small fraction of an [ɛ] for example. There are, however, some questionable items here. Why, for example, do we treat the sequences [dʒ] [eɪ] and [ɪə] as minimal units?

We take [dʒ] first. The interpretation of [dʒ] as a unit phoneme is suggested by the test of *commutation*: if we try to make English words by commuting, or exchanging, each part of the affricate [dʒ] with other sounds, we find that in such a word as *Jane* the [ʒ] can commute with *zero*, giving *Dane*, or with [ɹ], giving *drain*, or with [w] giving *Dwayne*. But the [d] cannot commute with anything. No consonant other than [d] can ever come before [ʒ] in English, i.e. there are no such words as */bʒeɪn/ or */gʒeɪn/ (the asterisk indicates a hypothetical or non-existent form). Nor can [ʒ] be preceded by zero—no genuine English word begins with [ʒ], i.e. there is no such word as */ʒeɪn/. It thus appears that the [ʒ] in [dʒ] is indissolubly linked with the [d] and the sequence must thus be regarded as a single, unitary, affricate phoneme.

Applying the commutation test to the corresponding voiceless affricate [tʃ] we find that both the [t] and the [ʃ] are commutable, so, from that point of view one might regard [tʃ] as a sequence of two phonemes, /t/ and /ʃ/. However, the parallelism with the unit phoneme /dʒ/ is obvious, and this suggests that we might well regard both as unit phonemes, and this interpretation is supported by other considerations, such as the historical origin of the sounds and certain phoneme alternances in modern English. Thus, most linguists regard these two affricates as unit phonemes, and partly because of this, often transcribe them as /č/ and /ǰ/. We will continue, however, to follow the principles of the IPA by using the digraphs /tʃ/ and /dʒ/.

The case of the diphthongs /eɪ/ and (in the British version) /ɪə/ is different. Here there are genuine options in the analysis. Depending, in part, on the purpose of the analysis, one may choose to regard the English diphthongs either as units or as sequences of two vowel phonemes, or (in the case of /eɪ/ /aɪ/, /aʊ/ /oʊ/ etc.) as a vowel followed by a semivowel, i.e. as /ej/ /aj/, /aw/ /ow/—the first two are usually transcribed by American linguists as /ey/ /ay/, a transcription which violates IPA practice, since the symbol [y] in the IPA system represents a rounded close front vowel.

These ambiguities apart, however, phonemes, as we have said, represent the smallest sequential contrastive phonological units into which we can divide up a text.

6. Distinctive features

It was necessary to make the point about phonemes being minimal *sequential* units, because a further subdivision into contrastive units of a different kind is possible. This is the division, or better, the dissection, of phonemes into *distinctive features*. But this, we must emphasize, is a dissection in a quite different dimension. All of the phonological units we have looked at so far—the intonation contour, the foot, the syllable, and finally the phoneme, are all *units that follow each other in time* throughout a spoken text. Distinctive features, on the other hand, are *simultaneous components* of a single unit, the phoneme.

If we look again at the words *bit pit* and *fit* we can see how the initial phonemes in these words, /b/ /p/ /f/, have certain things in common, but also differ from each other. All three are *consonants*, as opposed to vowels; all three are, broadly speaking, *labials* (neglecting the fact that /f/ is actually labiodental); the first two resemble each other, being *stops*, while the third is a *fricative*; /b/ is (slightly) *voiced*, but /p/ and /f/ are both *voiceless*. We tabulate these facts as shown in Table 7 indicating presence of a feature by a + sign and absence of a feature by a – sign.

Table 7

Phoneme	Feature						
	cons.	vowel	labial	stop	fricative	voiced	voiceless
b	+	–	+	+	–	+	–
p	+	–	+	+	–	–	+
f	+	–	+	–	+	–	+

Obviously we could tabulate this information more economically by thinking of each feature as representing a binary choice: a sound is either a consonant or not a consonant, a vowel or not a vowel, voiced or not voiced. So we can reduce the number of features that we have to list here to *cons., labial, stop*, and *voiced*; see Table 8.

We can thus say that the phonological form of a word consists of a *sequence* of phonemes, and that every phoneme consists of a *set* of (simultaneous) distinctive features. The phonological forms of words are differentiated from each other by the occurrence in them of different phonemes: the phonemes are differentiated from each other by the existence in them of different distinctive features.

In the last forty years a great deal has been written about distinctive features and several scholars have sought to discover the minimum number of distinctive features that are used to differentiate phonemes in the languages of the world. Three works dealing with distinctive features are named in For Further Reading, at the end of this book. Readers are referred to these publications for more information on features, since we will not make use of a formal set of distinctive features in our further discussion of the English sound systems.

Table 8

Phoneme	Feature			
	cons.	labial	stop	voiced
b	+	+	+	+
p	+	+	+	–
f	+	–	–	–

Since this book is a practical introduction to general phonetics we do not intend to give a full account of the phonetics and phonology of English. Nevertheless, it will be useful to survey some aspects of the English sound system, and this we will do, beginning with consonants.

7. English consonant phonemes

English has a total of 24 different consonant phonemes, or, as we say, it has a consonant phoneme inventory of 24 items. These consist of 6 stops: /p b t d k g/, 2 affricates: /tʃ dʒ/, 9 fricatives: /f v θ ð s z ʃ ʒ h/, 3 nasals: /m n ŋ/, 2 approximants: /l ɹ/ and 2 semivowels: /w j/.

That is the overall inventory; but we have to note that not all items in this inventory occur in all positions in syllables. In initial position only 22 items occur in genuine English words, since /ʒ/ occurs only in a few incompletely assimilated foreign words or names, like *jabot* and *Jeanne*, and the velar nasal never occurs in this position. In syllable final position the semivowels /w/ and /j/ never occur, nor does /h/; this reduces the inventory for final position to 19 in those varieties of English that admit final /ɹ/ (called 'rhotic' varieties) such as most types of American English, Scottish and Irish English, etc. In varieties with no final /ɹ/ ('non-rhotic' varieties), such as British RP and other varieties of English in England, in the US, Australia, New Zealand, etc., only 18 consonants occur at the ends of syllables.

The full inventory is found only intervocalically—for here we have both the non-initial consonants, e.g. /ʒ/ in *pleasure, vision*, /ŋ/ in *hanger, longing*, and also the non-final consonants, e.g. /w/ in *away*, /j/ in *beyond*, /h/ in *ahead*, /ɹ/ in *around*.

It is important to be aware that phonemes are abstractions or generalizations: they are, that is to say, abstract phonological units, each of which is manifested, or realized, in speech in a number of different ways. You cannot *pronounce* a phoneme. You can only pronounce a specific *sound* which may be the realization of a phoneme. If you say, for instance, the English word *cat* you are producing a quite specific sequence of sounds. That sequence of sounds is not itself a sequence of phonemes: it is the outward or concrete manifestation, or realization, of the sequence of phonemes that we represent in transcription as /kæt/. Say *cat* a number of times: every time you say it you are obviously producing a different sequence of sounds—you may even hear slight differences in your pronunciation of them. But each utterance of *cat* is a realization of one and the same sequence of phonemes: /kæt/.

So, every utterance of a phoneme is a different sound—whether you are aware of a difference in pronunciation or not. The actual sounds you make are concrete, physical, events: the phoneme is, as we have said, an abstraction.

8. Allophones

Apart from the fact that obviously every single realization of a phoneme is a different sound, there are particular types of realizations of phonemes that are systematically related to particular contexts, or, as we say, to particular phonological environments. We have already noted some environmental variants of English stops, namely, that initially before stressed vowels English voiceless stops are noticeably aspirated: in syllable final position, particularly in American English, they are often unreleased and may be preceded and accompanied by glottal closure, and there are still other noticeable variants. Such systematic environmental variants of phonemes are called *allophones*. Allophones, just like phonemes, are abstractions— which are concretely realized in speech as particular sounds. We might tabulate some of the allophones of the English phoneme represented by /t/ as in Table 9.

It is a not uncommon practice to transcribe allophones, such as we have listed here, within square brackets, as [tʰ] [ʔt̚] [t-] [t̪], as if they were purely phonetic entities rather than phonological ones. Strictly speaking, however, since they are abstractions made from the environmentally constrained systematic realizations of variants of phonemes, they are part of the phonology of the language, and should thus be enclosed within slant lines. However in the notes on English consonants that follow we will transcribe allophones within square brackets.

Stops. Voiceless: /p/ /t/ /k/: all noticeably aspirated when initial, especially

Table 9

	Initial + stress	Final	Before /ɹ/	Before /θ/ or /ð/
/t/ =	tʰ	ʔt̚	t-(retracted)	t̪ (dental)
Example	tea	eat	tree	eighth

before stressed vowels (except in English of Scotland and Northern England).

Generally, in American English, and sometimes in RP, final voiceless stops are unreleased and often accompanied by glottal stop, i.e. [ˀp̚] [ˀt̚] [ˀk̚]. In British English they may be released when absolute final (before pause) = [pʰ] [tʰ] [kʰ].

Voiced: /b/ /d/ /g/: all partially (or completely) voiceless when initial, [b̥b]- [d̥d]- [g̥g]- or [b̥]- [d̥]- [g̥]-, or final -[bb̥] -[dd̥] -[gg̥] or -[b̥] -[d̥] -[g̥].

In American English, medial /t/ and /d/ after a stressed vowel are commonly realized as alveolar tap [ɾ], as in *latter* or *ladder*.

/t/ and /d/: additional allophones as in list above for /t/.

/k/ and /g/: noticeably fronted (palatalized) before [j] and front vowels, particularly /i/.

Affricates: /tʃ/ and /dʒ/: usually lamino-postalveolar affricates, but with the tongue-point raised (i.e. articulation is not far back on blade). Often with wide lip-rounding /dʒ/ has partially or wholly voiceless allophones, as for the voiced stops.

Note that we describe /b d g dʒ/ as 'voiced', even though they may be (partly or even fully) voiceless: this is because they are always *capable* of being voiced, i.e. are always potentially voiced, and in addition they have the rather lax articulation characteristic of voiced stops. In fact some authors describe both the voiced stops and the voiced fricatives as 'lax' as opposed to 'tense' voiceless ones. We prefer to call them 'voiceless' and 'voiced', since the 'lax' fricatives are virtually always at least partially voiced, the voiced stops are always potentially voiced, and the lax vs. tense opposition is no doubt merely caused incidentally by the aerodynamic effects of the different glottal configurations for the two classes of sound.

Fricatives: the voiced fricatives have partially voiced initial and final allophones: /v/ = [v̥v]- -[v]- -[vv̥], /z/ = [z̥z]- -[z]- -[zz̥], etc.

/f/ /v/: endolabio-dental (i.e. inner part of lower lip makes contact with edges and fronts of upper teeth).

/θ/ /ð/: apico-dental: in American English perhaps somewhat interdental (i.e. with tongue-tip slightly protruding through between the upper and lower teeth), in British English perhaps more commonly slightly postdental (i.e. with tongue-tip and rim behind or barely touching the inner edges of the upper teeth).

/s/ /z/: most commonly lamino-alveolar.

/ʃ/ /ʒ/: usually lamino-postalveolar, but with the tongue-tip noticeably raised: may also be apico-postalveolar. Usually with some degree of lip-rounding.

/h/: usually described as a glottal fricative: it has little in the way of a turbulence-generating stricture in the mouth, the fricative sound being mainly generated by turbulent flow through the glottis, but noticeably modulated by oral articulations. /h/ is often described as essentially a voiceless version of whatever vowel follows: thus, he /hiː/, had /hæd/, hall /hɔː/ might be transcribed allophonically as /i̥iː] [æ̥ædd̥] [ɔ̥ːɬ].

Nasals: /m/ /n/ /ŋ/: bilabial, apico-alveolar, and velar with few notable allophones, though note that /n/ undergoes slight shifts like those of /t/ and /d/ before postalveolars and dentals.

Approximants: /ɹ/ and /l/: both are normally voiced, but have wholly or partly voiceless allophones after voiceless stops, as in *pray* [pɹ̥eɪ], *play* [pl̥eɪ], *cry* [kɹ̥aɪ], *clay* [kl̥eɪ].

/ɹ/: I have up to now retained the transcription /ɹ/ as a reminder that the English r-sound is practically never a trill (represented in phonetic transcription as [r])—even in Scotland, where trilled [r]s are popularly imagined to be common! It is, however, normal practice to represent the /ɹ/ phoneme of English simply as /r/. This is in accordance with a principle of typographical simplicity, whereby the typographically simpler of alternative transcriptions is used whenever there can be no possible ambiguity. From now on I will represent the English /r/ phoneme as /r/, but will use [ɹ] in transcribing allophones.

In American English, /r/ can be pronounced in several different ways. It is virtually always an approximant—i.e. neither a trill nor a fricative, except that after /t/ or /d/ in such words as *try dry* it may be a postalveolar fricative—wholly or partly voiceless in *try*: thus [t-ɹ̥aɪ] and [d-ɹaɪ] (where [t-] and [d-], you remember, represent the retracted allophones of /t/ and /d/ that occur before postalveolar [ɹ]). One pronunciation is simply that of a retroflex approximant, i.e. an approximant made with the main body of the tongue in roughly an [ə]-type posture, but with the tip curled up somewhat.

A commoner variety seems to be a peculiar sound like the rhotacized vowel described on pp. 161–2. In this type of /r/ the body of the tongue is bunched up into roughly the position of an [ɤ] vowel. At the same time the root of the tongue is slightly retracted into the pharynx (slight deep pharyngalization) and there is a short longitudinal furrow in the dorsal surface of the tongue roughly opposite the uvula, or a little forward from there. Rather surprisingly at first sight, those who do not already use this type of /r/ can sometimes learn it by starting with a uvular trill (the 'gargling' sound) [ʀ], and then very slightly moving the tongue-body forward until the trilling ceases: further slight trial and error adjustments often lead to a reasonably good American /r/ of the type in question. The resemblance of the articulation of this American /r/ to a uvular [ʀ] is not really surprising, since both involve a rather similar dorsal furrow in the tongue.

/l/: apico-alveolar lateral approximant, voiced, except after the voiceless stops /p/ and /k/, as mentioned above. In addition to these voiceless (or partly voiceless) allophones there are two principal allophones, [l], a slightly palatalized variety of [l], often called 'clear l' occurring before vowels as in *leaf* [liˑf] *lie* [laɪ] and, in RP at least, before /j/ as in *million* [mɪljˑn], and [ɫ], a velarized variety of [l], often called 'dark l' occurring at the ends of syllables, as in *feel* [fiːɫ] *field* [fiːɫd], and when syllabic, as in *battle* [bætɫ̩] *middle* [mɪdɫ̩].

Semivowels: /w/ and /j/ (the latter often transcribed as /y/ in American publications—but, as mentioned earlier, this 'anglo-centric' usage violates IPA practice).

/w/: bilabial (rounded) + velar semivowel, and /j/: dorso-palatal semivowel.

Both semivowels are normally voiced, but have partly (or wholly) voiceless allophones after voiceless stops, as in *twelve* [tw̥ɛɫvy̥], *queen* [kw̥iːn], *Cuba* [kju̥ˑbə]. The sequences /hw/ and /hj/ as in *why* and *Hugh*, as spoken by persons who pronounce the /h/, may be realized as [hw], [hj], [hw̥], [hj̥], or as [ʍ], that is, in fact, a voiceless labial + velar fricative, and as [ç], voiceless dorso-palatal fricative.

9. Consonant clusters

By consonant clusters we mean those sequences of consonants that occur initially or finally in syllables. For example both /pl/ and /nt/ are consonant clusters in the word *plant*, because they occur in one and the same syllable. But we would not call the sequence /p-l/ in *stop-light* a consonant cluster, because the sequence crosses a syllable boundary: /p/ is the final consonant in the first syllable and /l/ is the initial consonant in the second syllable.

In Chapter 9, on Prosodies, we cited some English syllable structures and referred to the fact that languages differ as to the types of syllable structure that they admit. These differences are chiefly a matter of the extent to which different languages permit consonant clusters to occur at the beginnings or ends of syllables.

English permits initial clusters of either two or three consonants, as in such words as *pray*, *sky* (CCV), *spray*, *screw* (CCCV), and either two, three, or four final consonants, as in *ask*, *apt* (VCC), *asked*, *elks* (VCCC), or four as in *waltzed* /wɔltstl/, *glimpsed* /glɪmpstl/ (C(C)VCCCC). Some English speakers, in fact, simplify some of the longer final consonant clusters by eliminating some of the consonants—saying, for example, /ast/ (or /æst/) in place of /askt/ (or /æskt/) for *asked*. You might check your own usage in these and other words.

Other languages have different rules relating to syllable structure: Classical Arabic, and many varieties of modern colloquial Arabic, for example, admit no initial consonant clusters at all, but allow final clusters of two or three consonants. On the other hand, the Caucasian language Georgian permits initial consonant clusters of from two to six items! Examples are /rts'q'va/ 'to water', /prtskvna/ 'to peel' (the ligatures on /ts'/ and /ts/ indicate that these affricates are unit phonemes).

Not only is the number of consonants that can occur initially and finally in syllables always subject to limitations imposed by the phonological structure of the language, the particular sequences of consonants that can occur in clusters is always limited. In English, for example, there are 22 initial consonants. This means that, if these could be combined quite freely, the total number of clusters of two different consonants would be $22^2 - 22$, that is, 462. In fact the rules of participation in consonant clusters in English permit only from 36 to 44, according to dialect, that is, only 7.8 per cent to 9.5 per cent of the theoretically possible number of clusters.

The English initial 2-consonant clusters are shown in Table 10.

Naturally, adjacent sounds in clusters influence each other in various ways (some of which have already been mentioned), in other words, noticeable allophones of consonant phonemes occur in some clusters. Thus, the aspiration of the voiceless stops carries over into following approximants and semivowels, so that the latter become partly voiceless, such words as *play* and *twelve* being pronounced as [pl̥eɪ] and [tw̥ɛlvy].

Sequences of C(onsonant) + /w/ and C + /j/ exhibit some degree of labialization and palatalization respectively of the first element in the cluster. If, for example, you pronounce the words *seat* and *sweet*, carefully listening to the sound of the initial /s/ in both words, you will clearly hear the auditory effect of the progressive labialization of the /s/ of *sweet*—as usual, you will

Table 10

	p	t	k	f	m	n	l	r	w	j	as in
p							pl	pr	(pw)	pj	play pray (pueblo) pure
t								tr	tw	{tj}	try twelve {tune}
k							kl	kr	kw	kj	clay cry queen cure
b							bl	br	(bw)	bj	blue brow (Buenos) beauty
d								dr	dw	{dj}	dry dwell {due}
g							gl	gr	gw	gj	glow grow Gwen (gules)
f							fl	fr		fj	fly fry few
θ								θr	θw	{θj}	three thwack {thews}
m										mj	music
n										{nj}	{new}
s	sp spy	st stay	sk sky	sf sphere	sm smooth	sn snow	sl slow		sw sweet	{sj}	{suit}
ʃ								ʃr			shriek
h									{hw}	{hj}	{why} {Hugh}
v										vj	view

In this table {} indicates a cluster not present in all varieties of English—thus dental or alveolar consonants are not followed by /j/ in most types of American English. Items with ( ) are rare—/pw/ and /bw/, for example, occur only in the words *pueblo* and *Buenos Aires*.

find the difference between the two /s/ sounds easier to observe if you whisper the words, and isolate the /s/.

Again, if you compare such words as *coo* and *cue* you may hear that the burst of noise on the release of the palatalized /k/ before /j/ in *cue* is noticeably higher pitched than that of the /k/ in *coo*, betokening a more advanced, slightly palatalized, place of articulation, and if you articulate the two words silently, or nearly so, you will probably feel the slight difference in the place of articulation. However, it is necessary to point out that the allophonic difference between the /k/s in these two words may be minimal. This is because many speakers of English have a very advanced (centralized) and somewhat diphthongal /uˑ/ vowel in words like *coo*, i.e. something of the type [üw] or even [ɨʉ]. If your /uˑ/ is of that type, a better comparison would be with *caw*, for example.

In addition to these 2-consonant clusters, English admits of 9, and only 9, different initial clusters of 3 consonants. These are /spl/ /spr/ /spj/ /str/ {/stj/} /skl/ /skr/ /skw/ /skj/, as in *splay spray spew stray {stew} sclerosis screw square skua*, of which one item, *stew*, is pronounced with initial /st/, not /stj/, in most types of American English in accordance with the American rule of non-occurrence of /j/ after alveolars.

As we said earlier, it is not our intention to give a full account of English phonology, but just to provide an illustration of the highly organized, systematic, nature of the sound systems of languages. We will therefore not enumerate the final consonant clusters of English, but pass directly to a brief discussion of English vowels.

10. The English vowels

The enumeration of the vowel phonemes of English is a little less straightforward than that of consonants, for two reasons. First, there is slightly more divergence between major dialects (e.g. British and American) with respect to vowels than with respect to consonants, and secondly, because there are different ways of making a phonological analysis of vowels.

There is one general remark to be made about English vowels and diphthongs in stressed syllables, namely that vowels are normally longest when final (e.g. [iː] in *see*), shorter in syllables closed by a consonant, particularly those closed by a voiceless stop (e.g. [iˑ] in *seed*, [i] in *seat*). This should be borne in mind as we enumerate the vowel phonemes of English, with brief descriptions. In every case readers should experiment with the English vowel that they use, pronouncing it both in the sample words, and in isolation, aloud and silently, and trying to feel where and how it is articulated in relation to the Cardinal Vowels.

Front vowels.

/i/ as in *see*, *seat*. Unrounded rather close front vowel, somewhat less close and tense than CV 1. Sometimes slightly diphthongal—i.e. starting as an opener and laxer vowel and rapidly becoming slightly closer and tenser. We can represent this as [ɪi] or [ij].

/ɪ/ in *sit*. A slightly retracted and laxer and more open vowel. In American English often at least as open as a retracted CV 2 [e], and sometimes somewhat diphthongized, gliding inwards and downwards slightly towards [ə], particularly before /d/ as in *did* [dɪəd]. In RP often somewhat closer.

/eɪ/ in *day*, *date*. In both RP and Midwest American this is normally a diphthong, but the extent of diphthongal movement is variable. Most commonly, perhaps, it starts between CVs 2 [e] and 3 [ɛ] and glides forwards and upwards, but seldom, if ever, as far as [i] (hence our choice of symbols /eɪ/ rather than /ei/). The starting point may be lower, at about the level of CV 3 [ɛ], and even somewhat retracted, thus [ɛɪ] or [ɛ̈ɪ]. In some varieties of American English, and in the English of Scotland and northern England, it may be a pure vowel of the CV 2 type—our sample words being pronounced [deː] and [det]. You should experiment with these variant pronunciations, and try to discover which type you normally use.

/ɛ/ in *set*, *said*. In many types of both British and American English, this is a vowel rather similar to CV 3 [ɛ], though usually a little closer in RP and often a little retracted in American English.

/æ/ in *sat*, *sad*. Traditionally this is generally described as a more open vowel than the preceding one, usually somewhat less than half-way from CV 3 [ɛ] to CCV 4 [a], and this is true for many varieties of British and American English. However, some speakers of American English commonly use a closer, [ɛ]-like vowel in *sat* etc., distinguishing it from the traditional /ɛ/ by length (and sometimes diphthongization), thus pronouncing the pairs *set*/*sat* and *said*/*sad* as something like [sɛt]/[sɛːt/] or [sɛət], [sɛd]/[sɛːd] or [sɛˑəd].

Indeed, in the Midwest (very commonly in the area of Detroit) what I have called the traditional relationship between these two vowels has been virtually reversed in the speech of young people. In this modern pronunciation, the old /æ/ is a very front, approximately Cardinal, and usually

Table 11

Pronunciation	sacks/sex	mass/mess
Traditional	[sæks]/[sɛks]	[mæs]/[mɛs]
New	[sɛˑəks]/[sæks]	[mɛˑəs]/[mæs]

diphthongal [ɛˑə], while the old [ɛ] is a short monophthong, lower than [ɛ] and considerably centralized, which we might transcribe phonetically as [æ̈]. This new pronunciation is particularly noticeable before voiceless stops and fricatives, as in such word-pairs as *sacks/sex mass/mess*. Table 11 shows the traditional and new pronunciations.

Open central to back vowels: the vowels of *father, cot, caught*.

In RP, the words *father*, *cot*, and *caught* contain three quite distinct vowel phonemes, which we represent as /ɑ/ /ɒ/ and /ɔ/. The first is a somewhat long rather back open unrounded vowel which can be represented phonetically as [ä:], meaning an open vowel somewhat advanced from the position of CV 5. The vowel of *cot* is short, very back, and very open and somewhat rounded: i.e. approximately the rounded equivalent of CV 5. The vowel of *caught* is close to CV 6, that is, [ɔ].

In phonemic transcriptions of American English one tradition (exemplified, for example, in the *American Pronouncing Dictionary* of Kenyon and Knott) represents the vowel of the first two words as /ɑ/, seeming to imply that this is, phonetically a *back* vowel. The vowel in these words, however, is never (I believe) very back, in the kind of Midwest American that I am representing here, and indeed, in the pronunciation of the young, may be quite front, approximating to CV 4 [a], so that there is no justification for representing it as /ɑ/. The vowel of *caught*, on the other hand, is a very open back vowel, with open rounding. It is commonly represented in phonemic transcriptions as /ɔ/. But it is important to remember that in the Midwest it is nowhere near CV 6 [ɔ], but much closer to CV 5 rounded, that is [ɒ], the vowel of RP *cot*, the word *caught* being pronounced as (approximately) [kɒːt]. Much closer vowels, often somewhat diphthongized, occur in New York, where *caught* may be pronounced [kɔːt], [kɔˑət], or even [koˑət].

Table 12 sums up the relationships between the two Midwest and the three RP phonemes with an indication of how they are pronounced.

Remaining Back Vowels.

/oʊ/ in *coat*. Most usually a diphthong starting as a somewhat rounded vowel, between CV 6 [ɔ] and 7 [o] but centralized and gliding towards [ʊ]

Table 12

Midwest phoneme	Pronunciation	RP phoneme	Pronunciation
/a/ father/cot	[a]	/ɑ/ father	[ɑ]
		/ɒ/ cot	[ɒ]
/ɔ/ caught	[ɒː]	/ɔː/ caught	[ɔ]

but varying a good deal both in terms of the height and the centrality of the starting point. In modern RP, commonly starting completely unrounded and central, type [əʊ], and sometimes virtually unrounded throughout, hence [əɣ]. May be realized as a monophthong [oː] in some varieties of American English, and in the English of Scotland and northern England.

/ʊ/ in *put*. A moderately rounded, highly centralized vowel at about the half-close level, i.e. a relaxed, and centralized CV 7 [ö], or a slightly retracted and lax half-close central rounded vowel [ɵ]. In the word *good*, particularly, but not only, in American English, this vowel may be totally unrounded, thus being a strongly centralized [ɤ].

/u/ in *boot*. Traditionally regarded as a close back rounded vowel, and hence transcribed phonetically as /u/. However, in virtually all types of English it is not fully back and not fully close. In American English, in particular, it is often articulated at least half-way from back to central, sometimes even more centrally than that—which is why Americans usually have some difficulty in acquiring a good CV 8. Moreover, as mentioned earlier, it is often somewhat diphthongized, the diphthongization usually taking the form of progressive lip-rounding, hence perhaps something approximating to [üü] or even [ɨu]. Readers should carefully check their own pronunciation of /u/.

Central Vowels.

/ʌ/ in *cut*. Traditionally represented in phonemic transcriptions of English by /ʌ/, which strictly speaking indicates CV 6 [ɔ] unrounded, that is, a fully back half-open unrounded vowel. A fully back [ʌ] vowel occurs in some dialects, in Scotland, for example, but in the types of English we are dealing with here the vowel represented by /ʌ/ is more central.

In the Midwest it tends to be a little below half-open and advanced in varying degrees from back towards central. In RP it is much more open, and may be slightly in front of central.

/ɜ/ or /ɝ/ in *bird*. The RP vowel is a straightforward unrounded central vowel, varying from half-open to nearly half-close. In Midwest American it is commonly a rhotacized vowel of approximately a half-close central to back type, sometimes with slight lip-rounding, represented by /ɚ/, in which the little hook, reminiscent of the hook of an *r*, suggests the rhotacization.

The actual tongue-configuration of this vowel is approximately as follows. The tongue is bunched up into an almost spherical shape (the apex being somewhat drawn back into the body of the tongue), coming rather close to the soft palate as if to articulate a dorso-velar approximant. Simultaneously, a rather short, but deep, longitudinal furrow is formed in the dorsum of the tongue, somewhat like the furrow in which the uvula vibrates in the articulation of a uvular trill [ʀ] but a little further forward. At the same time, the root of the tongue is slightly retracted into the pharynx. Readers who are Midwesterners should experiment, isolating the vowel of words such as *bird, curt, fur, her*, and articulating it voiced, voiceless, and silently. Others may produce it by meticulously trying to replicate the tongue-configuration just described.

Major Diphthongs.

We have already described the two minor diphthongs /eɪ/ and /oʊ/—'minor' because they do not usually involve a very extensive movement of the articulators, and may, indeed, be represented by monophthongs in some varieties of English.

/aɪ/ in *high height*. A diphthong starting at, or a little behind, CV 4 [a], and gliding towards [ɪ]. The precise starting point and ending point of the diphthongal glide vary somewhat from one individual to another, and to some extent allophonically, i.e. from one phonological environment to another: thus, the /aɪ/ of *high* is longer than that of *height*, and the end point of the diphthongal glide may be lower. The reader can determine her/ his own variants of /aɪ/ by experiment.

/aʊ/ in *how out*. This diphthong starts at about the same place as /aɪ/ and glides upwards towards [ʊ], the lips, starting from a neutral position, becoming more closely rounded as the glide proceeds. Analogous variants, as for /aɪ/.

/ɔɪ/ in *boy*. This diphthong starts at a point between half-open and open, with rounded lips, and glides towards [ɪ].

American English has an additional diphthong /uɪ/, in *buoy*, absent in RP.

Centring, or /r/ diphthongs.

In RP there is a set of diphthongs ending in a central vowel of [ə] type, occurring in such words as *idea, beard* /ɪə/; *bare, Baird* /ɛə/; *poor gourd* /ʊə/;

and, for some speakers, *pour board* /ɔə/ (others simply have /ɔ/ in the last two words). In those cases where there is an orthographic *r* in the word, Midwest American has, in fact, an /r/, that is, the typical American /r/ described on pp. 161–2, 194–5. This /r/ is, in fact, virtually identical with the rhotacized vowel /ɚ/ described on pp. 201–2, so that we may represent such words as *beard, Baird, gourd, board* as /bɪrd/ /bɛrd/ /gʊrd/ / bɔrd/ or possibly /bɪɚd/ /bɛɚd/, etc.

The sound system of English consists, of course, of much more than we have looked at here. There are, as we hinted above (pp. 187, 188) units larger than the segmental phoneme, such as the syllable, the foot, and the tone group (or intonation contour) which have to be incorporated into a description of the phonology of English. And phonology is concerned also with rules relating stressed to unstressed forms of syllables, to rules relating the different phonological forms of word groups such as *photograph, photography, photographic* and so on.

But these matters go beyond the scope of this book. All we intended to do here was, by looking at some of the details of English phonology, to illustrate the point made at the beginning of the chapter, that languages make an orderly selection from the human sound-producing potential, and organize sounds in a highly systematic and rule-governed way into the phonological forms that are the outward and audible manifestations of the words and sentences that make up language.

11

Review

We have covered a good deal of ground in this book, and looked closely at many aspects of the production of speech. At times, while the reader was learning, by experiment, the various taxonomic categories of phonetics, it may have seemed difficult to see the wood for the trees. For that reason, it seems desirable to give here a brief review of most of the matters we have dealt with.

A speech act, or speech event, as we saw in the first chapter, can be studied in any one or more of a series of stages, or phases, starting with neurolinguistic programming and passing on through neuromuscular, organic, aerodynamic, acoustic, and neuroreceptive phases to the final stages of neurolinguistic identification of sounds and ultimate decoding and comprehension.

The actual production of the sounds of speech is, as we saw, an aerodynamic process—all vocal sounds are generated by the passage of a stream of air through the vocal tract, driven by the movements of various organs, and modulated to produce specific types of sound by movements and postures of others. The categories used in phonetics for the description and classification of sounds are, therefore, based very largely on the organic and aerodynamic phases of speech.

From now on we carry out our review of the phonetic categories mainly in the form of an extended list or glossary with brief explanations.

Productive components of speech

Initiation. An activity in the vocal tract which compresses or rarefies the air in the tract, and hence initiates, or tends to initiate, an air-stream. The organ or organ-group involved in initiation is an *initiator*.

Articulation. An activity in the vocal tract (chiefly in the part of the vocal tract above the larynx) which interrupts, or modulates, the air-stream in such a way that a specific type of sound is generated. The organ involved in articulation is an *articulator*.

Phonation. An activity in the larynx which is neither initiatory nor articulatory in which the air-stream is modulated by its passage through the glottis (the space between the vocal folds) before being finally 'shaped' into a specific sound-type by the articulation.

Types of initiation

Pulmonic Pressure. The air-stream is initiated by the lungs (hence 'pulmonic'), which contract to generate positive pressure and thus to initiate an outflowing, *egressive*, air-stream. By far the commonest initiation type, and the only one regularly used in most languages, including English.

Pulmonic Suction. The air-stream is initiated by expansion of the lungs, generating negative pressure (suction) and hence an inflowing, *ingressive*, air-stream. A sharp, hissing, intake of breath, caused by a sudden pain, for instance, is initiated in this way. In speech, occasional words may be uttered with pulmonic suction initiation, and more extensive talking on a pulmonic suction air-stream may be done for fun, or to disguise the voice.

Glottalic Pressure. The initiator is the larynx, with the glottis closed. The larynx is thrust upwards, compressing the air contained between the initiatory closure at the glottis and some closure or narrow stricture in the mouth. Glottalic pressure sounds are also called ejectives, and most commonly are stops or affricates, more rarely fricatives. The IPA diacritic for ejectives is an apostrophe, as in [p'] [t'] [ts'] [f'] etc. Glottalic pressure sounds are particularly characteristic of languages of the Caucasus and of many African and American Indian languages.

Glottalic Suction. As with the preceding, the initiator is the larynx, with closed glottis. Unphonated glottalic suction sounds are, in fact, 'inverse ejectives' (sometimes called 'injectives'). A downward thrust of the larynx generates negative pressure (suction) between the initiatory closure and an articulatory stricture in the mouth. The commonest glottalic suction sounds (and they are not very common) are what are called *voiced implosives*. In these, the glottis is not tightly closed, but disposed as for the production of voice, so that as the larynx suddenly jerks downwards, considerably lowering the air pressure above it, there is a brief leakage of air *upwards* through the glottis producing voice. Voiced implosives are represented as [ɓ] [ɗ] [ɠ]. They occur in Sindhi, and in a number of African and American Indian languages.

Velaric Suction. The initiator is the tongue, which forms an airtight closure at the velum (hence 'velaric') trapping a small quantity of air between that and an articulatory closure further forward. A slight downward motion of the tongue rarefies the trapped air so that when the articulation is released there is a sudden, noisy, influx of air into the mouth—the mechanism of *click* sounds, e.g. [ǃ], dentalveolar click, the sound represented by 'tsk tsk' or 'tut tut' in English; and [ǁ], lateral click. Velaric suction sounds are regular speech-sounds in Bushman, Hottentot, and a few other languages of southern Africa.

Phonation types

Voiceless. Glottis wide open, as for [p] [t] [k] [f] [s] [ʃ] [h] etc. and voiceless lateral, nasals, vowels, etc.: [l̥] [m̥] [i̥] etc.

Whisper (whispered sounds). Glottis narrowed so that the air-stream produces a rich hushing sound as it passes through. Glottal narrowing also occurs in *prephonation* during the pre-release phase of voiceless unaspirated stops and affricates.

Voice (voiced sounds). Glottis narrowed, vocal folds vibrating, as in [b] [d] [v] [z] [ʒ] [l] [m] [i] etc.

Creak. Glottis closed along most of its length but with a very small vibrating segment near the front end through which low-frequency bursts of air escape, producing a crackly sound, sometimes also called 'glottal fry'.

Breathy voice. Glottis rather wide open but very high velocity airflow so that the vocal folds are 'flapping in the breeze'.

Whispery voice. Vocal folds vibrate to produce voice, but air is also escaping through a narrow, whisper-type, chink: also called 'murmur'.

Glottal stop, tightly closed glottis, is sometimes included among phonation types, but is more properly regarded as either a type of *articulation* (in glottal stop [ʔ]) or as simply a concomitant of glottalic initiation.

Articulation: stricture types

Maintainable stricture types: i.e. those in which the essential articulatory posture can be held for a considerable time.

Stop. Articulators come together (approach), forming and holding a complete closure (hold) with buildup of (positive or negative) pressure behind it, sudden release of closure resulting in a noise-burst. A stop may lack *approach* or *release*, but the intervening *hold* is the one absolutely essential feature, and it can be maintained for some time. This is why stops must be classified as *maintainable* sounds, even though the noise of the air escape on their release is only momentary. Examples: [p] [t] [b] [d] [p'] [t'] [ɓ] [ɗ] etc.

Fricative. Sound formed with very narrow articulatory channel, such that airflow through it is turbulent, generating a hiss noise, whether voiced or voiceless. Examples: [f] [s] [v] [z] [x] [ɣ] [ɬ] [lʒ] etc.

Affricate. Sequential articulation—stop released into homorganic fricative (within one and the same syllable). Examples: [pf] [ts] [dz] [tʃ] (sometimes written in non-IPA [č]) [dʒ] (non-IPA [ǰ]) [kx] [gɣ] etc.

Approximant. Sound formed with slightly wider articulatory channel than fricative—turbulent flow when voiceless, non-turbulent when voiced. Examples: [ɹ] [l] [i] [e] [u].

Resonant. Sound with very wide articulatory channel—no local turbulence, even when voiceless. Examples: some vowels, such as [ɛ] [a]. The term is not much used, because the only examples are vowels, and they are classified in a different way.

Trill. One articulator taps repeatedly against another (usually at a frequency of about 25 to 35 Hz). Trills are *maintainable* because they require a static articulatory posture to be held for an appreciable time: the repeated tapping of the trilling organ is entirely caused by the air-stream causing it to 'flap in the breeze'. Examples: [r] [ʀ] and bilabial trill.

Obstruent and non-obstruent. These are useful cover terms for classes of sounds: stops affricates and fricatives are *obstruents*, the rest are generally regarded as *non-obstruents*, though the position of trill may be somewhat ambiguous.

Momentary (non-maintainable) stricture types: i.e. those whose articulation is *essentially* a momentary gesture, not a maintainable posture—that is, an *approach* and/or a *release* with no intervening *hold*.

Tap and Flap. One articulator makes momentary contact with another, either in a 'flicking' movement, e.g. the apico-alveolar tap [ɾ], or by momentarily striking it in passing, e.g. the retroflex flap [ɽ].

Semivowel. A momentary approximant-type articulation—an approach and/or release with no hold, e.g. [j], an approach and/or release, or departure from, a palatal approximant articulation (which, if maintained, would be an [i] vowel) [w], approach and/or departure from an [u] position.

The transverse dimension of articulation

Median articulation. Most oral articulations require the formation of an obstruction along the sides of the mouth, leaving open an articulatory channel along the centre, or *median*, line of the mouth—or, in the case of stops, a total, side-to-side obstruction usually followed by a median release, e.g. [p] [b] [f] [v] [s] [z] [k] [x] [j] [i] etc. Since median articulation is by far the commonest type it is normally not explicitly indicated in descriptions of sounds.

Lateral articulation. There is an obstruction somewhere along the median line of the mouth, leaving open a *lateral* channel or channels along one or both sides of the tongue. Examples: lateral approximants [l] [ʎ], lateral fricatives [ɬ] [ɮ].

Articulation: Locations

Articulatory Areas

Nasal area. Involving lowering of the soft palate, so that air passes out through the nose: *nasal* articulation, e.g. [m] [n] [ŋ] [m̩] etc.

Nasalized, with air passing out through both mouth and nose, e.g. [ɛ̃] [ã] [õ] etc.

Oral area. Articulation in the mouth, e.g. [p] [b] [t] [d] [s] [z] [l] [i] [e] etc.

Pharyngeo-laryngeal area. Articulation in the *pharynx*, [ħ] [ʕ], and *glottis* [ʔ] [h] [ɦ].

Principal oral articulations

Bilabial: e.g. [p] [b] [ɸ] [β]; *Labiodental*: e.g. [f] [v]; (*Apico*) *dental*: e.g. [θ] [ð], [t̪] [d̪]; *Alveolar*: e.g. [t] [d] [s] [z] [l] [r] [n]; *Postalveolar*: [ʃ] [ʒ] [ɹ]; *Retroflex*: [ʈ] [ɖ] [ʂ] [ʐ] [ɭ]; *Palatal*: e.g. [c] [ɟ] [ç] [ɪ] [ʎ] [ɲ] [j]; *Velar*: [k] [g] [x] [ɣ] [ŋ]; *Uvular*: [q] [ɢ] [χ] [ʁ] [ɴ] [ʀ].

Co-articulation and sequential sound-types

Co-ordinate or Double Articulation: simultaneous articulations of same stricture type at two different locations, e.g. simultaneous [p] + [k] = [p͡k], [p] + [t] = [p͡t], [ɸ] + [x] = [ɸ͡x]. There are special symbols for simultaneous approximant articulations at the *labial + velar* locations, [w], and at the *labial + palatal* locations, [ɥ].

Secondary Articulations: an opener articulation (usually of approximant type) superimposed on a simultaneous closer articulation.

Labialized. Simultaneous lip-rounding, e.g. [tʷ] [dʷ] [sʷ] [xʷ] etc.

Palatalized. Simultaneous raising of tongue dorsum towards the hard palate, e.g. [pʲ] [dʲ] [sʲ] etc. also symbolized as [ƥ] [ɗ] [ş] etc.

Velarized. Simultaneous raising of tongue dorsum towards the velum, e.g. [ŧ] [đ] [s̴] [ɫ] etc.

Pharyngalized. Simultaneous compression of pharynx—symbolized as [dˤ] [lˤ] [aˤ] etc.

Sequential sound-types: these are *homorganic sequences* which can be regarded as units, and may function as units (unit phonemes) in languages.

Geminate. Sequence of identical sounds, within one and the same word or morpheme, e.g. [tt] [ll] in Italian *notte, bello*, Arabic [ɬ] in *Allah*, etc.

Affricate. Stop released into homorganic fricative, e.g. [pɸ] [ts] [ts'] [dz] [tʃ] [dʒ] etc. within one and same syllable and morpheme.

Lateral affricate. Stop released into homorganic lateral fricative, e.g. [tɬ] [tɬ'] [dlʒ].

Lateral plosion. Release of a stop into a homorganic non-fricative lateral, often syllabic, e.g. [tⱡ] and [dⱡ] in English *bottle, middle*.

Nasal plosion. Release of a stop into a homorganic, often syllabic, nasal, e.g. [tn̩] and [dn̩] in English *button, sudden*.

Prenasalized stops. Homorganic sequence of nasal + stop at the beginning of a syllable and functioning as a unit phoneme, e.g. [mb-] [nd-] [ŋg-], rather common in Austronesian languages.

Non-homorganic sequences

Heterorganic sequences. The articulators used for the successive sounds are completely different, e.g. [kp] and [sp] in *back part* and *lisp*.

Contiguous sequences. Articulations of successive sounds made by adjacent parts of the same organs, [tɹ] in *tree* and [kj] in *backyard*.

Diphthong. Sequence of two vowels within one and the same syllable, e.g. [aɪ] in *high*, [aʊ] in *how*, and, in many types of English, [eɪ] in *day* and [lʊ] or [əʊ] in *go*. Diphthongs such as these have decrescendo or diminishing stress and are called *falling* diphthongs. We can indicate them by marking the last part of the diphthong, the weaker element, with [˘], thus [aɪ̆] [aʊ̆] etc. Diphthongs with crescendo or increasing stress are called *rising* diphthongs, and are indicated by placing the mark [˘] over the first element. The English words *yes*, *yawn*, *you*, etc. might be transcribed: [ĭɛs] [ĭɔˑn] [ĭuː], but these sequences are usually regarded as made up of semivowel + vowel, and are transcribed [jɛs] [jɔˑn] [juː].

Close and open transition between consonants

Close transition. Successive consonants articulated as closely together as possible. In *heterorganic* sequences there is articulatory overlap, i.e. the second articulation is formed before the first is released, e.g. [pl] in *play*, [kt] in *actor*. In *contiguous* sequences, there is articulatory accommodation, i.e. the articulation of one consonant accommodates to the articulation of the other, e.g. [k] + [j] in *backyard*, where the [k] is slightly palatalized to accommodate to the palatal [j], thus [kʲ], or [t] + [θ] in *eighth*, where the [t] becomes dental to accommodate to the dental [θ], and thus [t̪θ]. In *homorganic* sequences the articulation is simply prolonged, e.g. [k] + [k] in *black cat*, where there is a single, long, velar closure.

Open transition. In open transition there is no such overlap, accommodation or continuity of articulation; instead there is a momentary release and re-articulation. One can hear contrasts between close and open transition in such English pairs as *back part* [bækpɑ(ɹ)t] with close (overlapping) transition [kp], and *back apart* [bækəpɑ(ɹ)t], where the ultra-short, often voiceless, [ə] is little more than a mere open transition between the consonants. Compare, also, [pl] in *plight* [plaɪt] with [pəl] in *polite*, or [kɹ] and [ks] in *cracks* with [kəɹ] and [kəs] in *Caracas*, etc.

Vowels

Parameters of vowel classification

Vowels are basically classified in terms of *lip-position*, *vertical tongue-position* (*tongue-height*), and *horizontal tongue-position*.

Lip-position. We distinguish *unrounded* vowels, e.g. [i] [e] [ɛ] [ʌ] [ɤ] [ɯ] from *rounded* vowels, e.g. [y] [ø] [œ] [ɔ] [o] [u] etc.

Tongue-height. The degree of convex 'bunching up' of the tongue, from very bunched up, coming close to the roof of the mouth—high or *close*, e.g. [i] [y] [u] [ɯ] to very low and rather flat (though still convex)—low or *open*, e.g. [a] [ɑ] [ɒ]. Intermediate positions—*half-close*, e.g. [e] [ø] [ɵ] [o] [ɤ], *half-open*, e.g. [ɛ] [œ] [ɔ] [ʌ].

Horizontal tongue-position: the location of the bunched-up tongue in the front-back dimension of the mouth. Vowels produced with the tongue thrust forward as far as possible and bunched up in the front of the mouth are *front* vowels, e.g. [i] [y] [e] [ø] [ɛ] [œ] [a] [œ]. Vowels produced with the tongue drawn back as far as possible and bunched up at the back of the mouth are *back* vowels, e.g. [ɑ] [ɒ] [ɔ] [ʌ] [o] [ɤ] [u] [ɯ]. Vowels produced with the tongue about half-way between the front and back extremes are *central* vowels, e.g. [ɨ] [ʉ] [ɵ] [ə] etc.

Cardinal Vowels. A set of universal reference vowels, invented by the English phonetician Daniel Jones, by comparison with which virtually any vowel of any language can be specified with some accuracy. The Cardinal Vowels (CVs) are derived from the idea of a 'vowel space' within the mouth, circumscribed by a 'vowel limit' beyond which vowels cannot be produced. For example, CV 1 [i] is the highest and most front possible vowel: if the tongue is bunched up any higher, or pushed any further forward, the sound produced will be a palatal or prepalatal fricative. The CV 1 [i] thus marks the closest and frontest point on the vowel limit.

All the CVs are on the periphery of the vowel limit, i.e. they consist of the most *front* possible vowels, at approximately equidistant points from highest possible to lowest—[i] [e] [ɛ] [a] and the most *back* possible vowels, at equidistant points from lowest to highest—[ɑ] [ɔ] [o] [u]. There is a set of secondary Cardinal Vowels, with exactly the same tongue-positions, but the opposite lip-positions. These are, front: [y] [ø] [œ] [œ]; back: [ɒ] [ʌ] [ɤ] [ɯ].

These reference vowels are all tense and absolutely monophthongal. Practically none is exactly the same as any vowel of English: so English speakers have to be particularly careful in learning the Cardinal Vowels.

Acoustics of vowels

The vibrating vocal folds in the larynx generate a complex sound rich in harmonics. The tongue- and lip-configurations for vowels shape the mouth into a series of resonators. As the sound of voice passes through the mouth resonators, they pick out certain bands of frequency within the complex sound-wave and emphasize those. For each vowel the acoustic energy is thus concentrated in a particular set of frequency bands, called *formants* (Fs). Most vowels can be pretty well characterized in terms of the two lowest frequency formants, F1 and F2. Thus CV 1 [i] can be described as having F1 at about 240 Hz, F2 at about 2400 Hz. CV 3 [ɛ] has F1 at about 610 and F2 at about 1900 Hz. CV 6 [ɔ] has F1 at about 500, and F2 at about 700 Hz.

Vowel sounds are usually *heard* as unified sounds of particular qualities, within which the individual formants cannot be separately perceived. However, it is possible to become aware of F1 and F2 as follows.

Tapping the throat, with the glottis closed, generally makes F1 audible. Secondly, though the hushing sound of whisper is complex, a frequency representing F2 is usually audible in whisper. It is easy to identify the 'whisper-pitch' (= F2) of various vowels with musical notes, and this is a useful aid to the learning of some vowel sounds.

Additional vowel modifications

Nasalization. If the soft palate is lowered while a vowel is being produced, nasalized vowels are generated, e.g. [œ̃] [õ] [ɛ̃] [ɑ̃] as in French *un bon vin blanc*.

Retroflexion. If the tip of the tongue is turned up while a vowel is being produced, the vowel is retroflexed, as in some varieties of Midwest American, particularly with [ɑ˞] as in *far*, [ɝ] or [ɜ˞] as in *bird*.

Rhotacization. Rhotacization, or 'r-colouring', is sometimes confused with retroflexion, but in fact it does not involve the upturning of the tongue-tip characteristic of retroflexion. Rhotacization is a rather common feature of the vowel [ɝ] of *bird* in Midwest American. It is produced by two simultaneous modifications of the configuration of a tongue which is rather bunched up into approximately a half-close central to back position—some retraction of the root of the tongue back into the pharynx (slight deep pharyngalization), and the formation of a hollow in the centre of the tongue about opposite the uvula.

Prosodic features

Prosodic features, or prosodies, are phonetic features that characterize relations between segmental sounds, or stretches of speech more than one segment in length.

Initiatory prosodies

Stress. Initiator power—the energy expended by (usually) the pulmonic initiator in pushing air up from the lungs against the loads imposed by phonatory and articulatory strictures. Stress is marked in IPA transcriptions by vertical lines placed before the relevant symbol: ['] means *very strongly stressed*, ['] means *stressed*, [ˌ] means *weakly stressed*, and absence of stress-marks means *unstressed*, or most weakly stressed.

Syllables. Minor power peaks usually separated from each other by articulatory strictures.

Rhythm. Distribution of durations and timing of initiator pulses.

Feet. Rhythm units—unitary bursts of initiator power. In English initiator power appears to be delivered in a series of bursts or pulses, each quickly reaching a major peak and then dying away. These 'feet' tend to be of very roughly equal duration, irrespective (within limits) of how many minor power peaks, or syllables, occur within each foot.

Phonatory prosodies

Intonation. Meaningful pitch variations (i.e. variations in frequency of vocal fold vibration) often characterizing long stretches of speech, which may be many syllables in length, and relatively large grammatical units, such as the sentence: often used to distinguish statements from (certain kinds of) questions in many languages, such as English, French, and many other languages in Europe and elsewhere.

Tone. Meaningful pitch variations characterizing short stretches of speech, often of only one syllable in length, and the shortest grammatical units— words and morphemes: used in many languages, such as Chinese, Thai, many African and American Indian languages, to distinguish one word from another.

Articulatory prosody

Duration. The length of time that an articulatory stricture is maintained, known as *length* or *quantity*. In IPA transcription duration is indicated as follows: long vowel or (less commonly) consonant: [aː] [sː], half long [aˑ] [sˑ], short [a] [s], ultra-short (or ultra-weak) [ă] [s̆].

Sound systems

Phonetics. The study of the physiological, aerodynamic, and acoustic characteristics of speech-sounds.

Phonology. The study of how sounds are organized into systems and utilized in languages.

The human sound-producing potential. A universal, differently exploited by different languages. For example, the continuum of possible vowel-sounds is differently dissected by different languages (e.g. English and Spanish). The continuum of different possible voice-onset-times (VOTs). VOT = time difference between release of articulatory oral stricture and onset of voicing for a following vowel.

Phoneme. Minimal *sequential* contrastive unit of phonology used in the buildup of the phonological forms of words.

Distinctive Feature. Minimal *simultaneous* contrastive component of a phoneme.

For Further Reading

CHAPTER 1 **Introduction**

Illuminating but quite different introductions to phonetics are given in Aber-crombie (1967), Chap. 1, and Laver (1994), Chap. 1.

On the phases of speech in general see Catford (1977), Chap. 1, and Ball and Rahilly (1999), Chap. 1, pp. 13–18. The *aerodynamic* phase is dealt with comprehensively in Catford (1977), and in a highly technical manner in Shadle (1997). For the *acoustic* phase, see Catford (1977), Chap. 4, Clark and Yallop (1995), Chap. 6, and Fry (1979).

There is a relatively simple description of the *vocal tract*, and of the functions of the organs within it, in Catford (1977), Chap. 2. A more detailed description is given in Clark and Yallop (1995) Chap. 6.

CHAPTER 2 **Basic Components of Speech**

Initiation types (air-stream mechanisms) are gone into in detail in Catford (1977), Chap. 5. See also Laver (1994), Chap. 6, and Ball and Rahilly (1999), Chap. 2.

CHAPTER 3 **Phonation**

Phonation is discussed in Catford (1977), Chap. 6. Numerous types of voice, whisper and voice quality are described in Catford (1964), Laver (1994), Chap. 7, and most extensively in Laver (1980).

CHAPTERS 4 AND 5 **Articulation**

Articulatory *locations* and *stricture types* are dealt with (generally as 'place' and 'manner' of articulation) in all manuals of phonetics. Both of these parameters of articulation are dealt with in great detail (including aerodynamic data) in Catford (1977), Chaps. 7 and 8.

Laver (1994) has excellent descriptions and diagrams of the articulations of *stops* and *fricatives* in Chaps. 8 and 9. Clark and Yallop (1995), Chap. 2, entitled *Segmental Articulation*, combines succinct descriptions of initiation, phonation and articulation. Ball and Rahilly (1999), in Chap. 3 on *Speech Articulation*, makes use of the category of *maintainability* or *prolongability* that was introduced in Catford (1977) and used in the present book.

CHAPTER 6 **Co-articulation and sequences**

Multiple articulations and sequences are dealt with in Catford (1997), Chap. 11, and Laver (1994), Chap. 11 on *Multiple articulations* and Chap. 12 on *Interseg-mental co-ordination*. See also Ball and Rahilly (1999), Chap. 7. The latter two contain useful diagrams of multiple articulations.

CHAPTERS 7 AND 8 Vowels

On *vowels* generally see especially the excellent survey in Laver (1994), Chap. 10. The *Cardinal Vowels* and the theory underlying them are well described in Aber-crombie (1967), Chap. 10, and Abercrombie (1985), and, with some criticism, in Ladefoged (1993), Chaps. 8 and 9, where the *acoustics* of vowels is also dealt with. For general introductions to the acoustics of speech see the references cited for Chap. 1.

CHAPTER 9 Prosodic features

Prosodic features are described in Chap. 9 of Clark and Yallop (1995). See also Lehiste (1970), and the detailed analyses in Chaps. 14 to 16 of Laver (1994).

CHAPTER 10 Sound-systems of languages

Some aspects of *phonology* are dealt with in Abercrombie (1967), Chap. 5, and Ladefoged (1993), Chap. 2. On feature systems see Clark and Yallop (1995), Chap. 9, Jakobson, Fant, and Halle (1963), and Chomsky and Halle (1968), Chap. 7. For general descriptions of English see Jones (1970) and Gimson (1989), on British English, and Bronstein (1960) and Kenyon (1997), on American English. The latter, the 12th edition of a standard work, includes spectrograms of the sounds of American English.

CHAPTER 11 Review

A compressed survey of the field of phonetics is provided by Catford (1994).

A topic that is not explicitly dealt with in this book is phonetic notation. For an excellent general and historical introduction to this subject see Abercrombie (1967), Chap. 7. See also Laver (1994), Chap. 19. For general information on the IPA and specimen transcriptions of 29 languages, see the *Handbook of the International Phonetic Association*.

Ladefoged and Maddieson, *The Sounds of the World's Languages* is an extremely useful reference work, which might be regarded as an application of everything that can be learned from the present book. It is the most comprehensive survey of human speech that exists, containing descriptions of sounds largely supported by instrumental data.

Sooner or later students of phonetics will be reading articles and books like the preceding one that make use of the findings of instrumental phonetics. It is therefore desirable that they have some knowledge of the techniques of instrumental investigation of speech and how to interpret instrumental data. A good introduction to such matters is Painter (1979), and Chap. 12 of Ball and Rahilly is a short and readable survey of the topic. A comprehensive, but very technical, survey of speech research methods is Lass (1996).

References

ABERCROMBIE, DAVID (1967), *Elements of General Phonetics*, Edinburgh University Press.

ABERCROMBIE, DAVID (1985), 'Daniel Jones Teaching' in Fromkin, V. A. (Ed.) *Phonetic Linguistics: Essays in Honor of Peter Ladefoged*, Orlando FL, Academic Press, 15–24.

BALL, MARTIN J. and RAHILLY, J. (1999), *Phonetics, the Science of Speech*, London, Edwin Arnold Ltd, USA, Oxford University Press.

BRONSTEIN, ARTHUR J. (1960), *The Pronunciation of American English*, New York, Appleton-Century-Crofts.

CATFORD, J. C. (1964), 'Phonation types: the classification of some laryngeal components of speech production' in Abercrombie, D. *et al.* (Eds.) *In Honour of Daniel Jones*, London, Longman, 26–37.

CATFORD, J. C. (1977), *Fundamental Problems in Phonetics*, Edinburgh University Press and Indiana University Press.

CATFORD, J. C. (1994), 'Phonetics, Articulatory' in Asher, R. E. (Ed.) *Encyclopedia of Language and Linguistics*, Oxford, Pergamon Press, 3058–3070.

CATFORD, J. C. and PISONI, D. B. (1970), 'Auditory vs. Articulatory Training in Exotic Sounds', *Modern Language Journal*, 54/7, 477–81.

CHOMSKY, N. and HALLE, M. (1968), *The Sound Pattern of English*, New York, Harper Row.

CLARK, J. and YALLOP, C. (1995), *An Introduction to Phonetics and Phonology*, Oxford, Blackwell Publishers.

FRY, D. B. (1979), *The Physics of Speech*, Cambridge University Press.

GIMSON, A. C. (1989), *An Introduction to the Pronunciation of English*, London, Edward Arnold Ltd.

Handbook of the International Phonetic Association (1999), Cambridge University Press.

HARRIS, JIMMY G. (1999), 'States of the glottis for voiceless plosives', *Proceedings of the 14th International Congress of Phonetic Sciences*, San Francisco (Aug. 1999), vol. 3, 2041–2044.

JAKOBSON, R., FANT, G. and HALLE, M. (1963), *Preliminaries to Speech Analysis*, Cambridge, Mass., MIT.

JONES, DANIEL (1970), *Outline of English Phonetics*, 8th edn., Cambridge University Press.

KENYON, JOHN S. (1997), *American Pronunciation*, 12th edn., expanded, Lance, Donald M. and Kingsbury, Stewart A. (Eds.), Ann Arbor, George Wahr.

KENYON, JOHN S. and KNOTT, T. A. (1944), *A Pronouncing Dictionary of American English*, Springfield, Mass., Merriam.

LADEFOGED, P. (1967), *Three Areas of Experimental Phonetics*, London, Oxford University Press.

LADEFOGED, P. (1993), *A Course in Phonetics*, New York, Harcourt Brace.

LADEFOGED, P. and MADDIESON, I. (1996), *The Sounds of the World's Languages*, Oxford, Blackwell Publishers.

LASS, NORMAN J. (1996), *Principles of Experimental Phonetics*, St. Louis etc., Mosby.

LAUFER, A. and CONDAX, I. D. (1980), 'The Epiglottis as an Articulator', *Journal of the IPA*, 9/2, 50–6.

LAVER, JOHN (1980), *The Phonetic Description of Voice Quality*, Cambridge University Press.

LAVER, JOHN (1994), *Principles of Phonetics*, Cambridge University Press.

LEHISTE, ILSE (1970), *Suprasegmentals*, Cambridge, Mass., MIT.

PAINTER, COLIN (1979), *An Introduction to Instrumental Phonetics*, Baltimore, University Park Press.

SHADLE, CHRISTINE (1997), 'The Aerodynamics of Speech', in Hardcastle, W. J. and Laver, J. (Eds.) *Handbook of Phonetic Sciences*, Oxford, Blackwell, 33–64.

SWEET, HENRY (1877), *A Handbook of Phonetics*, Oxford, Clarendon Press.

Index